AF078994

The British Horse Society

BHS Equine Excellence Pathway

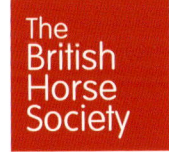

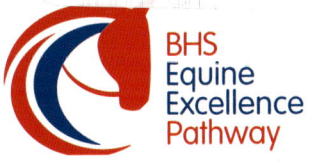

Complete Horsemanship Volume 2

Supporting you through every stage

Complete Horsemanship
Volume 2

KENILWORTH PRESS

Copyright © 2017 The British Horse Society

First published in the UK in 2017 by Kenilworth Press,
an imprint of Quiller Publishing Ltd

British Library Cataloguing-in-Publication Data
A catalogue record for this book is available from the British Library

ISBN 978 1 910016 17 6

The right of The British Horse Society to be identified as the author of this work has been asserted in accordance with the Copyright, Design and Patent Act 1988.

The information in this book is true and complete to the best of our knowledge. All recommendations are made without any guarantee on the part of the Publisher, who also disclaims any liability incurred in connection with the use of this data or specific details.

All rights reserved. No part of this book may be reproduced or transmitted in any form or by any means, electronic or mechanical including photocopying, recording or by any information storage and retrieval system, without permission from the Publisher in writing.

Edited by Martin Diggle
Design by Arabella Ainslie

Printed in China

Appointed GPSR EU Representative: Easy Access System Europe Oü, 16879218
Address: Mustamäe tee 50, 10621, Tallinn, Estonia
Contact Details: gpsr.requests@easproject.com, +358 40 500 3575

Kenilworth Press
An imprint of Quiller Publishing Ltd
The Hill, Stroud, GL5 4EP
Tel: 01453 847800
Email: info@quillerbooks.com
Website: www.kenilworthpress.co.uk

Contents

ACKNOWLEDGEMENTS 6
INTRODUCTION 7

SECTION 1 HORSE CARE AND STABLE MANAGEMENT 11

- Chapter 1 Working with Horses 13
- Chapter 2 Horse Behaviour 25
- Chapter 3 Health and Welfare 31
- Chapter 4 Horse Anatomy and Physiology 53
- Chapter 5 Feeding 69
- Chapter 6 Fitness Training 85
- Chapter 7 Horse Walkers 93
- Chapter 8 Clipping, Plaiting and Shoeing 101
- Chapter 9 Transporting Horses 115
- Chapter 10 Stable Design 127
- Chapter 11 Care of Horses at Grass 135
- Chapter 12 Tack and Equipment 147
- Chapter 13 Lungeing 157

SECTION 2 RIDING 173

- Chapter 14 Flatwork 175
- Chapter 15 Jumping 199

SECTION 3 COACHING 213

- Chapter 16 Coaching Concepts 217
- Chapter 17 Coaching in Practice 239

WHAT'S NEXT? 319

Complete Horsemanship Volume 2

Acknowledgements

The British Horse Society acknowledges with thanks permission to use the following images within this book, all of which are copyright of the individuals and organisation who kindly supplied them.

Chapter 3

Mud fever courtesy of *Equi-Med Ag Ltd*.
Dark red gums courtesy of *Redwings Horse Sanctuary*.

Chapter 4

Images courtesy of Gillian Higgins, who also contributed text for this chapter.

Chapter 5

Bagged Cool Mix and Competition Mix courtesy of *Spillers Horse Feed*.
Bagged Healthy Hooves and Healthy Tummy fibre feeds courtesy of *Dengie Horse Feed*.
Top Line conditioning cubes, Senior Mix and an example of ingredients listed on a feed bag, courtesy of *Baileys Horse Feed*.

Chapter 6

Dr David Marlin provided assistance with the text.

Chapter 7

All images in this chapter courtesy of *Claydon Horse Exercisers Ltd*, Southam, Warwickshire, CV47 1BG.

Chapter 9

Keep the horse steady and central going down the ramp courtesy of *Ifor Williams Trailer Ltd*.

Chapter 10

A purpose-built outdoor courtyard; A window with a louvre board design; A rug rack; An automatic water drinker; Furnished stable door. All courtesy of *Monarch Equestrian*.

Chapter 16

SkillBase First Aid provided the text for 'What to do in the event of an accident/rider fall'.

The British Horse Society also acknowledges with thanks the assistance of the following riding centres and their staff in the production of photographs for this book: Wellington Riding Ltd, Warwickshire College (Moreton Morrell), Pittern Hill Stables, Berkshire Riding Centre, Spanish Bit Riding School and Livery, Lyne House Livery, Brampton Stables and Millfield School. Pictures throughout this publication supplied by Tara Taylor and Jon Stroud.

Introduction

Introduction

Welcome to the *Complete Horsemanship Volume 2* from the British Horse Society (BHS). If you are new to our series, we welcome any reader who is passionate about horses. Within our second volume we further explore the foundations of caring for horses and continue to discuss how a rider can develop their flatwork. We introduce the foundations of jumping, the basics of lungeing a horse and the fundamentals of coaching. We believe that learning about all of these key areas of equestrianism will give you a comprehensive understanding of horses, or as we like to reference it, you are on your way to becoming a complete horseman.

In *Volume 2* you will find chapters on how to:

- Understand the basics of working with horses.

- Understand in more detail why horses behave the way they do and how to handle their behaviour.

- Look after the health and welfare of horses. This introduces both how to treat and prevent common health problems.

- Manage feeding — from what to feed to monitoring diet for effectiveness.

- Manage fitness training — from types of work to practical tips on handling a horse walker.

- Prepare horses for plaiting, clipping, shoeing or transportation (including how to load and unload).

- Consider the suitability of the horse's environment both in the stable and out in the field.

- Tack up with basic equipment.

- Lunge — introducing the key foundations.

- Further develop foundations of flatwork from understanding the aids to exploring the scale of training.

- Jump — introducing the basics of jumping from pole work to basic gridwork.

- Coach — introducing the theory of coaching as well as welfare considerations.

- Coach — putting theory to practice covering preparation techniques and developing different riders.

Introduction

Volume 2 still encourages you to have fun developing your riding and horse management skills, whether you want to enjoy this wonderful sport recreationally, or whether you're now dedicated to pursuing a career with horses. The training tips within the sections are there to further develop and enhance your knowledge.

The BHS education system is one of the best and most widely-respected in the world. The *Complete Horsemanship* series supports anyone wishing to study qualifications within the BHS Equine Excellence Pathway. There are a number of bespoke professional career pathways available, depending on your long-term goal. Whether it is becoming a successful groom or a stable manager, a professional rider or a specialist coach, there is a pathway to choose from.

Equestrian qualifications show potential employers of the skills accrued for a career with horses. The BHS qualifications framework is internationally recognised, with some of the best instructors, riders and grooms coming through the BHS Equine Excellence Pathway, including Fellows Carl Hester and Yogi Breisner.

The BHS Equine Excellence Pathway gives each student the opportunity to gain qualifications and awards in their chosen profession. The Pathways have been specially developed through extensive consultation with the equine industry to incorporate the latest research and thinking, with current practices and friendly assessment methods.

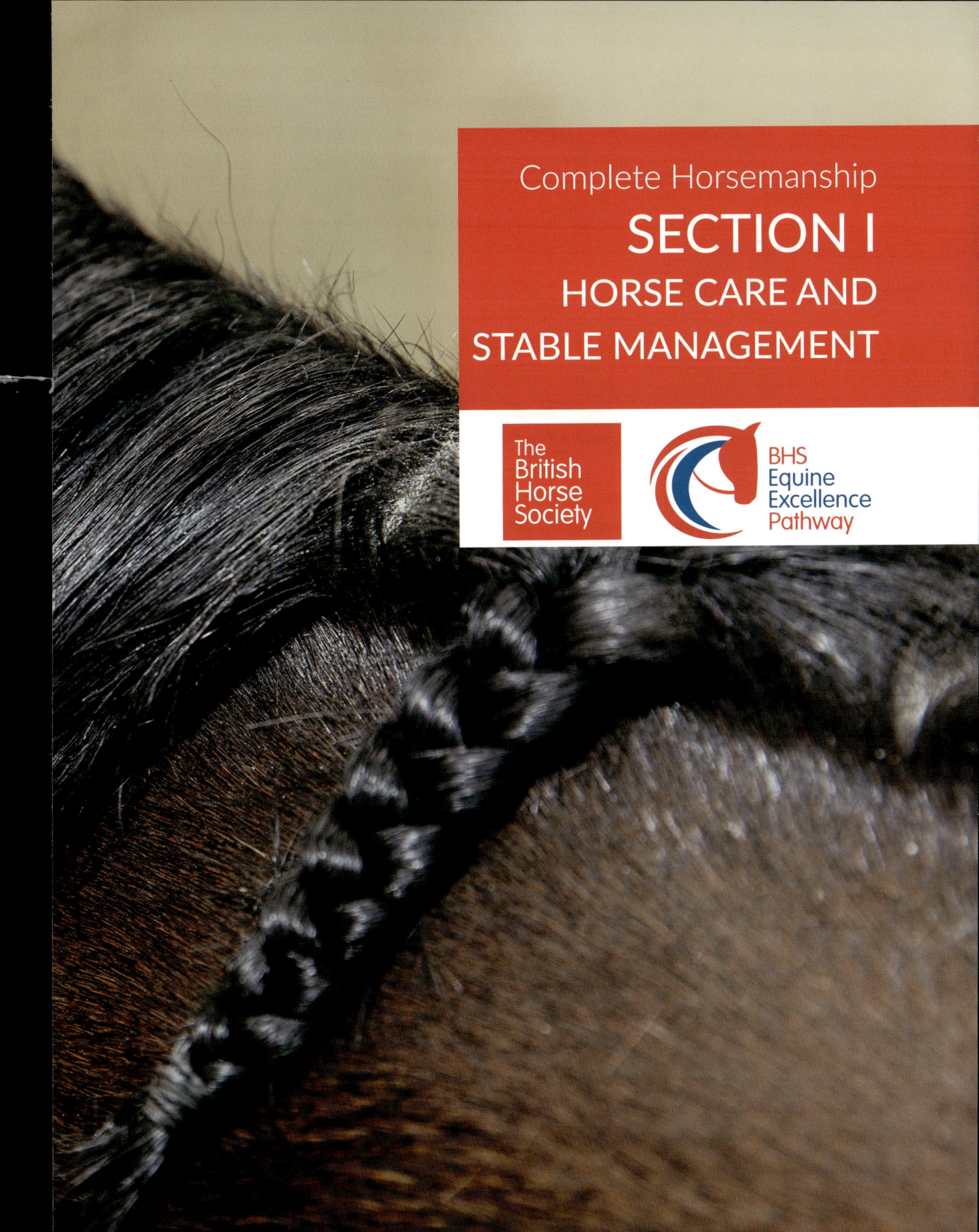

Chapter 1
Working with Horses

Legal requirements of an employee

General responsibilities

Valued qualities and skills to develop

Your employment rights

Summary

Working with Horses

Who does not want a career doing something they truly love? A career with horses can therefore be attractive, but you need to be aware of the realities. While being rewarding and enjoyable, it does have its pitfalls. Yard work involves a certain amount of hard physical labour and you may be expected to work long hours in all weathers. You should expect to start your career at the bottom and work your way up, and only a small proportion of your working day, if any, will include riding, which may form only part of your training. Most daily duties will revolve around caring for horses; mucking out and less enjoyable tasks such as removing droppings from fields and sweeping and tidying the yard may be unavoidable. But if you can embrace all this cheerfully, horses can give you a hugely rewarding career, and help you develop skills that will set you up for life.

Most daily duties will revolve around caring for horses.

> *There may be some tasks that cannot be undertaken by an employee unless they have received appropriate training — e.g. driving a tractor to level the arena.*

Legal requirements of an employee

As an employee you must adhere to the legal requirements of working on a yard:

Health and Safety. By law you are required to take reasonable care of your own and others' health and safety. This means following your employer's or supervisor's instructions, wearing appropriate personal protective clothing (PPE) and reporting any safety concerns to a senior staff member.

Safeguarding. Any business that involves activities with children (i.e. under-18s) or adults at risk is required to have measures in place to keep people safe when they are at their centre or yard. This includes protection from abuse or harm from things like bullying, neglect, or physical, emotional and sexual abuse. There should be someone on every yard trained in safeguarding to whom you can report concerns.

Clear policies and up-to-date training are the best way to keep all those involved fully informed of their safeguarding responsibilities.

The British Horse Society has a template Safeguarding Policy for Approved Centres, Affiliated Riding Clubs and Accredited Professional Coaches. As a member body of the British Equestrian Federation (BEF) the BHS adheres to The BEF Safeguarding Policy (Children and Young People) and The BEF Safeguarding Policy (Adults at Risk). These policies are available to download from the BHS and BEF websites. You should make yourself aware of the Safeguarding Policy and Codes of Conduct that the organisation you are working for has in place.

As a Trainee Coach you may be in a 'position of trust' with the under-18s whom you coach or instruct. The BHS and BEF have specific guidelines regarding position of trust. As a coach you must ensure that you maintain a healthy, positive and professional relationship with participants. When you are in a position of trust you must not engage in a sexual relationship with an under-18 participant as this will be classed as an abuse of trust.

Remember, it is everyone's responsibility to make sure that children and adults at risk are safe. If you have a concern, you must report it to the most appropriate person in your organisation, for example your Club Safeguarding Officer, line manager or senior instructor. If you consider that a child is in immediate danger you must report this to the police.

You may be approached by a child or an adult at risk about something that is concerning them. If this happens, remember to:

- Create a safe environment.

- Be honest — never promise to keep secrets.

- Record all information provided.

- Maintain confidentiality but do not take on sole responsibility.

There are many safeguarding topics with which you may need to familiarise yourself:

- Online safety.

- Criminal record checking.

- Photography guidance.

- Relationships with parents.

- One-to-one situations.

- Physical contact.

- Bullying.

All these topics are covered in the Safeguarding Training provided by the BHS. Online refresher training is available after three years. The BHS Safeguarding Team provides guidance documents, which are available on the BHS website.

Data Protection. This refers to personal information about staff and clients. By law this must be kept confidential, with measures in place to ensure that it is kept secure, e.g. by use of computer protection software or a locked cabinet. Personal data must not be shared with any third party without the correct consents being in place.

It is also good practice to avoid talking openly about horses or people in any forum, including social media. This has the potential not only to damage someone's reputation but also to spread false rumours, and may be used against you in the future.

Equality and Diversity. These rules exist to ensure that you can work without being worried that you will be discriminated against in any way. Businesses are required to follow practices that prevent discrimination in the workplace, and to ensure equal treatment for all. Employees should always treat colleagues with respect and, if you feel that you or someone else is being discriminated against, you should report this to a senior staff member. If it is your employer who you feel is being discriminatory, you can contact an organisation outside of work for advice — e.g. Citizens Advice, Equality Advisory Support Service or the Advisory, Conciliation and Arbitration Service (ACAS).

Horse Welfare. Animal welfare acts ensure that the basic needs of animals are met. This legislation requires horses to have:

1. A suitable environment to live in.
2. Access to sufficient food and clean water.
3. Appropriate company.
4. Adequate exercise (or turnout).
5. Protection from pain, suffering, injury and disease.

These basic needs should be the underpinning ethos of everybody who works with horses: their well-being must be at the heart of everything you do.

General responsibilities

In the early stages of your career you are likely to be supervised by a senior staff member in your daily care of horses and routine yard activities. Although you may not be supervised directly as you work, there should be someone to whom you can report problems and who should provide you with tasks and instructions. If you are asked to exercise a horse on the lunge, for example, you should be briefed about how long for, and what work should be included within that session.

It is your responsibility to follow instructions and to report any concerns you have to your supervisor. Remain observant as you work, and your knowledge should enable you to recognise signs that a horse is unwell, or spot changes in behaviour that may indicate a problem.

It is also important to report health and safety concerns you may notice, e.g. unstable hay bales, so that measures can be put in place to prevent accidents. It is also important to report incidents, even if they do not appear serious at the time. An example of this would be to report if someone slips on an icy patch on a winter's day — even if they are unhurt, so that a sign can be put up to warn others of the hazard and make sure the affected area is gritted.

You should also be able to act in the event of an emergency by having knowledge of emergency procedures (such as the fire drill) at your yard and what to do in the event of an accident, even if you do not lead the emergency response yourself. Your role could include calling emergency services, catching loose horses or assisting a first-aider.

All accidents, no matter how minor, should be reported to your supervisor and recorded. You may be asked to fill out an accident report form if you are involved with any incident.

Valued qualities and skills to develop

In order to do well and progress in your career you should be aware that there are certain qualities that employers value, and skills beyond your current technical knowledge and riding ability that need developing.

Valued qualities

Reliability

Most yards carry out a range of practical tasks both for their horses' welfare and their continued income, e.g. feeding, mucking out, catching in, turning out and getting horses ready for lessons. In most cases such tasks must be done within a strict time-frame. Although work can be postponed to another day in many workplaces, this is often not the case on a yard. Consequently, if someone is late or does not turn up for work, it has a huge impact on the other staff, who must pick up the slack. There will always be instances when a person is unwell and this cannot be helped. However, on all other occasions, employers require you to turn up for work and arrive on time and be prepared to complete the work being done within a reasonable time-frame.

Honesty

Honesty is always important in matters both small and large. Everyone makes mistakes, and your employer or supervisor will respect you more for owning up if you have made one.

Good work ethic

Yard work is hard work, and requires a good work ethic. In other words, it needs employees who take their work seriously and have pride in it. Attention to detail is a crucial skill when you are working with horses, as any abnormal signs may be an indication that all is not well with a particular horse. This can be especially significant in competition/racing yards in contexts such as reporting any slight heat/swelling in a horse's limb during routine picking out of feet, etc.

Flexibility of work hours

Working with horses is not a nine-to-five job. It is common to find a late night is required if you work at a riding school that offers evening lessons. If you work as a groom, travelling to competitions may involve very early starts and late returns, or even stays away overnight. If you aspire to working in a stud you will find that most foals are born in the early hours of the morning! Most employers will support and acknowledge extra hours with extra pay or time off, but flexibility is key on both sides.

Professionalism

In addition to covering the qualities listed above, professionalism extends to your appearance, conduct, behaviour towards others and more. You should dress for work according to guidelines set by your yard, and you should always be polite and respectful to both clients and your colleagues. The latter may also be your friends, but it is important to distinguish how you interact with them in a social setting and how you do so at work — for example, in the language you use. Most people have access to social media and it has fast become a part of our daily routine to check posts. However, during work hours you should not be using your phone for personal purposes without permission from your supervisor. In addition, take care about what you post on social media. Many employers will check a person's social media comments when they apply for a job to help them get a feel for the applicant, but employers may also check current employees' social media activity for any signs of unprofessionalism.

Skills to develop

Being a team player

In most yards you will work as part of a team, so it is essential to be a team player, collaborating with others to achieve common goals. This may involve stopping what you are doing to help others, or taking on some of their work if they are called away to another task. Throughout your career, you will undoubtedly come across people whose personalities clash with your own. Working as a team is about putting differences aside and focusing on the work to be done.

Communication skills

It is essential to have good communication with superiors, colleagues and clients, by passing on messages, providing information where required, generally being friendly and so on. It is easy for busy people to keep their heads down and get on with their work without making polite conversation with clients arriving at the yard, but a smile and greeting can go a long way to helping a yard achieve a friendly and welcoming atmosphere. Communication is not just about speaking to but also listening to others and focusing on the message being relayed.

Empathy

Life on a busy yard can become stressful and sometimes frustrating, especially if people or horses do not behave as expected. However, it is important to be patient and tolerant of all, especially the horses in your care. Empathy is about trying to see things from the point of view of other people or horses, to help you understand their behaviour and respond appropriately.

Efficiency

As mentioned previously, yards often have a lot of work to be completed within a fairly tight timescale. It is therefore essential for workers to be efficient and to work to industry-accepted timescales. While you may be efficient at mucking out, there may be some tasks where you need more practice before you can do them to an acceptable standard and speed, e.g. plaiting up for a competition.

Practice often makes perfect, and each time you tackle such a job you can time yourself to check your improvement. There are many other things you can do around the yard to ensure efficiency, such as multi-tasking, e.g. depositing feed buckets back at the feed room as you cross the yard and filling water buckets while mucking out rather than standing and waiting while they fill. (Also, carrying two buckets will be more economical than just one, as well as helping to prevent back problems.)

Physical fitness

Working on a yard is physically demanding, and if you are insufficiently fit you will struggle to be efficient and to complete tasks on time. Lack of fitness may also result in injury, as may incorrect lifting and handling techniques. While working day-to-day will increase your fitness, if you have a period without working (e.g. between seasonal employment) it is useful to prepare yourself in advance.

Efficiency and physical fitness are useful skills to develop.

Your employment rights

Contracts in principle

If you are employed you should have a contract of employment. This should include:

- The names of you and your employer.
- The date on which you started work.
- What you will be paid.
- Your hours of work.
- Your holiday entitlement.
- Details of notice periods, i.e. how much notice you are required to give if you decide to leave your job.
- Your sick pay entitlement.
- Details of the disciplinary, dismissal and grievance procedures.

Some contract details

The following are some criteria that an employer must address when producing your contract of employment.

National Minimum Wage and National Living Wage

You must not be paid less than the National Minimum Wage (NMW), and if you are aged 25 years or older you should be paid the National Living Wage. The NMW varies depending on your age, and you will be paid a different rate if you are on an apprenticeship scheme. You can find more details of what you should be paid on the Government website, www.gov.uk.

Hours of work

The hours you work must adhere to the Working Time Regulations. These state that on average (usually over 17 weeks) you should not work for more than 48 hours a week. If you are under 18 years old you should not work more than 8 hours a day or 40 hours a week. There are some exceptions to these rules; if you require further advice you should contact the Advisory, Conciliation and Arbitration Service (ACAS).

Holiday entitlement

If you are employed you will be entitled to paid holiday. Your statutory holiday entitlement depends on how many days a week you work. If you work five or more days per week you are entitled to 28 days holiday a year; this includes bank holidays. Your employer may state how much notice is required for you to request a holiday and may have a policy as to when you can take holiday.

Sick pay entitlement

If you are ill for four or more consecutive days and you are an employee you should receive Statutory Sick Pay in place of your normal pay. If you are not eligible to receive this you may be able to claim Employment and Support Allowance. You can find more details, including your eligibility on the Government website, www.gov.uk.

Details of the disciplinary, dismissal and grievance procedures

Your employer should have a disciplinary procedure laid down to deal with situations where they have concerns about your work. These concerns may be in relation to your behaviour at work, your standard of work or absence from work. It is likely that your employer will try to resolve these problems by talking to you informally. However, dependent on the severity of their concerns your employer may choose to take disciplinary action, which may ultimately lead to dismissal. For further information, including codes of practice in relation to disciplinary and dismissal procedure, you can contact ACAS or visit their website.

Useful contacts in relation to employment rights

The UK Government's website provides current information in relation to Government services including employment rights and state benefits, www.direct.gov.uk.

Citizens Advice is an independent charity in the UK that gives free, confidential information and advice to help people with legal, consumer and other problems, www.citizensadvice.org.uk.

The Advisory, Conciliation and Arbitration Service (ACAS) provides information and advice for employers and employees on all aspects of workplace relations and employment law, www.acas.org.uk.

The Equality Advisory Support Service provides advice and assistance to individuals on issues relating to equality and human rights, www.equalityadvisoryservice.com.

The British Grooms Association is a professional body for people who work with horses. It is a social enterprise and is non-profit making. It brings together all who work hands on with horses offering support and dedicated career advice, and it promotes professionalism and good horsemanship, www.britishgrooms.org.uk.

Summary

- Working with horses can be very sociable and fun, and it is a fantastic way to earn a wage from doing something that you love.

- Wages vary widely in the equestrian industry (apart from racing, which has a wage structure), although some jobs include accommodation that can vary from shared hostel rooms, to luxury cottages. Food, free livery for your own horse, riding lessons and the chance to compete are also sometimes included as part payment.

- Working with horses can include early mornings, late nights and weekends, but no two days are the same!

- A contract of employment is an agreement that governs the employment relationship between an employer and employee.

TRAINING TIPS

To get the most out of a career working with horses make sure you:

1. Are physically fit.

2. Are willing and able to work outside in all weather conditions and have a good general knowledge and experience of horse care and stable duties.

3. Whilst working on a yard it is very likely that you will be working with children, the BHS Safeguarding and Protecting Children courses will provide you with the necessary information to protect yourself and others from harm.

4. The British Grooms Association is a useful organisation to contact in relation to information about working in the horse industry.

Chapter 2

Horse Behaviour

Signs that a horse is unsettled in the stable

Signs that a horse is unsettled in the field

Summary

Horse Behaviour

Horses have evolved to eat forage little and often and can spend up to 16 hours a day grazing, while travelling up to 65–80km (40–50 miles) per day in the wild. They are also very social animals and live in large family groups. Domesticated horses have very different lifestyles but they still have the same behavioural needs. Modern husbandry practices can deny horses the freedom to live as they would in the wild and the behaviour observed in horses who spend most of the day stabled with limited turnout or exercise and an unnatural feed regime, is therefore very different. If domesticated horses have limited access to turnout this not only limits foraging and social interaction opportunities, but also self-exercise.

Signs that a horse is unsettled in the stable

Horses can become unsettled for a number of reasons. For example, some horses become anxious if they are left alone on the yard or cannot see other horses, while others may become unsettled if there is something happening out of the ordinary, e.g. loud noises from workmen, as this may trigger their innate flight or fight instinct. This anxiety can be displayed by the horse calling, barging up against the door, or moving around the stable excessively. Some horses can develop anxiety and display abnormal behaviours if they have been stabled for long periods. These behaviours are often referred to as 'stereotypical'.

Stereotypical behaviour

Stereotypical behaviour is a repetitive pattern of behaviour with no obvious goal or function. Stereotypical behaviour is rarely seen in animals in the wild but is often displayed by various species of domesticated animals and seems to occur as a result of an animal's living environment not meeting their psychological needs. Stereotypical behaviour in horses includes crib-biting, wind-sucking, box-walking and weaving. Horses may initially develop these behaviours as coping mechanisms when put into an environment that does not meet their needs but, over time, the behaviour may develop into a habit that can still be displayed even if the horse is moved into a suitable environment.

A horse crib-biting.

Crib-biting/wind-sucking

When crib-biting, the horse will grasp an object (usually a stable door or a fence) with his teeth, and pull back, also making a grunting noise as he gulps in air. Wind-sucking is similar but does not involve the horse holding on to an object with his teeth.

Box-walking

Box-walking is when a horse repeatedly walks around his stable in a circle. As stated earlier, horses in the wild will cover long distances each day in search of food and water. Domesticated horses have this need to walk too, but stabling limits the amount of exercise a horse can take. Lack of exercise and confinement cause horses stress and frustration and thus they may develop box-walking as a means of coping by releasing their frustration and energy.

Weaving

Weaving is where a horse stands, often with his head over the stable door, and shifts his weight from one leg to the other while swinging his head from side to side. Again, the cause is often being stabled for a long time. This behaviour can cause stress and injury to the bones and internal structures of the forelegs.

Possible solutions

For some of the behaviours mentioned above there are products available that may, to some extent, provide short-term solutions. These include collars for wind-sucking and crib-biting and weave grills to prevent weaving. However, these products do not address the root cause of the horse's anxiety and can, themselves, cause the horse stress. If a horse shows any stereotypical behaviours the best solution is to increase turnout and allow the horse access to ad lib forage. If there is limited turnout, it is essential that the horse has sufficient forage when stabled. As mentioned earlier, horses in the wild graze for up to 16 hours a day, and domesticated horses also have a natural desire to chew. If they are prevented from performing this function it can lead to anxiety and the consequent lack of saliva production has also been linked to conditions such as stomach ulcers. To make hay rations last longer, you can provide hay in a small-holed haynet. In addition to this you can provide 'stable toys' such as food balls, licks or a 'horse safe' mirror that is positioned on the stable wall to help keep the horse occupied.

Signs that a horse is unsettled in the field

Signs that a horse is unsettled in the field can include running around, spooking, sweating and calling excessively — and we should try to avoid this to help prevent stress and injury.

A horse can become unsettled for a variety of reasons, many of which hinge on the fact that horses are prey animals: an excessively windy day, a low-flying aircraft, fireworks, a hunt going past, local shoots or crop-scarers all create noise that may frighten a horse and cause him to take flight. Horses will usually settle after a short time, but if they continue to gallop about it may be necessary to bring them in, to prevent them injuring themselves. If you have local shoots or hunts going past frequently, you may find that the horse is frightened initially but becomes more accustomed to the noise, sights and smells if they happen on a regular basis.

Horses, as stated earlier, naturally want to be with their herd mates for safety and companionship. A horse may become unsettled in the field if he is the last one to be brought in, cannot see other horses, or if a friend is removed from the same field. The response may be to pace the fence line, gallop up and down, and start calling.

An unsettled horse may canter up and down the fence line in a field.

In the summer months, biting flies may unsettle an especially sensitive horse. You may see him galloping around to try to stop the flies from biting, in which case you may want to stable him during the day and allow him turnout at night, or spray him with fly repellent, or put him in a fly rug or fly mask.

In the winter months, horses may become unsettled if there isn't enough grazing, leaving them hungry. It is important to provide supplementary forage in this case. If you put piles of hay around the field instead of offering a large bale, try to ensure there are more hay piles than there are horses. Especially if there isn't much grazing, horses within a group may bicker and fight over food.

Horses may also become unsettled if the grouping is inappropriate, for example, a particularly submissive horse may not be allowed to drink from the trough or eat from the hay provided if there is an over-dominant horse present.

Why horses may be difficult to catch

A horse who is difficult to catch can be very frustrating. To tackle the problem, it is important to consider the causes. These may include:

- The horse is anxious about going back to the yard to be stabled.

- The horse doesn't want to leave his field companions, possibly because of separation anxiety.

- The horse is not well handled, or lacks trust in humans.

- The grass is just too good to leave!

There are various potential solutions to this problem:

- Put the headcollar behind your back when you approach the horse.

- Take a friend with you so you can bring two horses in together. This allows the one who is harder to catch to be brought in with another one, so he does not have to leave the field alone.

- You may consider leaving a headcollar on while the horse is out in the field, so it is easier to catch him. However, there are risks involved with this as horses can injure themselves if the headcollar becomes caught on a gate or fence. If leaving a headcollar on you should use either a field-safe headcollar (with a quick-release buckle) or a basic leather headcollar that will break if the horse becomes caught on something.

- Take time to catch the horse, reward him with food afterwards (making sure that this is done out of the sight of other horses or you may get mobbed) and then release him straight away. This will help him understand that being caught doesn't always mean being taken out of the field, ridden and stabled. You can also catch the horse, bring him in, feed him and then turn him straight out to show him that coming in brings rewards.

- Handle the horse as much as possible, as well as completing ground work to build the horse's trust.

Summary

- Horses have an innate need to be outdoors to socialise, forage and exercise in line with the type of lifestyle they would have led centuries ago, before domestication. When a horse exhibits certain behaviours or responds to situations in a certain way, this is usually relates back to his natural instincts.

- Horses can develop stereotypical behaviours if they have been stabled for long periods or left without access to enough forage. Stereotypical behaviour is a repetitive pattern of behaviour that has no obvious function. These behaviours include crib-biting, wind-sucking, box-walking and weaving. The best solution for these behaviours is to increase turnout and to provide sufficient forage for the horse to chew while stabled.

- Horses can also become unsettled in the stable if they feel they are being left behind, for example if other horses are being turned out.

- Horses can become unsettled when in the field; this is most likely to happen when the horse is startled, triggering a flight response. However, horses can also become unsettled when they are irritated by flies, if there is a lack of food, or if they have been grouped with horses they do not get on with.

- Some horses are difficult to catch, which can be very frustrating. If this is the case then you need to think about why they are behaving this way. For example, is the grass just too good to leave; are you taking them away from their friends; or do they lack confidence and require more handling to build their trust in humans?

TRAINING TIPS

1. Spend as much time as you can observing the horses in your care in all of their environments, interacting with them whenever you can. This way you will build up a relationship and rapport with them and learn to read their body language more readily.

Chapter 3

Health and Welfare

Routine health procedures

Common health problems

Veterinary emergencies

First aid procedures

Care of a sick or injured horse on box rest

Summary

Routine health procedures

Keeping your horse happy and healthy is one of your most important roles as an owner or carer. Prevention is better than cure, so by following simple health procedures you will hopefully avoid unnecessary problems.

Worm control

Parasitic worms can cause significant and irreversible damage to the horse's gut and other organs, and cause a loss of body condition, colic and even death. The importance of effective worm control can never be underestimated. But worming programmes have evolved in recent years and the blanket use of wormers (scientifically known as 'anthelmintics') is no longer recommended as it is thought to contribute to drug resistance.

The main strategies for effective worm control are pasture management, worm burden monitoring and following a recommended worming programme.

Pasture management

Managing grazing paddocks can greatly contribute to effective worm control by preventing the worms from completing their life cycle.

- Remove droppings daily — this helps to remove any parasites or their eggs within the faeces.

- Rotate paddocks — by allowing a paddock to rest over the winter months, the majority of larvae will die off in the colder weather. Rotation also prevents a paddock from being over-grazed.

- Cross-graze — sheep or cattle will ingest equine worm larvae, which cannot survive in their new host.

- Don't overstock paddocks — when there are too many horses in a paddock, more droppings are produced and less grass is available, creating a higher risk of infection by ingestion.

- Do not use horse manure as fertiliser — there is a risk of spreading parasites within the faeces across the pasture.

Worm egg count and tapeworm blood test or saliva test

To minimise the risk of worm resistance, it is now advisable to use a more targeted approach to worm control. Worm Egg Counts (WEC) can be used to identify if a worm burden is present and whether a wormer is required. A fresh sample of faeces can be tested at a laboratory and if the WEC is more than 200epg (eggs per gram of faeces) a wormer may be recommended, depending on other factors such as the age of the horse or whether he has underlying disease or illness, etc. However, if the WEC is less than 350epg, treatment may not be required, so unnecessary use of a wormer should be avoided. WEC test kits can be bought from a testing laboratory or a local retailer, and most vets also offer this service.

Unfortunately there is not yet a test available for encysted redworm, so you may need to take advice on the best course of treatment if a burden is suspected. Tapeworm eggs do not show up on WECs either, so to test for a tapeworm burden your vet will do a blood test or use the relatively new saliva test kit. The blood test measures levels of antibodies present, which are associated with levels of infection. Therefore, if a horse has a tapeworm infection, he is likely to have high levels of related antibodies in his blood. The saliva test kit is simple to use and can be done at home. A sample of saliva is taken from the horse's mouth using a swab, which is then sent to the laboratory for testing, and a course of treatment can then be recommended.

Worming programme

It is likely that after using WEC and tapeworm testing, your vet or SQP will advise on the best worming programme for the particular horse. An SQP (Suitably Qualified Person) is the legal term given to a qualified animal medicine advisor who is entitled to prescribe certain veterinary medicines. SQPs are qualified and regulated by AMTRA (Animal Medicines Training Regulatory Authority).

How to administer a wormer

Please be aware of legislation outside of the UK on administering wormers and other medication.

Wormers are most commonly available in syringes, but can also come in tablet, liquid or granule form. The amount needed will vary according to the horse's weight, e.g. one syringe will hold enough for a 600 or 700kg (1,320 or 1,540lb) horse (the amount varies depending on the type of wormer), or a tablet usually treats 100kg/220lb (so a 500kg/1,100lb horse would need five tablets). With any wormer, it is important to follow the instructions on the packet. The weight of the horse can be calculated using a weigh-tape or by standing the horse on a weighbridge. Some vet's surgeries or equestrian centres may have a weighbridge available, and this is the most accurate way to weigh a horse. Some yards use a weighbridge regularly as part of their health and condition monitoring.

Using the type of wormer recommended by the vet or SQP, first check the expiry date on the packet. You need to set the dose to the correct weight, which can be done on a syringe by turning the stopper round until it moves down to the correct weight. It is best to do this out of sight of the horse, as many will see the wormer and try to hide at the back of the stable.

For this reason it can be a good idea to put the headcollar on and tie the horse up in his stable before you approach with the wormer. Consider also removing the cap before you enter the stable. This can then be left in a safe place outside and replaced after worming.

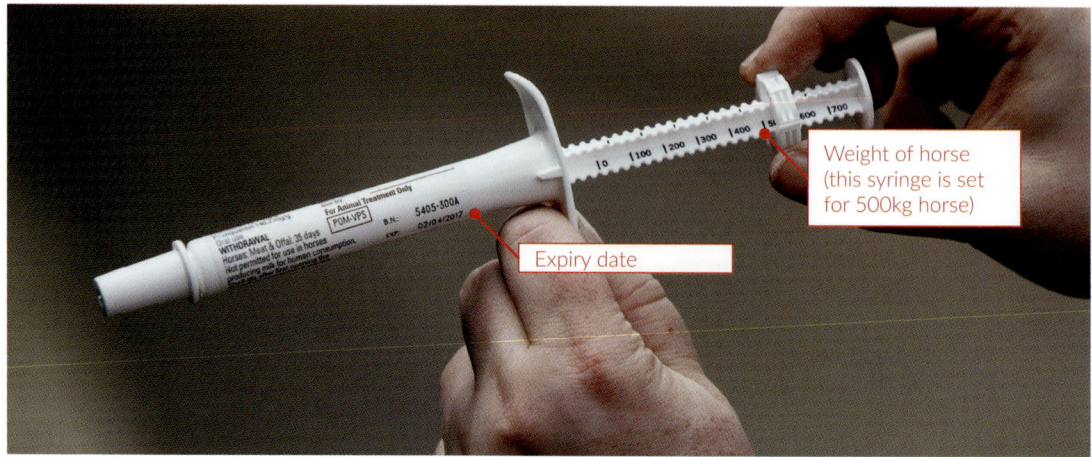

Wormer syringe set to use for a 500kg (1,100lb) horse.

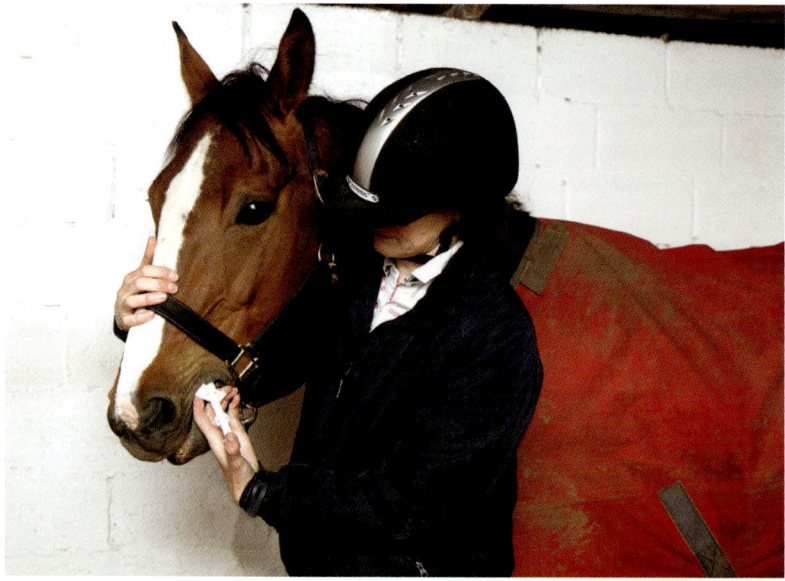

One hand can hold the horse's head steady while the other hand places the syringe into the corner of the mouth. Aim the syringe towards the back of the mouth and press the plunger down until it reaches the stopper.

Make sure the door is closed properly behind you. If the horse is tied up, untie the knot before worming in case he pulls back. You will need to hold the horse's head steady either by keeping one hand on the headcollar (making sure your fingers are nowhere they can get caught) or gently placing your hand under the horse's chin and over the top of his nose. This can be done from either side, depending on whether you are left- or right-handed. With the other hand you can gently place the syringe into the corner of the horse's mouth.

The syringe needs to be as far into the horse's mouth as you can get it without putting your fingers into the mouth. With the syringe aimed towards the back of the mouth, press the plunger down until it reaches the stopper, to ensure the correct dose is dispensed.

Some horses will try to spit the wormer back out so, once it is dispensed, hold the horse's head up a little until he has swallowed. If the horse spits out even a tiny amount of wormer, it is important to tell your supervisor as this will mean that the horse has not had his full dose, which could render the wormer ineffective.

Syringing allows you to make sure that the horse receives his full dose as it goes straight into the mouth. However, there may be times when you use other forms of wormer (e.g. granules that are mixed into the feed). It is essential for the horse to get the correct dose, so if he is a fussy eater and the wormer used is in liquid or granule form, you may need to syringe these straight into the mouth (granules would need to be made into a solution by adding water). Worming tablets are a relatively new concept, and can be fed on their own as a 'treat' (as you would a mint), mixed in with the horse's feed or 'disguised' inside a piece of apple or carrot. Some horses will eat this readily, whereas others may require other inventive solutions.

Vaccinations

Vaccinations can help reduce the risk and spread of disease and decrease the severity of the disease in affected horses. The most important diseases to vaccinate against are tetanus and equine Influenza. Tetanus is debilitating and often fatal, and horses are particularly susceptible to it because of the environment they live in and their susceptibility to injury. Equine influenza is highly contagious, so vaccination is essential in reducing the risk of outbreaks. Equine herpes virus (EHV) is also commonly vaccinated against on competition yards and studs as this is a common virus that can cause respiratory disease in young horses, abortion in pregnant mares and paralysis in horses of all ages and types.

Vaccinating against equine influenza involves an initial course of three injections with the second one 21–92 days after the first, and the third one 150–215 days after that. The initial course is then followed by an annual booster, which must be given within 365 days of the previous injection, otherwise the vaccinations will need to be restarted. They should all be recorded by the vet in the horse's passport. At some competition venues, you will be expected to present your horse's passport on arrival and will not be allowed to compete (or possibly not even enter the venue) if the vaccinations are not fully up to date.

Dental care

A horse's teeth continually erupt and are worn down by chewing. This can sometimes lead to uneven wear or sharp edges, which can cause soreness, lacerations or ulcers on the inside of the mouth or tongue. Eating may then become painful and the horse may start to drop or spit out half-chewed pieces of food (called quidding) or even avoid eating altogether. A sore mouth may also affect the horse when being ridden, and you may notice him holding his head differently or becoming resentful of the bit. Therefore it is essential to have the teeth checked regularly. If you notice any problems, such as lumps of half-chewed food on the floor or the horse becoming resistant to having the bit in his mouth, you should report this to a senior member of staff.

The vet will use a speculum (gag) to hold the mouth open when checking and rasping the teeth.

The horse's teeth should be checked and rasped every 6–12 months, although some horses (e.g. older horses or those with ongoing dental issues) may need checking more often. It is advisable to have the horse's teeth checked by the vet, but someone fully qualified with the BAEDT (British Association of Equine Dental Technicians) may be recommended by the vet for future checks or maintenance.

Foot care

The horse's feet should be trimmed or shod every 4–6 weeks by a farrier registered with the Farriers Registration Council in the UK, or the Irish Farriery Authority in the Republic of Ireland. Barefoot trimmers (other than registered farriers doing this work) are not regulated so are not recommended for trimming the horse's feet.

Regular foot care is necessary to stop the feet from cracking or becoming too long or unevenly shaped, which can alter the foot balance and cause problems in the tendons, ligaments and joints of the leg.

3 | Health and Welfare

Regular visits by a registered farrier will help to keep your horse's feet healthy and well-balanced.

Common health problems

Mud fever

Causes and recognition

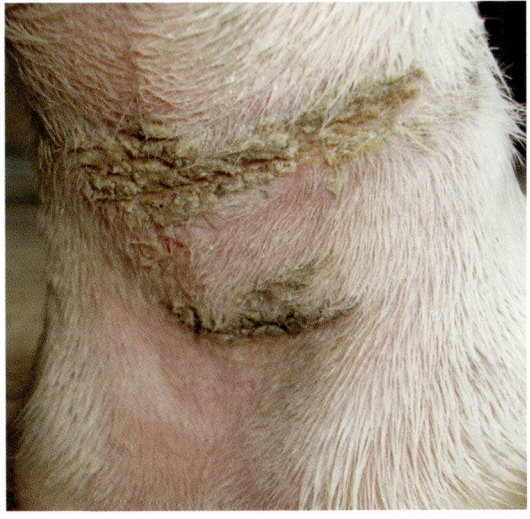

Mud fever.

Mud fever, or equine pastern dermatitis, is a bacterial skin infection that affects the lower legs. It is common in horses standing in wet, muddy fields or in dirty bedding where the skin has been softened by constant moisture. Mud fever can also be caused by trauma (e.g. a boot rubbing, or a wound), poor grooming, sandy surfaces and parasitic infection, where the integrity of the skin has been compromised. Horses with white legs seem to be particularly susceptible to it, as are horses who are heavily feathered (where moisture can be trapped under the hair). The signs of mud fever may vary slightly for each case but the skin will usually be dark pink and inflamed, with general swelling in the affected area. The hair becomes matted and there are usually numerous tiny scabs, particularly around the heels and the back of the pasterns. This can be a very painful condition and will cause varying degrees of lameness depending on the severity.

Prevention

It is not always easy to avoid mud (particularly in winter) but the legs need time to dry off, e.g. in the stable with plenty of clean, dry bedding. Keeping the legs dry is the key to prevention. Avoid over-washing them but, if you do have to, dry them off with a towel or similar. Alternatively, you could allow the legs to dry and then brush any dirt or mud off. If the horse has lots of feather, clipping this off will help to reduce the moisture trapped by the hair. Leg protection (e.g. turnout boots) can help keep the legs drier and cleaner, although these should only be used for short periods (i.e. daily turnout). Leaving them on for longer could cause further skin problems or rubs.

Mite infestation

Cause and recognition

Mites are tiny parasites that live on the horse's skin, the most common of which affect the lower legs. They cause irritation and horses with mites can often be seen stamping, scratching their legs against each other or biting at their legs. Scabs can often be seen and sometimes oozing lesions as well.

Prevention

Keep the horse well groomed, check through his coat daily and maintain a good level of hygiene. Horses with thicker coats or feathers are more at risk of mites, so clipping could decrease the risk. Mites pass from host to host by direct contact or via the immediate environment (e.g. bedding). Therefore, if mites are present, prevent them spreading by keeping each horse's tack and equipment separate, not sharing stables and avoiding direct contact between horses.

Thrush

Causes and recognition

Thrush is a common infection of the frog, often associated with wet or damp conditions (e.g. deep litter style bedding or a badly poached field) and thus is usually seen more in winter. However, poor foot conformation such as long heels, or poor hygiene (feet not picked out regularly) may make the horse more susceptible to thrush. It can affect any foot, although hind feet are more commonly affected. Thrush produces a foul-smelling, black discharge from the frog, and pressure applied to the affected area causes pain. Occasionally it will also cause general swelling of the lower leg. If left untreated, it can affect deeper tissues of the foot, and cause permanent damage.

Prevention

Prevention centres around good stable management and regular foot care. The horse should be stabled on clean, dry bedding or, if living out, should not be constantly in wet, muddy conditions. The feet should be regularly picked out and inspected, and regular farrier visits will also help keep the frogs healthy and the feet balanced. The feet may also benefit by being scrubbed with an antibacterial agent.

Capped elbows/hocks/knees

Causes and recognition

A capped elbow, hock or knee is an inflammatory swelling or distension of the bursa overlying the relevant joint. It is usually caused by trauma or prolonged contact with a hard surface, e.g. the stable floor when lying down, the trailer's rear ramp or the projecting heel of a shoe. The 'capping' is a soft, fluid-filled swelling that can be felt just beneath the skin. The horse is not usually lame.

Prevention

When a horse is stabled, rubber matting and a deep enough bed will help protect him when lying down. Capped knees or hocks can be caused by repeatedly striking the stable door or walls, so padding them may help prevent these problems. Legs in general, but knees and hocks in particular, should be protected when travelling by travel boots, bandages or knee and hock boots.

Knocks to bony areas

Causes and recognition

This can happen anywhere bone is close to the surface, e.g. hips, shoulders or skull. For example, a horse may catch a hip when walking through a doorway, may bang his head on a hayrack or door frame, or be kicked on the shoulder or cannon bone by another horse. The trauma could cause swelling, skin abrasions and even fractures.

Prevention

Opening stable doors and gates wide enough for a horse to pass through comfortably will help prevent bangs. Stable doors should be high enough for horses not to bang their heads on the top of the frame, but if the horse is still likely to bang his head, you could place padding around the door frame. Some occurrences are difficult to prevent (e.g. a kick in the field) but you can try to minimise the risk by placing horses in suitable groups when turned out or separating a horse if necessary.

Veterinary emergencies

There are numerous health conditions that require a visit from the vet, but some conditions will require immediate attention and the vet should be called straight away. These conditions include:

- Colic.

- Suspected broken limbs.

- Non weight-bearing lameness.

- Significant bleeding.

- Respiratory distress (the normal respiration rate of a healthy horse at rest is 8–16 breaths per minute).

- Injury to eyes.

- Injury or puncture wound to joints.

- Wound that needs stitching.

- Horse with a high temperature and showing signs of distress – the normal temperature of a healthy horse is 37.5–38.5°C (99.5–101.3°F) and the normal resting pulse rate is 28–44 beats per minute.

It is not practical to discuss here all possible emergencies and some, such as eye injuries, may require specialist treatment. Respiratory distress and high temperature may be signs of a variety of conditions/diseases that require expert diagnosis. What follows are notes on some conditions for which prevention or treatment may involve more junior workers on a yard.

Wounds

Horses are generally susceptible to injury however much we try to minimise the risks. Although veterinary advice should be sought for every wound, it is important to be able to describe one accurately so that the vet can advise you on the best treatment procedure.
There are four main types of wound, each of which require varying treatment.

Puncture wound

A puncture wound is caused by penetration by a sharp object, such as standing on a nail, or a thorn in the leg. These wounds may often appear small on the surface but could run deep into the underlying tissues, so should not be underestimated. Debris (e.g. a thorn) could be left inside the wound, which would then cause further problems. Puncture wounds are particularly serious if close to a joint or tendon, as they can puncture the synovial fluid capsule and potentially result in a life-threatening infection. Therefore it is important to call the vet out to thoroughly assess and clean the wound and give advice about any further treatment needed.

Open wound

An open wound could be a tear or a cut with straight edges. These wounds often bleed heavily and can involve deeper tissues, so a veterinary visit is always advised. They may need to be stitched.

Graze

A graze is a superficial wound where the top layer of skin has been removed as a result of friction. Grazes often contain debris such as grit or dirt, and will require a thorough surface cleanse. A vet will be needed for more serious grazes, e.g. caused by a horse falling on the road or on to concrete.

Bruise

A bruise can be found anywhere and can be caused by a trauma, such as a kick from another horse or by standing on a stone. The skin is not usually broken, but the underlying tissues and blood vessels could have been damaged, causing localised pain and swelling. The severity of the bruising will depend on the location as well as how big and deep the damage is. It is important to consider which structures underlie a bruise. If the wound is on a joint, on or near the eyes, tendons, or where bone is close to the surface, it is imperative to call the vet.

Lameness

Lameness is a common occurrence in horses and it is important to be able to recognise signs that a horse is lame. Some signs may be harder to see, but the most obvious ones to be aware of are:

- An abnormal stance such as pointing a foreleg.

- Not placing weight on a leg when standing. When relaxing many horses will rest a hind leg and this is normal, but the horse should stand equally on all four legs when alert.

- Reluctance to walk.

- Not placing weight fully on a limb when walking.

- Shuffling in walk, or a shortened stride length.

- Nodding the head when walking or trotting.

- An uneven rise of the hips when walking or trotting.

- An irregular rhythm of walk or trot.

If you suspect a horse may be lame you should report this to a senior staff member or, if one is not available, ask the vet for advice.

Colic

Colic is the general term given to abdominal pain or discomfort, and is the most common equine emergency and cause of death in horses. Therefore it is vital for horse owners or carers to be able to recognise the early signs of colic; calling the vet straight away will increase the horse's chance of recovery.

Signs

The most common and important signs are:

Restlessness or agitation

- Repeatedly attempting to lie down.

- Frequent rolling.

- Box-walking.

- Unexplained sweating.

Eating or drinking less than normal, or reduced droppings

- Eating or drinking less than normal or not eating or drinking at all.

- Passing fewer droppings than normal or not passing any.

- Changes to the consistency of droppings.

Abdominal pain

- Pawing at the ground.
- Kicking at the belly.
- Watching or looking at the flanks.

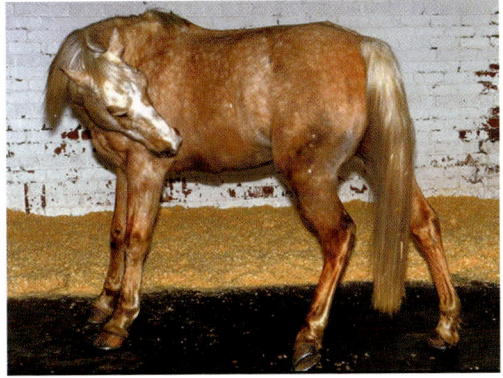

Flank watching.

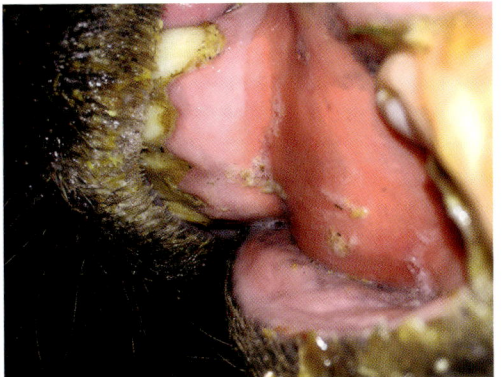

Dark red gums.

Clinical changes

- Increased heart rate.
- Rapid breathing rate.
- Changes in the colour of the gums.
- Reduced gut sounds or no gut sounds at all.

Tiredness or lethargy

- Lying down more than usual.
- Lowered head position.
- Dull and depressed.

The horse may display one or any combination of these signs, and each sign can vary in severity. Even the smallest change in behaviour could indicate a problem, so if you are in any doubt it is best to report it so that the vet can be called straight away.

Prevention

There are many potential risk factors associated with colic, but some simple steps will help reduce the risk of it occurring.

1. Follow the rules of feeding:

- Provide fresh clean water at all times.

- Ensure feed is correctly prepared, such as soaking sugar beet.

- Always weigh feeds.

- Feed little and often.

- Feed plenty of forage.

- Feed good-quality feeds.

- Make changes to feed and forage gradually.

- Do not work the horse straight after a bucket feed.

- Feed according to body weight, work done and temperament.

2. Routine health care:

- Follow a worm control programme.

- Ensure that the horse has regular dental checks.

3. Lifestyle and turnout:

- Make changes gradually — it is ideal to provide turnout all year round, however this may not always be possible in the winter months. If turnout has to be reduced, gradually increase the time spent stabled before stabling fully and, when reintroducing turnout, gradually increase the time turned out. This allows the horse time to become accustomed to the new routine and the reduced or increased amount of grazing.

- Do not graze the horse on sandy surfaces — ingesting sand particles can cause an accumulation in the gut, leading to colic.

- Ensure that the horse is not fed grass cuttings. It is easy for horses to gorge on a pile of grass clippings and as soon as the grass is cut it starts to ferment.

4. Exercise:

- Make gradual changes to the intensity and duration of exercise.

- Ensure that the horse is cooled off properly after work and before feeding.

First aid procedures

Cleaning a minor or superficial cut

The very nature of horses and the environment they live in means a wound is likely to need cleaning. Use plenty of clean and fresh water — either from a hosepipe or a bowl. Start by cleaning the area around the wound. If using the hosepipe, aim it above the wound so that a steady stream of clean water runs over it, ensuring you have enough pressure to wash any dirt out and away. If using a bowl of clean water, have several pieces of clean gauze swabs ready (cotton wool is not advised as it can leave fibres in the wound). Using a piece of gauze you should clean the cut from the middle outwards (wiping rather than dabbing), so any dirt is moved out of the wound. To reduce any contamination, it is best to use a clean piece of gauze for each wipe, and plenty of water.

Tubbing

Put very simply, tubbing is placing the horse's (clean) foot in a bucket of hot, salty water for veterinary purposes (e.g. in the case of a foot abscess). You will need:

- A shallow, clean bucket with no handle, or a clean rubber skip bucket — ideally kept specifically for this purpose.

- Boiling water that has been cooled slightly (still hot but cooled enough so that you can hold your hand in it).

- Epsom salts.

Put in water to a suitable depth, up to or over the horse's coronet band, but follow the instructions given by your supervisor as this will depend on the ailment (e.g. if an abscess is suspected the water should cover the coronet band). Epsom salts can then be added until no more can be dissolved and you start to get a sludge forming.

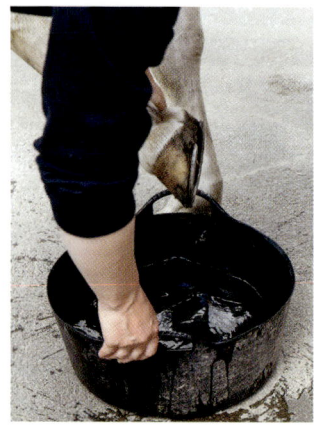  

i. You first need to make sure the foot is picked and scrubbed out, and the lower part of the leg is clean. Then, pick the horse's foot up and move the bucket into place.

ii. Steer the horse's foot into the bucket.

iii. Once the horse has placed his weight on to the foot, make sure you have sufficient depth of water.

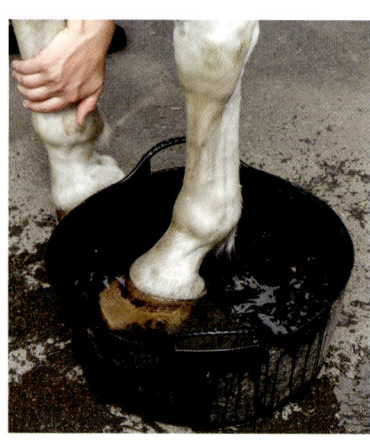

iv. You may need to hold the opposite leg up to prevent the horse from moving his foot out of the bucket. He will need to stand in the water for five minutes.

Cold hosing

In addition to being used to clean a wound, a hosepipe can be used to reduce heat and swelling. It is a good idea to introduce the hosepipe as a slow trickle, starting at the hoof until the horse is used to it, before moving up the leg and gradually turning up the pressure. The hosepipe should be held above the site of the wound or swelling, aimed down the leg so that the water runs across the area. If the flow is not aimed downwards it can sometimes 'bounce' back off the horse, rather than creating a steady stream. The duration of cold hosing can vary, so follow the vet's advice (although usually it will be roughly 5–10 minutes). Cold hosing will need repeating at intervals, but the vet will advise you.

Foot poultice

A foot poultice can be used when an abscess is suspected or there is a puncture wound to the foot, to draw out any infection. The poultice should be cut to a size slightly bigger than needed, to ensure the whole area is covered. If it is for the bottom of the foot, either cut a hoof-sized piece off a larger piece or use a pre-made hoof-shaped poultice. Poultices can be applied wet or dry. A hot wet poultice is more effective at drawing the infection out, but a dry poultice may be better if pus is flowing out freely already, or to dry the foot out after a wet poultice has been used. If using a wet poultice, put it in a clean bowl and cover with boiled water that has cooled enough to let you handle the poultice before gently squeezing out any excess water.

The poultice should be cut bigger than needed and placed with the shiny side facing away from the foot.

Before applying a poultice, the whole foot needs to be thoroughly cleaned out. Have everything you need ready within reach before you start.

Place the poultice on the foot with the shiny side away from the foot and then cover the whole foot with a layer of padding material (e.g. Gamgee) to provide a cushion, in particular covering soft tissue areas such as the heel bulbs. If you are applying a wet poultice, put a layer of plastic (such as a plastic bag without handles) over the top to help keep the moisture inside.

The poultice and padding then need securing with a self-adhesive bandage, which is tight enough to keep everything on but not so tight that it may damage the soft tissue areas. Finally cover the whole bandage in tape to help prevent the hoof from wearing through the bandage, particularly at the toe.

A poultice boot can be used over the top of the self-adhesive bandage to help keep the poultice secure, although this needs to be well-fitted so that it does not rub. The boot may also help protect the poultice and bandage from contamination.

General poultice

A poultice, in theory, can be used anywhere that you can secure it with a bandage, although it should not be used on or near a joint because of the risk of drawing out synovial fluid. The principles are the same as for applying a foot poultice — prepare the poultice as required. The area should be thoroughly cleaned before the poultice is applied, with the shiny side facing outwards, away from the horse. The area should be covered with a layer of padding, and an adhesive bandage used to secure it all. Take care that the bandage is not applied too tightly, which could restrict circulation and cause soft tissue damage.

Care of a sick or injured horse on box rest

A horse who is ill and on box rest needs to be kept warm and as comfortable as possible, and checked regularly throughout the day. Records of temperature, pulse and respiration should be kept, listing any observations made and treatments given so that any differences or abnormalities can be picked up easily. Gentle grooming can promote circulation and skin health, which can be affected by limited movement on box rest. Provided the horse's condition permits this, the feet should be picked out at least twice a day, to help keep them healthy. A deep bed should be provided, as long as the horse's condition does not mean that this would prevent him being able to move easily around the stable. The stable should be skipped out more regularly than usual to keep the horse's environment as clean as possible. A dust-free environment should be provided where viable (or at least dust kept to a minimum) because a horse is particularly sensitive to dust when his movement is limited. The stable should offer good ventilation, although not be draughty. Cobwebs should be removed from the stable, as these can harbour large amounts of dust. The water supply should be clean and changed regularly to encourage the horse to stay well hydrated, which is particularly important for maintaining normal health and digestion while on box rest.

Box rest limits the horse's movement and the opportunity for social interaction and stimulation. As horses are herd animals it is a good idea to provide companionship for them while on box rest, in the form of another horse nearby. It might be that a stable mirror does the trick, but it will depend on the individual horse. It is important to keep the horse as settled as possible during box rest, to avoid worsening any injury or illness.

Stable bandages

Stable bandages are used for a variety of reasons, including support, warmth and to minimise swelling. Padding (e.g. Fibregee or Gamgee) is used underneath non-elasticated bandages that are usually made of wool or man-made fibre with Velcro fastenings. They should always be applied in pairs to offer even support on both sides.

Putting on a stable bandage

Before you start, check that the bandages are clean and dry, and have been rolled up correctly, with the Velcro fastening in the middle and not around the outside. The bandage needs to be tightly rolled, making it easier to put it on. Using padding and bandages that are all the same will mean that each leg is bandaged with the same level of support and tension. The leg also needs to be clean before bandaging to avoid irritation or rubbing.

3 | Health and Welfare

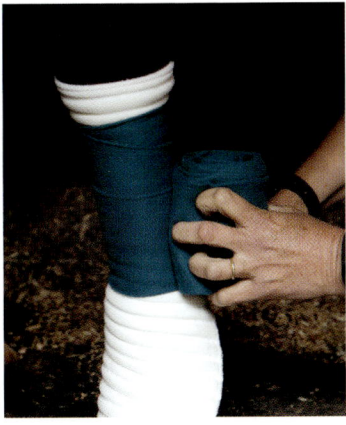
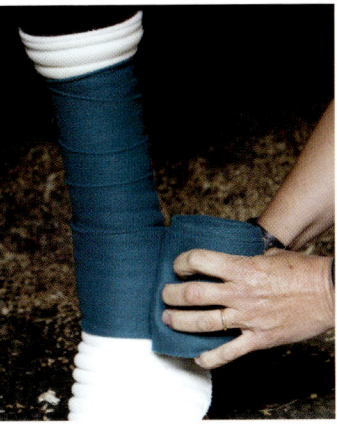

i. Place the padding around the leg, overlapping on the outside of the leg, with the outer overlap facing backwards. Wrap it closely around the leg to avoid any wrinkles or folds. The padding should cover from the knee down to just above the coronet band.

ii. Holding the padding in place, the bandage should start roughly a third of the way down the leg. Wrap it round the leg anti-clockwise on the left leg and clockwise on the right leg. This will make sure the tension is maintained against the bony front of the leg rather than against the tendons at the back of the leg.

iii. The bandage continues down the leg, with each layer overlapping the previous one by roughly half (this may vary slightly depending on the length of the bandage — a longer bandage may require more overlap and a shorter bandage may require less). The bandage should be tight enough to stay up and offer support, but not so tight that you cannot fit a finger comfortably inside it.

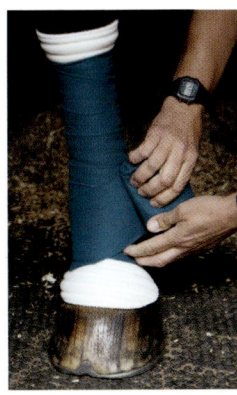
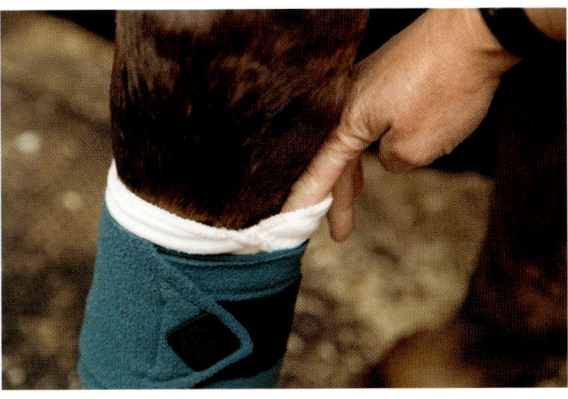

iv. The bandage should continue down the leg, wrapping round under the fetlock, before going back up to just under the knee. The overlap and tension should stay constant throughout the bandage, and take care to avoid any wrinkles or folds in the padding or bandage. The Velcro should ideally be secured on the outside of the leg, facing toward the back of the horse.

v. When you have secured the bandage with the Velcro, check it for tension and positioning. If it is not as you would like it, remove the bandage and start again rather than leave one on that is going to cause problems.

Putting on a stable bandage.

Removing a stable bandage

When removing the bandage, unfasten the Velcro before unwrapping the bandage by passing it from hand to hand, gathering it in a ball as you go. It is not safe or time-efficient to try to roll the bandage as you remove it. Re-roll the bandage once it has been removed, provided it is still clean. Do not reuse dirty padding or bandages, as this can irritate the horse's legs.

Consequences of poor bandaging

Poor bandaging can cause significant problems, as well as impacting on the horse's comfort. Too tight a bandage will restrict the circulation and could injure the leg (particularly the tendons). A bandage that is too loose will not provide sufficient support, could slip down the leg (causing further problems if it bunches round the leg) or come off completely (which could cause further damage). Uneven tension will result in pressure points and could injure or damage the leg. If the padding comes too low down and touches the floor the horse might stand on it when moving or getting up or down, which could again cause injury.

Summary

- Worm control involves good pasture management, carrying out worm egg counts and tapeworm testing, and following a recommended worming programme from a vet or SQP.

- Wormer should be administered carefully, following the instructions on the packaging and dosing according to the horse's weight. It is important that the horse receives the full and correct dose.

- Horses should be vaccinated against equine influenza and tetanus annually.

- Horse's teeth should be checked and rasped every 6–12 months.

- The horse's feet should be trimmed and/or shod every 4–6 weeks.

- It is important to be able to recognise signs of ill health and know when to call the vet.

- The normal TPR of a healthy horse is: temperature 37.5–38.5°C, resting pulse rate 28–44 beats per minute, resting respiration rate 8–16 breaths per minute.

- There are four types of wounds — puncture wounds, open wounds, grazes and bruises.

- Use plenty of clean fresh water when cleaning a superficial cut, using a gauze swab to wipe from inside to outside of the cut.

- It is important to be able to recognise signs of lameness, such as an abnormal stance, not weight-bearing on one leg, reluctance to walk, not fully weight-bearing when in walk, shuffling in walk, a shortened stride length, nodding of head in walk or trot, an uneven rise of hips in walk or trot, an irregular rhythm in walk or trot.

- For more information on the signs of colic, please refer to the REACT leaflet, which is available on the BHS website.

- There are different treatments that can be used to treat minor injuries such as tubbing, cold-hosing and poulticing.

- Stable bandages can be used to provide warmth and support and reduce swelling.

- Poor bandaging can injure or damage the legs, restrict the blood supply or cause discomfort to the horse.

TRAINING TIPS

1. If you get the opportunity, assist or observe at veterinary or farrier visits.

2. Offer to help when it is worming time on the yard.

3. Watch a variety of horses' movement — a sound horse can allow you to see 'normal' movement, and a lame horse can show you 'abnormal' movement.

4. Practise putting on stable bandages and ask an experienced person to check them, until you are confident you can put them on correctly.

Chapter 4

Horse Anatomy and Physiology

Key organs

The digestive system

Major bones of the skeletal system

Summary

Complete Horsemanship Volume 2

Horse Anatomy and Physiology

Anatomy is the study of parts of the body. Physiology explains how the parts (systems) work together in harmony. Learning about anatomy and physiology helps us understand how our horses function so we can get the best from and do the best for them. (Photo: Matthew Roberts).

There are eleven interrelated systems of the horse. For ease of understanding, the systems are generally divided up and explained in 'compartments'.

You will learn more about each of them as you develop your knowledge and will be able to:

- Identify the location of key organs.

- Describe the function of the digestive system.

- Identify the main bones of the skeletal system.

Key organs

The heart

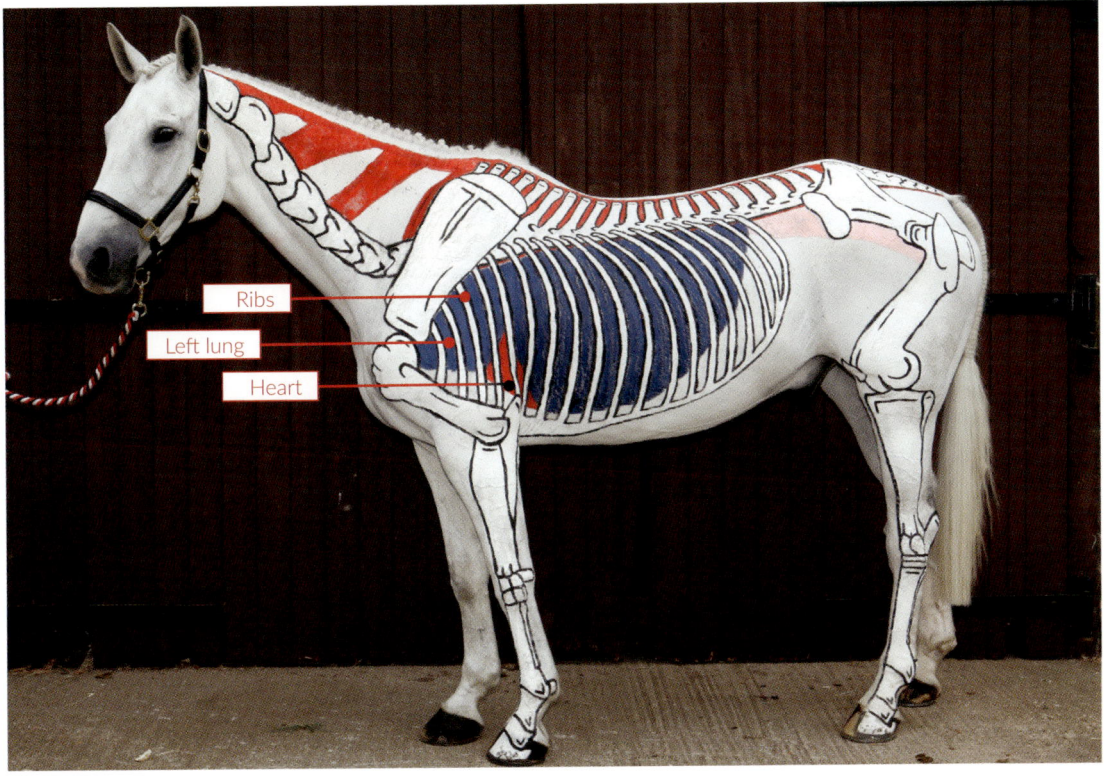

The heart, which is the powerhouse of the circulatory system, is located between the lungs to the left of the chest and within the protective walls of the rib cage. (Photo: Gillian Higgins).

- The heart is a cardiac muscle weighing approximately 4.5kg (10lb).

- The main function of the heart is to pump blood around the body.

- Resting heart rate in a horse is between 28 and 44 per minute (bpm) although, as with people, this varies.

- The heartbeat can increase up to around 200bpm during strenuous exercise.

Note: it is useful to practise using a stethoscope to locate the heart and to become familiar with counting the heartbeat.

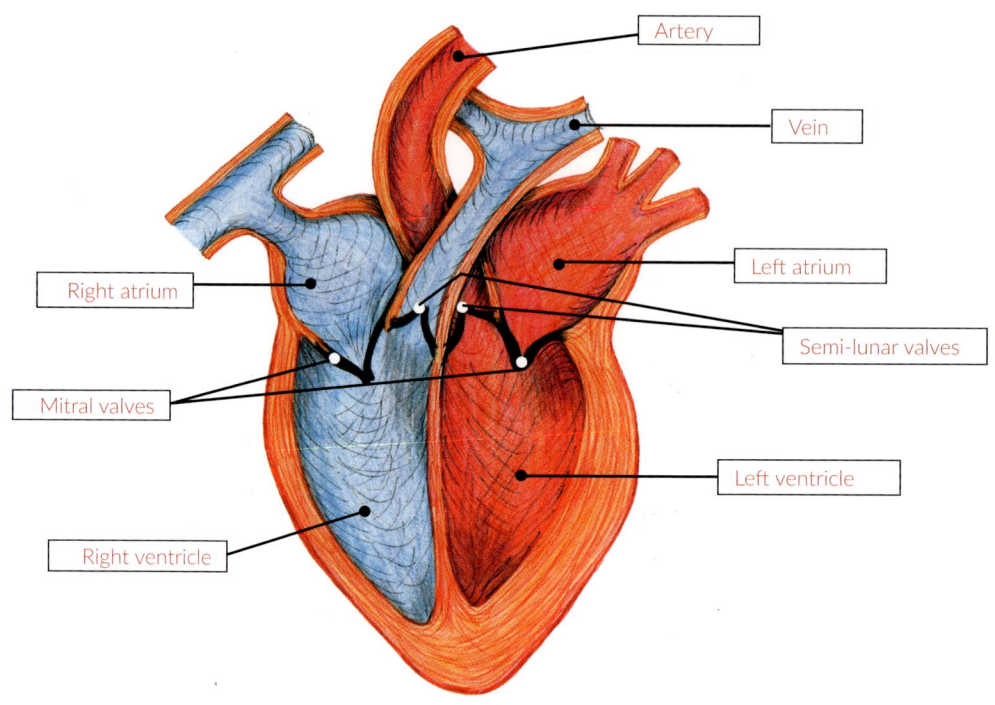

The heart, is divided into four parts. The top two parts are the right atrium and left atrium. The bottom two sections are the right and left ventricles. (Illustration: Gillian Higgins).

You will learn much more about the how the heart works when studying the circulatory system by reading about this in more depth in *Volume 3* of *Complete Horsemanship* but in brief its function is to pump oxygen-rich blood taken from the lungs around the body and return blood laden with carbon dioxide to the lungs to be exhaled.

The lungs

The horse breathes by inhaling oxygen into the lungs. This is then absorbed into the blood, pumped around the body by the heart, returned to the lungs and exhaled as carbon dioxide. This is known as gaseous exchange.

- The lungs are the largest organ in the body.

- The lungs fill the thorax — a large cavity enclosed by the ribs, sternum, spine and diaphragm.

- The diaphragm is a forward-facing bowl-shaped structure that separates the chest and abdomen.

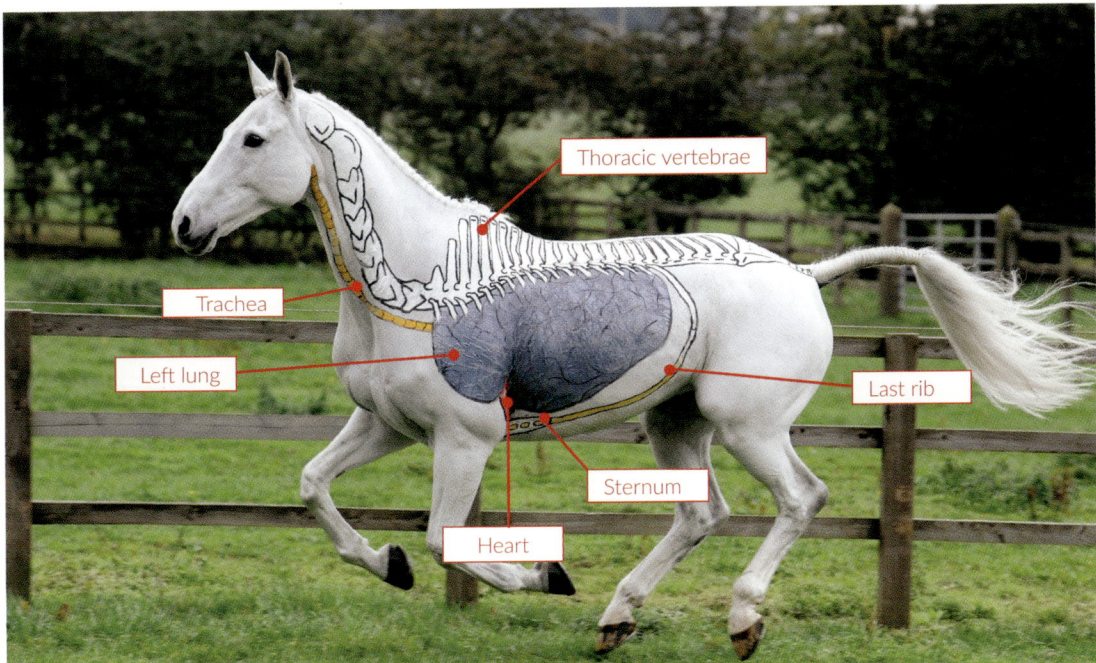

The lungs are part of the respiratory system and are responsible for processing air. They are larger than often realised and are located within the thorax in front of the last rib. (Photo: Matthew Roberts, taken from Horse Anatomy for Performance *by Gillian Higgins).*

- At rest the horse breathes air into the lungs at 8–16 breaths per minute. This can increase significantly as the horse exercises!

- If human lungs were to be spread out they would each cover the size of a tennis court. Horses' lungs are larger!

The kidneys

- Each kidney weighs about 700gm (25oz) and is approximately 15cm (6in) in length.

- Each kidney is protected by a 'kidney capsule' of tough fibrous tissue.

- The main function of the kidneys is to cleanse the blood, remove toxins and excrete liquid waste as urine.

- The horse needs to drink plenty of water for the kidneys to work well.

Many people think the kidneys are both situated just behind the saddle. Anatomically that is not completely accurate as their actual location is partly under the thoracic spine.

Complete Horsemanship Volume 2

The kidneys form part of the urinary system. The right kidney is located beneath the ribs of the last two thoracic and first two lumbar vertebrae. (See the diagram in the section on the skeletal system later in this chapter). The left kidney is slightly further back beneath the last rib and the first few lumbar vertebrae. (Photo: Gillian Higgins, taken from *Horse Anatomy for Performance* by Gillian Higgins).

The digestive system

- The horse's stomach is small — about the size of a rugby ball. It is located within the abdomen slightly to the left.

- It is because the horse has a very small simple stomach and because he is a 'trickle feeder' that he needs to have continuous access to grass or hay.

- If he is having 'hard feed' he needs to have two or three small feeds per day rather than one large one.

- The large intestine is very large and heavy and fills the abdominal cavity.

- The strong spine evolved partly to support the weight of the heavy digestive system.

The horse is a browsing herbivore. Left to himself he will graze for about 16 hours per day. (Photo: Gillian Higgins).

The function of the digestive system is to take in, break down and digest food, absorb the nutrients (goodness) and expel the waste. (Photo: David Higgins).

Mouth and teeth

Strong lips sort through and grasp the food, which is then sheared by the incisor teeth. The food is then moved further back in the mouth where it is chewed in an elliptical (circular type) motion by the premolars and molars, mixed with saliva, then swallowed.

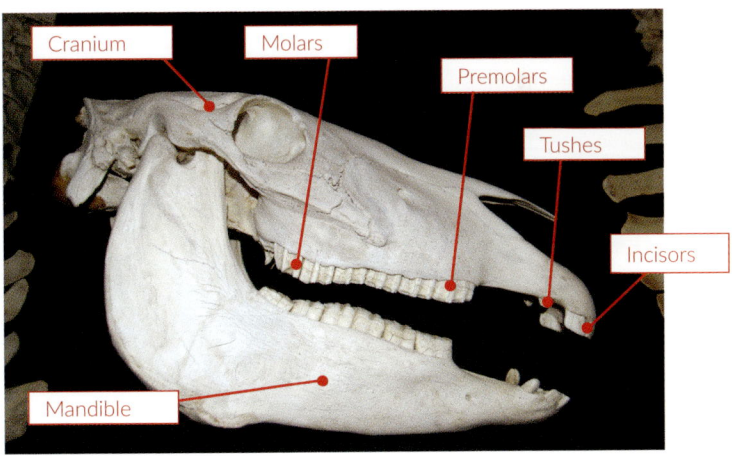

Horses usually have between 36 and 42 teeth. (Photo: Gillian Higgins).

Saliva

Unlike human saliva, horse saliva does not contain enzymes! This means that the only form of digestion that occurs in the mouth is mechanical (broken down by chewing).

Oesophagus

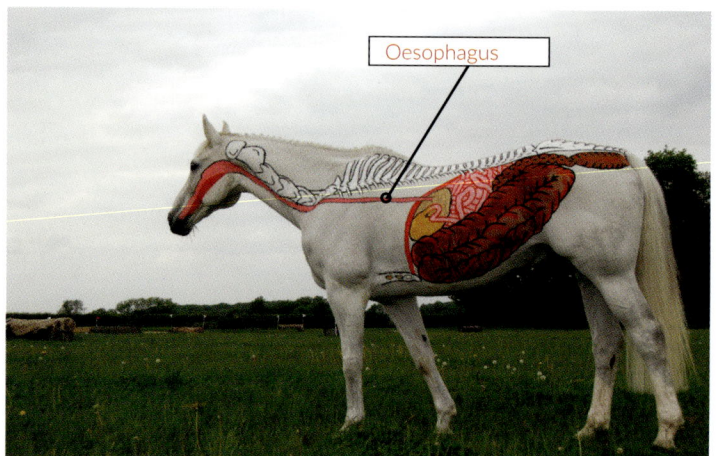

Food is propelled through the oesophagus to the stomach by strong waves of muscular contractions known as peristalsis. This process occurs throughout the digestive system. (Photo: Gillian Higgins, taken from Horse Anatomy for Performance by Gillian Higgins).

Stomach

Because the horse's stomach is so small (about the size of a rugby ball), he is only able to process small feeds. If feeds are too large, undigested food will pass out of the stomach after about 20 minutes. This is very wasteful both in terms of utilising the goodness, and cost. It also means the digestive process, which should take place in the stomach, has to be dealt with in the small intestine.

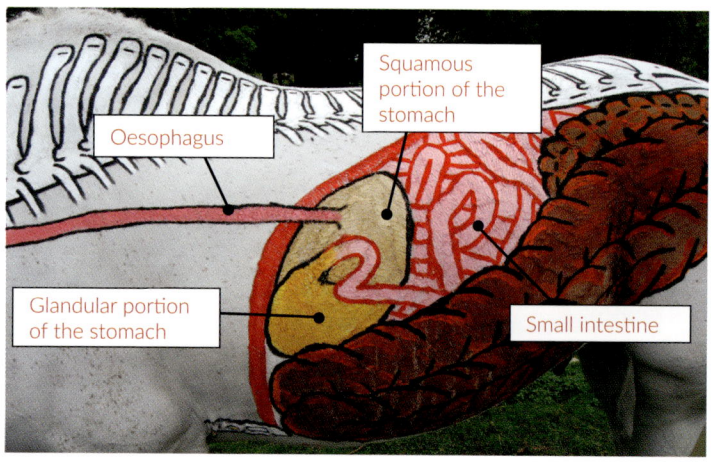

The stomach, which is located within the abdomen, is divided into two parts. It works best when there is a constant flow of food passing through it. Food remains in the stomach for about 2 hours. (Photo: Gillian Higgins).

> **Useful tip**
>
> *We are generally taught that horses should not be ridden on a full stomach. But, nor should they be ridden on an empty stomach! The reason for this is that if the stomach is empty the hydrochloric acid that is continually produced in the lower glandular section can 'splash' up on to the top part of the stomach. This can cause ulcers! The way to avoid this is to feed a handful of hay or chaff before riding.*

Small intestine

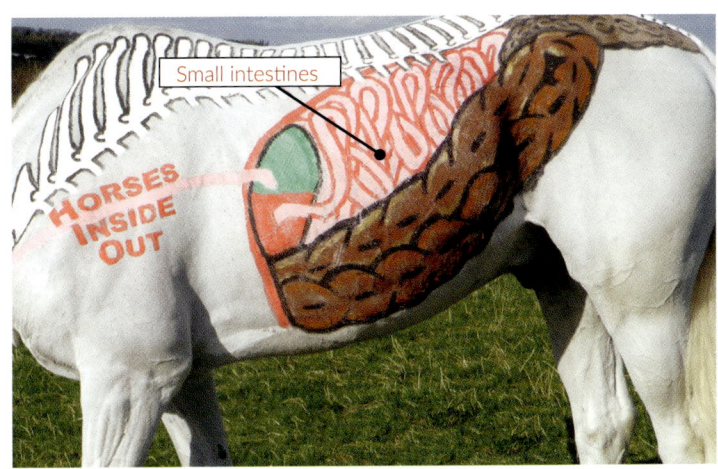

The small intestine is approximately 21m (68ft) long. Most of the digestion (breaking down of the food by enzymes) and absorption of nutrients occurs here. Food stays in the small intestine for about 90 minutes before it passes into the large intestine. (Photo: Gillian Higgins).

Large intestine

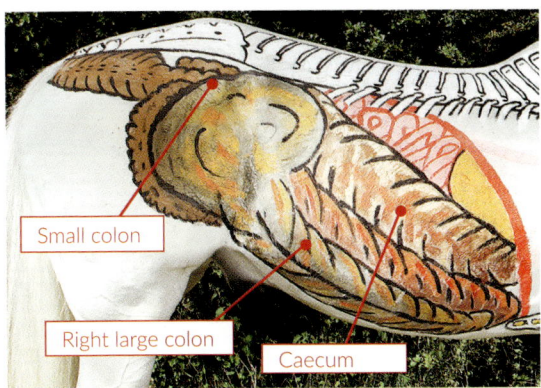
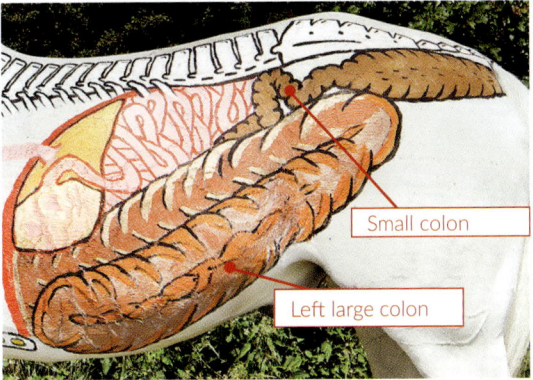

The large intestine, which forms part of the hind gut, is very large and very heavy. It is approximately 8m (26ft) long, forms 60 per cent of the digestive tract and accounts for about one-third of the horse's body weight. It is divided into three sections; the caecum, large and small colons. (Photos: Gillian Higgins, taken from Horse Anatomy for Performance by Gillian Higgins).

The hind gut, from which the horse absorbs most of his energy, is where the bulk of digestion takes place. It is the most important part of the digestive system. Hind gut digestion is performed by billions of micro-organisms, friendly bacteria and protozoa. Without them the horse would not be able to digest and absorb cellulose, the tough insoluble carbohydrate present in grass, hay and roughage, which is the main fuel for survival and performance.

Because of the length and all the folds of the large intestine, food can take several days before it passes into the rectum, forms balls of faeces and exits through the anus.

Note: The twists of the hind gut can result in an accumulation of undigested food, which can lead to a blockage in the intestine. This is one of the causes of colic.

Major bones of the skeletal system

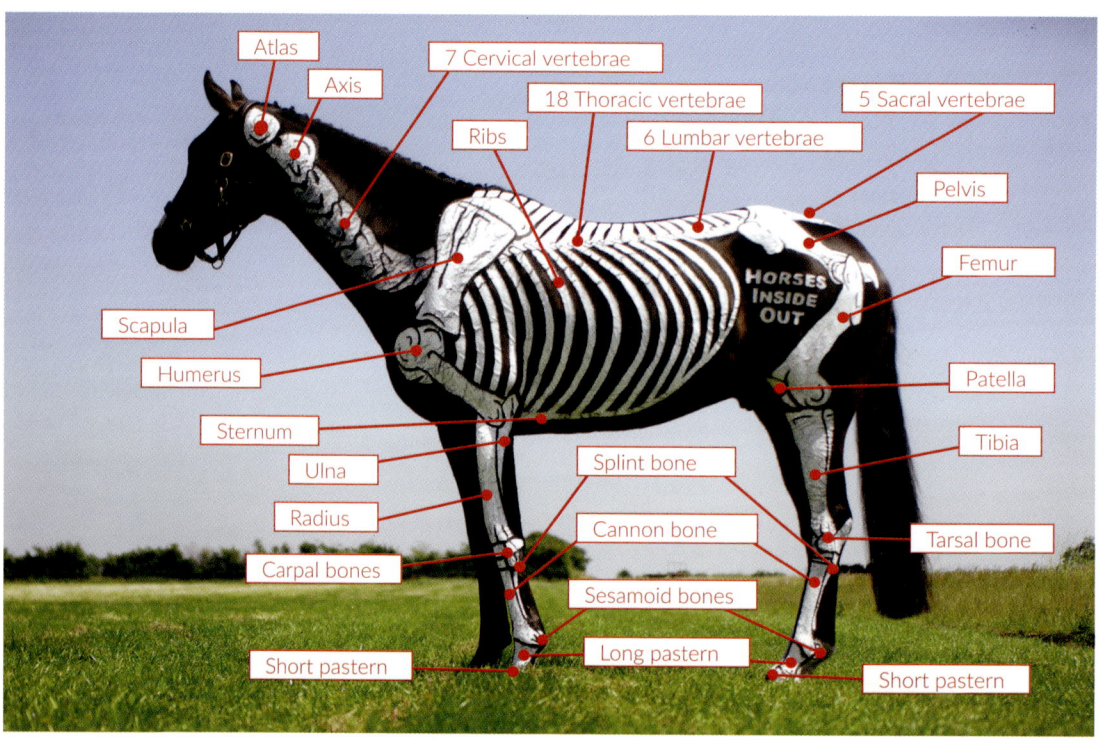

The skeletal system provides a strong framework that supports and shapes the body. You can see the position of some of the major bones in this photo. (Photo: Gillian Higgins).

The skeleton consists of approximately 205 bones. It is divided into two parts:

1. The axial skeleton, which includes the skull, the vertebrae of the spine from the skull to the tail, the sternum and the ribs.

2. The appendicular skeleton, which consists of the forelimbs from the scapula to the hoof and the hind limbs from the pelvis to hoof.

Types of bone

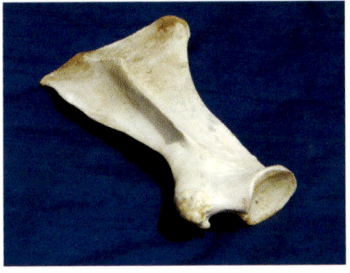

The flat bones, which include the scapula, skull, pelvic bones and ribs, have broad, flat surfaces to enclose and protect the organs and provide a large area for muscle attachment. (Photo: Gillian Higgins).

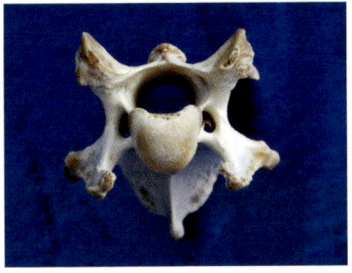

The spinal column is made up of irregular bones, as you can see in more detail below. (Photo: Gillian Higgins) .

Short bones are strong and compact and are found in the short pasterns, knee and hock. (Photo: Gillian Higgins).

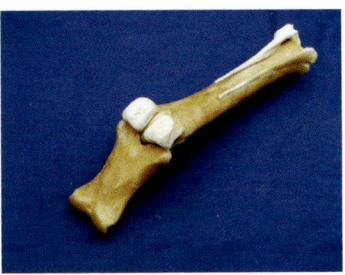

Sesamoid bones lie within the tendons and ligaments to add strength. A good example is the navicular bone in the hoof. (Photo: Gillian Higgins).

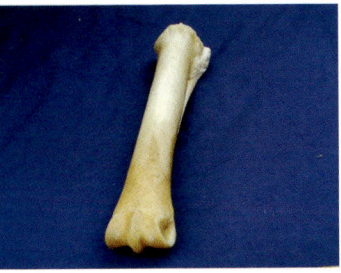

Long bones act as levers and have joint surfaces at either end. They are found in the appendicular skeleton. Examples are: the femur, radius and ulna, humerus and cannon bones of the lower leg. (Photo: Gillian Higgins).

Bones come in a variety of different shapes and sizes, as shown in the following photos.

The skull

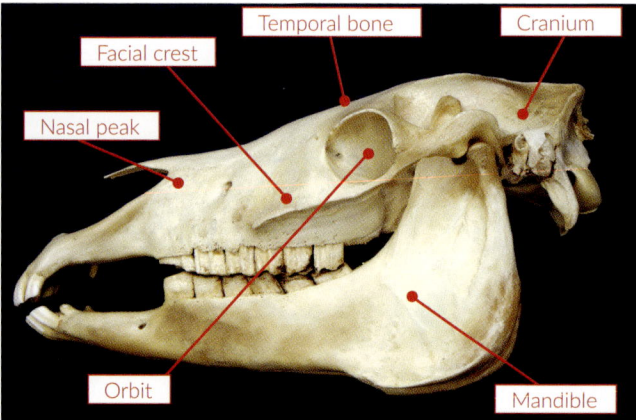

The skull, which is made up of thirty-four flat and irregular bones, provides protection for the brain, eyes, inner ear and nasal passages. The skull also houses the teeth, forty in a male horse and between thirty-six and forty in a mare. The poll is the highest point of the skull and it is attached to the cervical vertebra at the atlas, which is the first bone of the cervical vertebrae. The wings of the atlas can be felt at the sides just behind the ears. (Photo: Gillian Higgins).

The spine

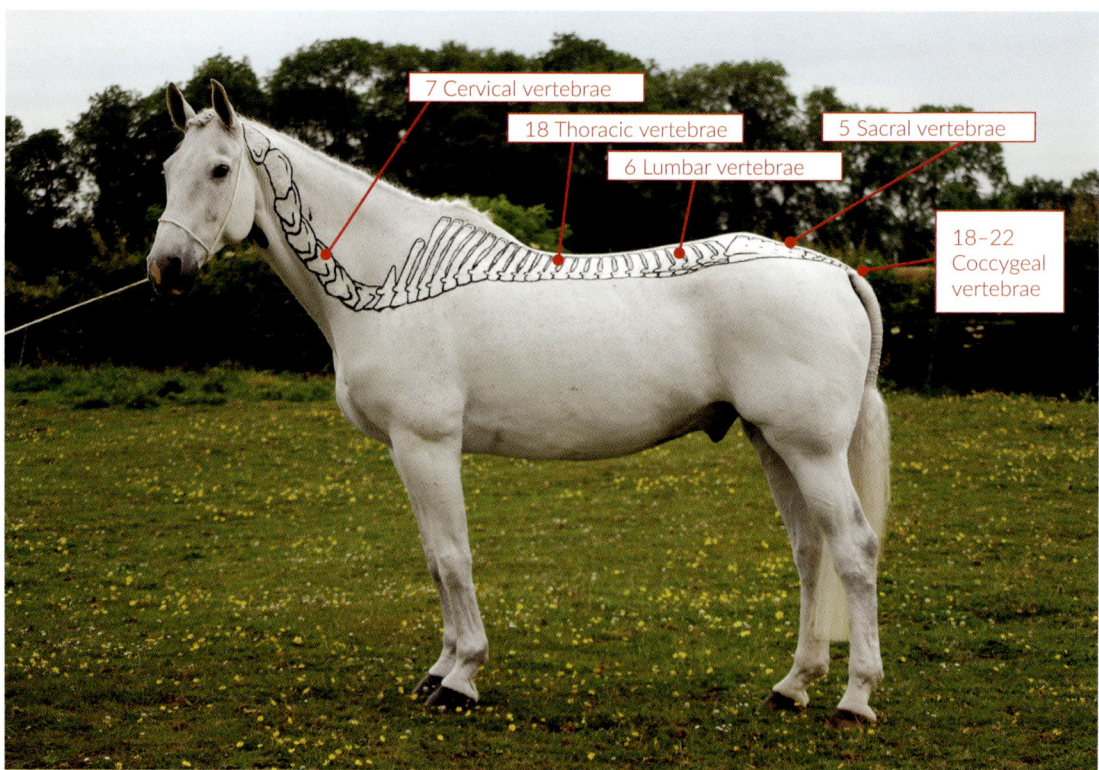

The spine is made up of irregular bones. Here you can see the different sections. The spinal cord, which carries messages between the brain and the rest of the body, runs through a hole in each vertebra. This hole is known as the vertebral canal. (Photo: Gillian Higgins).

The cervical or neck vertebrae are compact and allow the horse to bend his head around towards his body. They are situated lower within the neck than many people think. The area between the cervical vertebrae and the topline is filled with the muscles and ligaments essential for supporting the heavy head.

The thoracic vertebrae have long extensions (spinous processes) protruding upwards. You can feel them if you run your finger along the midline of the horse's back. These spinous processes provide areas for muscle and ligament attachment. Ribs emerge from between the bodies of adjacent thoracic vertebrae. This is the area on which we sit. There is very little movement between these vertebrae.

The lumbar vertebrae, which are located just behind the saddle, form the least flexible area of the back. These vertebrae are not supported by ribs, but are characterised by wide bony projections (transverse processes) that extend from the side of the vertebrae and add extra stability.

The sacrum consists of five bones (sacral vertebrae) fused together. They function as one bone and are immensely strong. They provide the attachment point that binds the pelvis and hind limb to the spine.

The coccygeal vertebrae (that form the skeletal tail) consist of between eighteen and twenty-two cube-shaped bones. Although the spinal cord peters out after the sacrum some nerves do continue into the tail, allowing the horse to carry and swish it.

Between the last lumbar and first sacral vertebra is a hinge joint. This is known as the lumbosacral junction. It is the most flexible part of the spine after the neck and tail and is the joint that allows the horse to round his back, and bring his hind legs well under in canter, gallop, in collected dressage movements and while jumping. (You can see it at its most extreme in the sliding Western halt.)

The forelimb

The forelimb of the horse consists of:

- *The scapula* is a large, flat bone that is an important area for muscle attachment. It has an important role in moving the forelimb and must not be restricted. Because of the way it moves it is important that at least two fingers can be inserted between it and the point of tree of the saddle.

- *The humerus* is one of the strongest bones in the body.

- *The radius and ulna*, which join with the humerus to form the elbow joint.

- *The cannon bone* is the main bone below the knee.

The hind limb

The hind limb is the powerhouse of the horse. It is made up of a series of large, strong bones. It consists of:

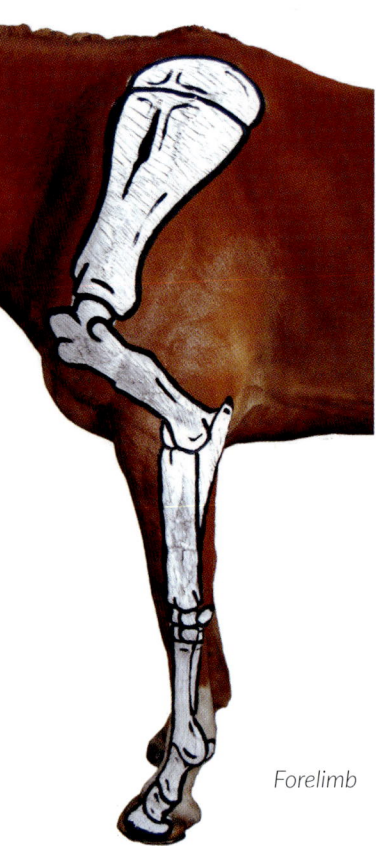

Forelimb

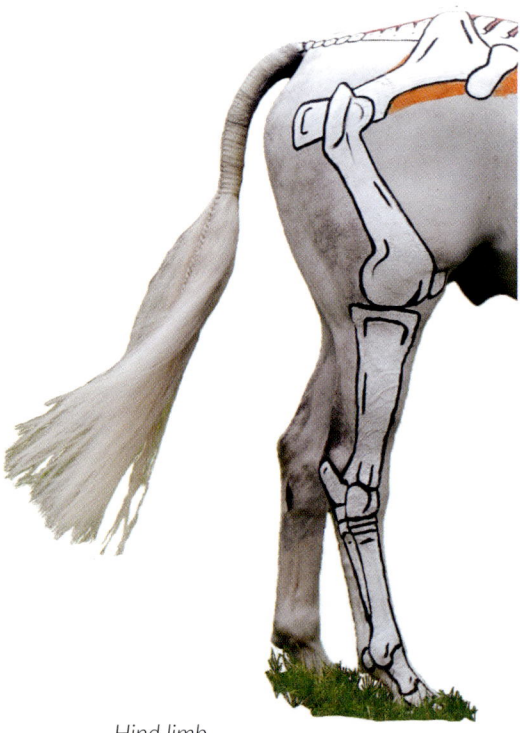

Hind limb

- *The pelvis* is an odd-shaped bone that forms the highest and widest points of the main skeleton, which can easily be felt. The widest points of the pelvis are known as the false hips (the actual hip is much further back).

- *The femur* is the strongest and heaviest bone in the horse.

- *The tibia* meets the femur at the stifle joint.

- *The patella* is equivalent to the human kneecap and can easily be felt.

- *The cannon bone*, as in the forelimb, is the main bone below the knee.

Note: It is important to practise identifying these bones on a live horse.

Summary

- Anatomy is the study of the parts of the body.

- Physiology explains how the parts work together.

- The heart pumps blood around the horse's body.

- The lungs process the oxygen breathed in.

- The kidneys cleanse the blood, remove toxins and excrete liquid waste.

- The digestive system is made up of: mouth and teeth, oesophagus, stomach, small intestine, large intestine, rectum and anus.

- The horse's skeleton is made up of 205 bones.

- The axial skeleton refers to the skull, vertebrae, sternum and ribs.

- The appendicular skeleton refers to the forelimbs from scapula to hoof and the hind limb from pelvis to hoof.

TRAINING TIPS

1. Practise locating and naming the key organs and main bones of the horse on diagrams and then try to locate them on the horse.

2. Practise labelling the bones on a horse using sticky labels.

3. Try carefully to feel the outline of bones such as the scapula, spine, pelvis, and the bones in the legs. They are usually easier to find on finer types of horse.

4. Observe or assist with vet visits and, if appropriate, ask to listen through the stethoscope if the vet is checking the heart or listening to the gut sounds.

This chapter has been written by Gillian Higgins, anatomist, sports and remedial therapist, anatomical artist, BHS senior coach and author. If you have enjoyed this introduction to anatomy and physiology visit www.horsesinsideout.com to look at the bookshop and the 'what's on?' page.

Chapter 5
Feeding

Weight estimation

How much to feed/energy requirements

What to feed

Monitoring diet for effectiveness

Summary

Weight estimation

Condition scoring

The aim of any feeding plan should be to keep the horse at the correct body weight. To evaluate a horse's weight, start by visually assessing the parts of the body that change when there is too little or too much body fat. This method is sometimes known as fat or condition scoring and is used widely by vets, nutritionists and researchers. For each part of the body they will give a score from one to five (one signifying no fat, five being lots of fat), then use this as a picture of how close to ideal body weight the horse is.

Start by observing and feeling the following body areas; is the horse too thin, too fat or hopefully just right?

Back (where a square numnah would sit). For an ideal body weight, you should not be able to see the horse's ribs, but you should be able to feel them if you run your hand gently over them. A fat horse's withers and spine will be hidden under fat and you may see a gutter along the spine.

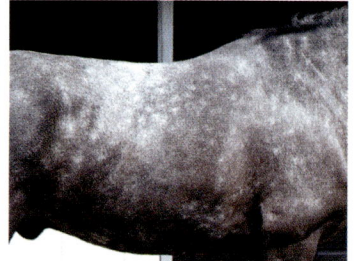 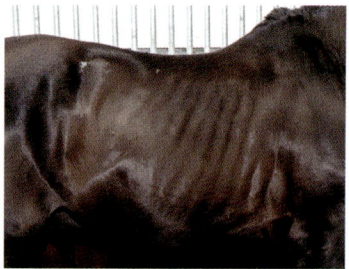 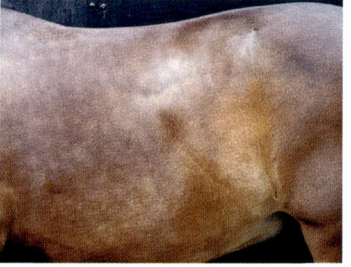

Horse's back at ideal body weight.   *Horse's back when too thin.*   *Horse's back when too fat.*

Neck (particularly the top of the neck or crest). At ideal weight the neck should be well covered and firm to the touch. The topline should be even, with no bulging up or out. Take care not to confuse a very fat crest that is solid to the touch with a correctly muscled one.

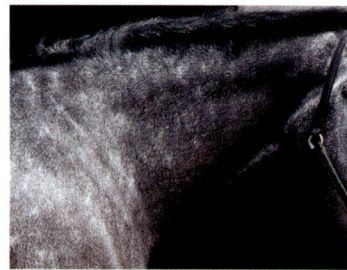 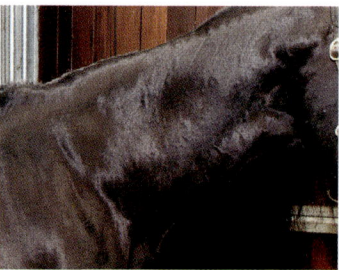 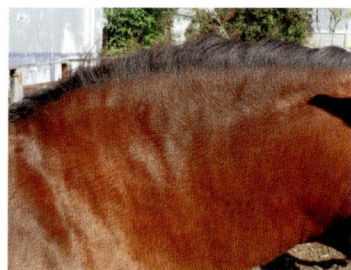

Horse's neck at ideal body weight.   *Horse's neck when too thin; the topline may look sunken.*   *Horse's neck when too fat; the crest may bulge up and out.*

Quarters (it's important to look from the side and from behind). The quarters should be well covered and you should not see any parts of the pelvis through the skin. You should be able to feel these bony points just under the surface.

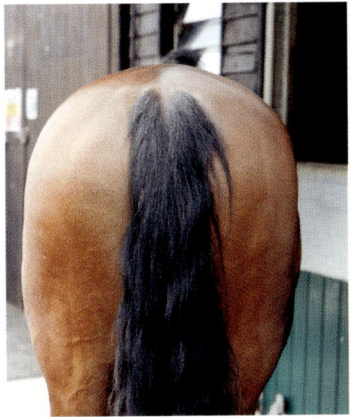
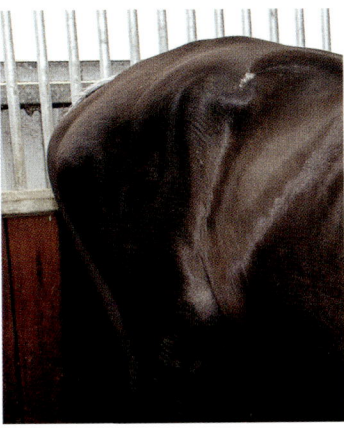
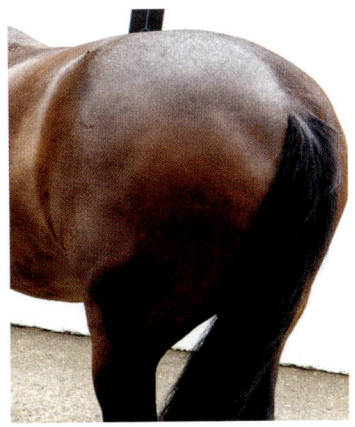

Horse's quarters at ideal body weight.

Horse's quarters when too thin; the backbone is obvious and the flesh on either side looks sunken.

Horse's quarters when too fat: the backbone is hidden, with an obvious gutter and the flesh either side is bulging. The pelvis can't be easily felt under the skin.

Assessing weight

Once you have established whether the horse is too thin, too fat or just right, it is important to weigh or estimate his weight. By knowing the weight you can accurately work out how much to feed, monitor weight loss or gain and work out correct doses of wormer, medication or supplement. There are several ways this can be done.

Weighbridge/scales

The best and most accurate method is to stand the horse on a set of scales in the same way you would weigh yourself. Some large yards and most veterinary hospitals have weighbridges that are really just very large scales that the horse walks on to and stands still so a reading can be taken. Many feed companies are willing to make yard visits and weigh horses in return for talking about their products. Some horses may take a little time to get used to them but the experience is very similar to going on to a loading ramp and it quickly becomes normal.

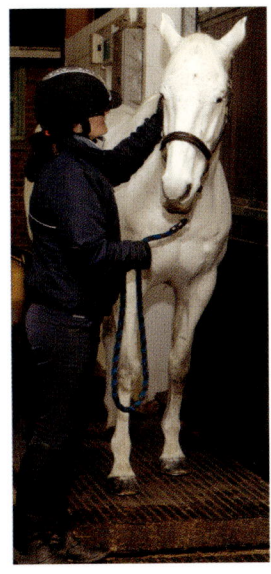

It is necessary that the horse stands still to take an accurate reading, so reassure him if he is a little fidgety.

Weigh-tapes

Most tack shops sell measuring tapes that are specially calibrated to calculate a horse's weight based on the measurement round his middle. Normally there is a separate scale for horses and ponies, so make sure you use the right one. The formulae used can differ so it's important to use the same one when you re-weigh. The tape should pass over the lowest point of the withers and, holding the tape snugly to the side, as close to the elbow as possible.

Formula

One drawback of using a weigh-tape is they are not always accurate for different breeds and builds as they just use one measurement. Breeds with a large middle in comparison to their height or length may not be well represented. Researchers have put together formulae that use an additional measurement lengthways to try to account for breed/type differences. Below is an example of one formula, although it may be sensible to chat with someone who has used this method before.

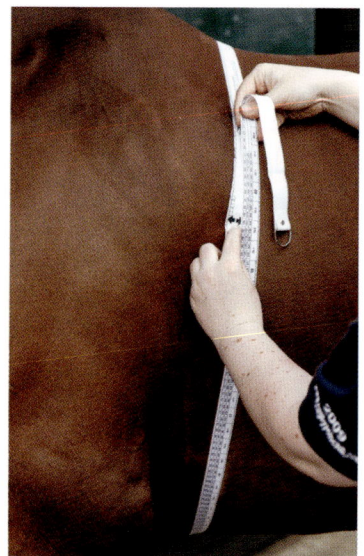

Make sure you follow the manufacturer's instructions as each tape may differ a little.

$$\text{Weight (kg)} = \frac{(\text{Girth})^2 \times \text{Length}}{11{,}877}$$

Where length is from the point of shoulder to the point of buttock. In this formula, both length and girth are measured in centimetres.

Accuracy

If using a weigh-tape simply to monitor how stable a horse's weight is, then the method chosen does not matter much so long as you use the same tape in the same position each time. The same goes for taking measurements using a formula. And when assessing weight by sight and feel, it is similarly important that the same person does it each time, as everyone will view things a little differently. It is a good habit to weigh and assess a horse's body condition regularly, so small changes can be picked up before they become a problem. Once a month would be a good starting point.

If weight is being calculated to work out wormer or medication doses then it is much more important to use scales for a highly accurate reading. As mentioned, weigh-tapes are known to underestimate weight for some types/breeds and thus you may under-dose for worming, with implications for the horse's health.

How much to feed/energy requirements

The starting point for working out how much to feed is to consider what the horse needs to stay at the correct body weight when doing nothing more active than moving around to graze. This is termed 'maintenance' and horses need to eat around two per cent of their body weight per day in fibre. Horses who are too fat or put on weight easily may need less than this, but no horse or pony should be fed less than 1.5 per cent of their body weight per day as fibre; any less could cause illness and gut problems like ulcers and colic.

It is important to point out that a horse kept in a stable with limited access to turnout will do less exercise than one able to move around freely, so the maintenance requirement of such a horse may be less than two per cent to avoid weight gain.

Besides having a sufficient volume of feed, all horses require a balanced diet that contains the correct nutrients, vitamins and minerals. This can be achieved by using a low-calorie balancer or a vitamin and mineral supplement to complement a forage-based diet. You may feed bagged feed that is already balanced, or combine it with a supplement as needed.

Approximate weight of different horses and ponies/feed needed per day if eating two per cent of their body weight

Type of horse	Approximate body weight	Feed needed (two per cent of body weight)
13.2hh Native pony	350kg (770lb)	7kg (15.4lb)
14.2hh Native x Thoroughbred	400kg (880lb)	8kg (17.6lb)
15hh Polo pony	450kg (990lb)	9kg (19.8lb)
15hh Cob	500kg (1,100lb)	10kg (22.0lb)
16hh Thoroughbred	550kg (1,210lb)	11kg (24.2lb)
16.2hh Sports horse	600kg (1,320lb)	12kg (26.4lb)
17hh Hunter	700kg (1,540lb)	14kg (30.8lb)

Once maintenance has been considered the next issue is what work the horse is doing and how likely he is to need extra energy in the form of calories. Defining work or exercise levels is tricky and people often overestimate the work their horse is doing, leading to an oversupply of calories and weight gain. The table below gives an overview of how different activities might be split into five different categories, where 'light work' is further split into three levels — low, medium and high. The table also gives an indication of how much trot, canter, jumping and fast work is anticipated in each category. This is very much a rough guide as each horse's work plan and routine will be different. If in doubt, opt for the lower level as the basis for feed requirements, and increase if needed. Horses in light work (low, medium and high) may well not need any feed in addition to forage. Those in medium work are likely to need some more energy-dense components added to their diet. High-energy fibres or some fat would be a good way to do this. Horses in hard work will almost certainly need additional energy-dense feeds; high-energy fibres, fats and cereals could all be used provided they are fed in small meals.

Analysis of work levels

Classification of Work	Number of hours worked per week	Work breakdown for an hour session (maximum time and percentage)	Example of activities	Riding school work per session (based on 1–3 hours daily 4–6 days a week*)
Light–low	1–3 hours	Up to 15 mins trot	Hacking Occasional schooling	
Light–medium	3–7 hours	Up to 25 mins trot Up to 10 mins canter Occasional jump	Hacking Occasional schooling Low-level dressage Low-level Riding Club/Pony Club Occasional showing	Beginner horses — mainly walk and low-speed trot, occasional canter

Classification of Work	Number of hours worked per week	Work breakdown for an hour session (maximum time and percentage)	Example of activities	Riding school work per session (based on 1–3 hours daily 4–6 days a week*)
Light–high	5–7 hours	Up to 30 mins trot Up to 12 mins canter Up to 3 mins poles/jumping	Faster hacking Regular schooling Low- to mid-level dressage Riding Club/Pony Club Low-level showjumping Schooling for polo Short sessions on the gallops Regular showing Endurance rides up to 40km (25 miles)	Intermediate horses — up to 30 mins trot, up to 10 mins canter, up to 10 mins poles/jump
Medium	5–7 hours	Up to 30 mins trot Up to 15 mins canter Up to 10 mins poles, jumping, fast work	High-level dressage (Advanced +), Riding Club/Pony Club Medium level showjumping (Newcomers +) Low- to medium level eventing (up to intermediate) Low-medium goal polo Early racing training Endurance rides up to 80km (50 miles)	Advance horses — equivalent of high-level recreation but more hours per week
Hard	5–9 hours	As medium plus up to 1 hour extra over the week of speed work; increase in galloping and jumping duration	High-level eventing High-goal polo Racing Endurance rides over 80km (50 miles)	

*Riding school: if the number of hours drops from 1–3 hours daily 4–6 days a week then the work should be dropped down a category. The type of work is very similar to that shown for a leisure horse; it is the number of sessions per week that causes it to be higher.

What to feed

The number of bagged feeds commercially available is colossal and it can be a challenge to select the right ones. It is helpful to understand different feeds and ingredients in terms of the calories or energy that they supply. You can broadly separate them into fibre feeds, cereals, fats and oils or commercially produced mixes and cubes.

Fibre feeds

Quality of fibre feeds

Feed/ingredient	Description	Energy or calories it provides (low-medium-high)	Might be useful for ...
Sugar beet	Highly digestible high-fibre by-product of sugar refining process. Comes as cubes, shreds or flakes; all MUST be soaked according to manufacturer's instructions before feeding to horses	High — but soaking means 'as fed' is about 80 per cent water and less energy-dense	• In small quantities good fibre/bulk source for any type of horse • In large quantities for horses in medium to hard work or those who need to put weight on • Older horses who can't eat long fibre
Alfalfa	Plant related to peas and beans (legumes), fed either as dried and chopped 'chaff' or as pellets. Also a good source of protein and some minerals	Medium	• Horses in light work-medium work • Part of the diet of horses in hard work

5 | Feeding

Feed/ingredient	Description	Energy or calories it provides (low-medium-high)	Might be useful for ...
Chaff/chop	Chopped dried fibre such as grass and straw. Often mixed with a little molasses or oil and may have extra vitamins/minerals added	Low — but can vary significantly dependent on type of fibre included — read the bag	• All horses to add bulk, help slow down rate of eating and hide supplements or medication
High-fibre nuts	Combination of a range of high-fibre, low-energy ingredients such as oat fibre, wheat feed, grass and straw	Low — but depends on company's formulation — read the bag	• All horses to increase fibre • Those who need a little more than grass and hay • Older horses who can't eat long fibre
Grass nuts	Grass harvested, dried and pressed into cubes	Low-medium (depends on grass used — read the bag)	• All horses to increase fibre • Those who need a little more than grass and hay (if using higher-energy grass nuts) • Older horses who can't eat long fibre

Fibre should always make up the biggest part of a horse's diet. For horses doing no work or leisure activities (light work) fibre alongside essential vitamins and minerals is often sufficient. When horses are doing medium work or struggle to hold their weight you may need to think about adding more high-energy fibre or add oil or cereals.

Fats and oils

Quality of fats and oils

Feed/ingredient	Description	Energy or calories it provides (low-medium-high)	Might be useful for ...
Oil	Variety of types – soya, corn, sunflower etc. Also found in high-oil pellets. Some horses may prefer the taste of one type to another	High	• Horses in medium to hard work or who need to put weight on
Linseed	Can be fed as extracted oil, pellets or meal	High	
Fish oil	Can be fed as liquid oil or a high oil supplement. As horses are naturally vegetarian, some people disagree with feeding them fish oils	High	

Fats and oils are a good way of adding energy to the diet with much less chance of horses becoming excitable than with cereals. They have the added benefit of improving the condition of the horse's skin and coat. Some oils such as linseed are high in omega-3, which has known health benefits. If you use large quantities of oil some vitamin E may need to be supplemented.

Cereals

Quality of cereals

Feed/ingredient	Description	Energy or calories it provides (low-medium-high)	Might be useful for ...
Barley	Needs to be treated before feeding to allow horse to use it fully (normally buy it treated – crimped, micronised, extruded, etc.): purchased as a 'straight'	High	• Horses in hard work or those who need to put weight on

5 | Feeding

Feed/ingredient	Description	Energy or calories it provides (low-medium-high)	Might be useful for …
Oats	Often cracked or crimped to allow the horse to use them fully, or can buy naked oats, which can be fed straight away: purchased as a 'straight'	High	• Horses in hard work or those who need to put weight on
Maize	Usually fed as part of a commercially available mix or cube in relatively small amounts; needs to be processed to help horse digest it fully	Very high	• Horses in hard work or those who need to put weight on
Peas/beans	Included as part of a commercially available mix or cube in relatively small amounts to provide protein; need to be processed to help horse digest them fully	High	• Found in small amounts in most commercial mixes

Cereals such as barley and oats should be used with care, as the starch they contain can be harmful to the digestive tract when fed in large quantities. They can make the pH of the gut more acidic, which can contribute to gastric ulcers, colic and laminitis. There are obviously situations where grass and hay may not provide enough energy on their own but, as a rule of thumb, it is much safer to use additional fibre-based feeds first (remember fibre feed can be high-calorie and high-energy too!). Oil is another good way of adding more energy to the diet before thinking about cereals. If feeding cereals, always continue to feed plenty of fibre, and the cereals should be split into several small meals to allow the horse's system to process them correctly and minimise the impact on gut health.

Commercially produced blends

To make life easy, many blended complete feeds are available, often named in a way that makes their function easy to understand. Common ones are:

- Cool or leisure — low-energy, high-fibre, low- (but not always) cereal.

- Competition — medium- to high-energy, dependent on the formulation.

- Conditioning — medium- to high-energy, dependent on the formulation.

- Senior — ranges in energy content. Will normally have vitamins and minerals balanced to suit the older horse's needs.

There are some important things to remember about ready-made feeds. First, always read the bag and ingredients list. Names may be a little misleading: just because a feed is named 'competition', does not mean it is suitable for any horse simply because he is doing a competition.

Feed bag labels list the ingredients contained within the feed. These feeds provide the correct levels of vitamins and minerals but only if you feed them at the quantities stated on the bag. If you are feeding less because your horse does not have such high energy needs, you may need to feed additional vitamins and minerals.

A range of feeds available on the market.

ANALYTICAL CONSITITUENTS		COMPOSITION	ADDITIVES (per kg)	
Protein	12.5%	Micronised Wheat, Nutritionally Improved Straw, Wheatfeed, Distillers' Grains, Micronised Soya Beans, Molasses, Soya Oil, Calcium Carbonate, Vitamins and Minerals, Calcined Magnesite, Sodium Chloride, ScFOS (Digest Plus prebiotic) 2.5g/kg, Grape Pip Solubles 6.5mg/kg	**Nutritional Additives**	
Oil	5.5%		**Vitamins**	
Fibre	9.0%		Vitamin A (E672)	12,500 iu/kg
Ash	6.0%		Vitamin D3 (E671)	1,500 iu/kg (as cholcaliferol)
Calcium	0.9%		Vitamin E (E306)	300 iu/kg (alpha tocopherol acetate)
Phosphorus	0.5%		**Trace Elements**	
Magnesium	0.3%		Iron (E1)	225mg (ferrous sulphate monohydrate)
Sodium	0.3%		Iodine (E2)	0.75mg (calcium iodate, anhydrous)
			Cobalt (E3)	0.30mg (cobaltous carbonate monohydrate)
		ZOOTECHNICAL ADDITIVE	Copper (E4)	40mg (cupric sulphate, pentahydrate 28mg, Copper chelate of amino acid hydrate 12mg)
		Saccharomyces cerevisiae sc47 (4b1702) 1.6 x 10⁹cfu/kg	Manganese (E5)	75mg (manganous oxide 53mg, Manganese chelate of amino acid hydrate 22mg)
			Zinc (E6)	130mg (zinc oxide 92mg, Zinc chelate of amino acid hydrate 38mg)
			Selenium (E8)	0.5mg (sodium selenite 0.3mg, Selenium enriched yeast (Sel-Plex®) 0.2mg)

An example of ingredients listed on a feed bag.

Before choosing one of these feeds you should ask how much energy the horse needs to stay at a healthy weight and perform his current work. Many older horses do not need a specialist 'senior' feed if they are healthy and maintaining their weight well.

Monitoring diet for effectiveness

Once a horse has his diet initially determined, it is important to monitor how effective it is. The easiest way initially is to measure the horse's weight and evaluate his body condition regularly, as described above. If the horse then loses or gains weight, the diet may not be quite correct. Horses all respond in slightly different ways and this is where feeding becomes an art, fine-tuning a basic feed plan into one that suits each horse.

Over or underfeeding your horse may also have an effect on his behaviour and temperament — it is always better to start with a high-fibre, low-protein diet until you know how he reacts to his feeding regime.

Factors to consider

Ingredients

Choosing the wrong feed ingredients for a horse may result in weight gain or loss.

Example 1 — A good doer in light work-high (see Analysis of work levels table, page 74–75) may put weight on despite being fed only a small amount of cool mix in addition to grass and hay. Although this does not appear to be a fattening or energy-dense feed, and the cool mix is primarily fibre-based, it may still provide excess calories for the horse's energy needs. Forage, plus a low-calorie vitamin and mineral balancer, may be the only feed he needs to stay healthy.

Example 2 — A horse who is hard to keep weight on through the winter is still not looking right despite being fed two bucket feeds a day containing a conditioning mix and some barley (in addition to grass and hay). It is possible that these energy-dense cereal feeds, while providing enough calories on paper, are giving the horse short bursts of calories that cannot be digested and used fully. It may be that, by reducing the conditioning mix and barley, and replacing them with energy-dense fibre such as sugar beet or some oil, energy would be released more slowly and more calories used to put on weight.

Another thing that must always be considered is the nutritional quality of grass and hay. These feeds can range from very low to very high energy content and sometimes, weight for weight, provide as many calories as a high-calorie concentrate mix. A fat horse left to graze round the clock on very high-energy grass will clearly put weight on.

Age

Age in itself may not make it harder to keep weight on a horse, but some older horses have dental problems that mean they can't chew and cope with long-fibre feed in the same way as younger horses. Similarly, there may be an underlying medical problem. If an older horse is losing weight it is always best to have the teeth and general health checked by a vet. Once the health status has been determined a change to the diet can be discussed.

Work

If a horse's workload changes it is essential to adjust the diet accordingly. If work decreases, less energy must be supplied or the horse will be likely to put on weight and may develop some unwanted behavioural traits. When increasing work, it is better to see how the horse responds before increasing or changing the diet, to avoid feeding unnecessary calories and wasting money.

Management

Depending on the time of year and the horse's home environment, more or fewer calories may be required to stay healthy. Cold weather requires more energy to stay warm and so extra food may be needed to maintain weight. By using rugs and shelter you can minimise the energy lost. Fibre feed helps keep horses warm since heat is released as a by-product of digestion. Diets high in fibre will keep horses warmer than those high in cereals. Horses who are not relaxed when stabled will use more calories through being alert and restless (they also spend less time eating). It's therefore important to find a calming environment for an excitable or nervous horse.

Medical issues

If there is no obvious reason for a horse losing weight then it is advisable to seek veterinary advice. Certain metabolic diseases and damage by intestinal worms can influence the ability to digest and use food efficiently. A horse who has a worm burden may lose weight despite being fed what should be enough good-quality food. Another major reason for

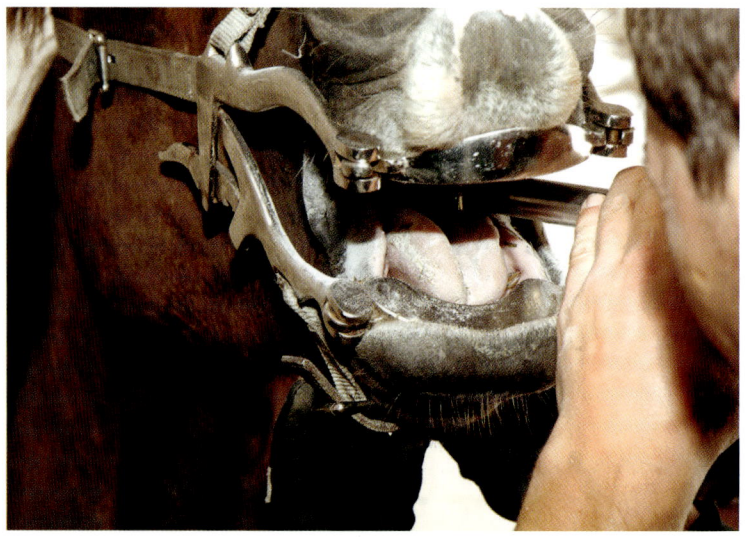

Your horse's teeth should be checked regularly for any problems.

inefficient food conversion is dental problems. Make sure the horse's teeth have been checked by a vet or a BAEDT-registered dental technician.

Individuality

Every horse is unique and the way horses digest and utilise feed varies. Feed two horses of identical size, build, type and workload the same diet and one may flourish while the other either loses or gains weight. Similarly, one horse may not tolerate a particular feed well and his behaviour may be affected. One size does not fit all when it comes to feeding horses and each horse should be monitored individually.

Summary

- The horse's digestive system works best with a steady stream of fibre, which starts breaking down in the stomach, continues in the small intestine where nutrients begin to be absorbed and finally undergoes fermentation in the large intestine by microbes to release and absorb remaining nutrients.

- It is important to know your horse's weight and body condition — scales or a weighbridge are the most accurate method, followed by formulae, then a weigh-tape.

- Weigh and fat score regularly to monitor changes.

- Horses need two per cent of their body weight for maintenance, plus essential nutrients, vitamins and minerals.

- Most leisure activities are classed as light work. Medium and hard work involve a high proportion of fast work and/or intensive jumping activity.

- When choosing feeds ask: 'How much energy (calories) does the horse need to maintain a healthy weight and do his work?' Then choose a feed that matches this need, while thinking about the health of his gut. Next monitor his weight and how he responds to see if it suits him.

- Always read feed bags as the energy/calorie content may not be what you expect.

TRAINING TIPS

1. Go to your local feed merchant and read lots of different feed bag labels; pay attention to how they are classified, then how much energy is actually in them, as well as reading the ingredient lists.

2. Try to assess the fat coverage on a number of horses and compare notes with someone more experienced.

3. If you have access to weighbridge or scales compare the real measurement with that of a weigh-tape and formulae for a number of horses. How accurate were the different methods?

4. Pick a horse on your yard, assess his body condition, find out how much work he is doing, then have a go at estimating how much and what type of feed would suit him. Compare this back to his normal diet and have a chat with the yard manager about any differences you find.

Chapter 6

Fitness Training

Reasons for improving fitness

Types of work

Factors to consider when working horses

Summary

Fitness Training

During your work you are likely to be involved with exercising horses to develop and maintain their fitness. Horses need to be properly prepared for the type of work expected of them; if they are not sufficiently prepared their performance will be affected. A lack of fitness also brings a much greater risk that they may injure themselves. Be aware of different types of work and surface conditions, and how these may affect the amount of effort the horse has to make. It is essential to be aware of the signs of when a horse is tired and needs a breather. In this situation you should always stop and either end the training session for that day or allow the horse time to see if he recovers before undertaking further training.

Reasons for improving fitness

Whether competing, working in a riding school or going out on a fun ride, horses need to be fit enough to carry out their work so they can perform at their best.

Inadequate fitness could lead to:

Risk of injury to the horse and rider. Tiredness can lead to a lack of coordination, which increases the chance of injury, particularly during faster work, jumping, work requiring frequent turning (e.g. mounted games or polo) and over varying terrain. Common injuries range from overreaches to tendon injuries, but there is also a risk to the rider — for example, a horse who becomes tired during a jumping session could refuse, peck on landing or fall.

Reluctance to work. A horse who is insufficiently fit for his work will struggle to perform. As a result he may become less willing and cooperative in his work.

Under-performing. An insufficiently fit horse will be unable to perform at his best, affecting not only his ability to compete but even the experience he may give a client during a lesson in a riding school.

Types of work

As part of your job you may be asked to exercise horses under the instruction of a senior staff member, perhaps as part of a horse's fitness programme. This may include hacking, lungeing, basic schooling or, in some cases, specific canter or gallop work. Before starting, remember to make general observations to check that the horse is in good health. If he shows any signs that he may be under the weather (e.g. not eating up, temperature, cough, nasal discharge, change in behaviour), working him could make his condition worse. In this situation you should always seek advice from a senior staff member before undertaking exercise.

At the start of any exercise session you will need to warm up the horse. This increases the blood flow around the body and allows the muscles to warm up, increasing the range of movement to prepare them for the work to be done and to reduce the risk of injury.

Horses should undertake a variety of work on a weekly basis. As well as preventing boredom, it can help to maintain soundness.

Hacking is an opportunity to unwind, whether it be relaxation between days of schooling sessions, or to let off steam and have a gallop. Hacking allows the horse to work over a variety of terrain, which helps coordination and balance. Riding up and down hills also builds up the muscles of his hindquarters, and is good for improving balance.

Schooling on the flat develops a horse's way of going, including suppleness, balance and responsiveness, and is the basis for most disciplines.

Some horses may no longer jump as a result of previous injuries, and some horses prefer not to jump. However, jumping is a valuable exercise even if the horse's competition specialty does not involve it. It provides variety, and can help develop suppleness and build strength in the hindquarters. Pole work can also be used during schooling sessions and is useful for improving coordination.

As well as providing variety, lungeing enables the horse to work without a rider. As lungeing mostly takes place on a continual circle, even without the weight of the rider it is hard work and 30 minutes is equal to approximately an hour of ridden work, so it is a time-saving method of exercise.

Some horses may not get the breadth of work described above, particularly some riding school horses. However, even there variety can be provided by hacking or varying their work to include a mixture of flat and jumping lessons, and lessons for novice or more experienced riders. In good weather and where facilities are available the location of lessons can also be varied (e.g. with some taking place in a field).

Factors to consider when working horses

General factors applicable to all

It's important to understand the factors that make work easy or hard for a horse:

Duration. Logically, 2 minutes trotting is easier than 5 minutes trotting.

Speed or gait. Usually the horse works harder the faster he is moving; gallop is harder work than trot. This is also true within a gait; if a steady canter becomes a fast canter, for example. The exception would be when a horse is schooling at a higher level, where a collected canter is harder work than a working canter.

Ground conditions. Softer ground is physically harder to work on than firmer ground, as you will have noticed yourself when running or walking on a beach. Bear this in mind, particularly when hacking and if the weather has been wet. In soft or boggy conditions, cantering over softer ground will be harder work, so take care and reduce the speed as there is a greater risk of injury to the horse. Similarly, some school surfaces can be deeper than others. Varying terrain and uneven surfaces also demand more coordination and greater effort from the horse.

Therefore, when introducing a horse back into work after some time off, it is usual practice to start with short walk hacks on roads or relatively firm, level bridleways. This involves a degree of concussion on the legs, and too much work on hard surfaces can jar the feet and joints and may cause damage to underlying structures. That said, lower-level concussion from roadwork can improve the strength of the horse's bones; this can be achieved by walking and short trots; five minutes of trot a day is sufficient to achieve this.

Inclines. Going uphill is much harder work for the horse than work on flat ground or riding downhill. Hill work can be used as part of a horse's fitness programme, and is useful for strengthening the muscles of the hindquarters as they push the horse uphill. Working downhill can also be harder than working on flat ground as the horse will have to use different muscles to maintain balance.

Weight. In most circumstances a horse will work harder carrying a heavier weight than carrying a lighter one. However, a horse will find it easier to carry a rider who is in balance compared to a novice rider of the same weight who has not yet established their balance.

Horses working up a hill.

Pattern of exercise. Some schooling exercises require a greater physical effort than others, e.g. frequent transitions between gaits are more tiring than staying in one gait. This is also true for transitions within a gait; any acceleration or deceleration will increase the effort required. Small circles require the horse to bend to a greater degree than large ones and thus greater physical effort. This should be considered particularly when lungeing the horse on a constant circle. Too small a circle may put undue stress on the horse; ideally aim for one of 18–20m in diameter (i.e. the horse should be around 10m from you). If your lunge line is too short to allow this, make sure you walk a small circle yourself.

Weather conditions. In hotter weather the horse will find work harder, but will need less time warming up physically. Similarly, riding into a strong wind can also be draining. In cold weather, allow a little longer for warming up as the horse will start colder.

Factors that may influence how an individual horse is exercised

Common factors include:

Overweight. The tendons and joints of an overweight horse will experience greater loading and may be at increased risk of injury when worked. Some lower-intensity work (e.g. walking on roads) until enough weight is lost is advisable. Other types of work then need to be introduced gradually. The feed should not be increased until the horse is working at a level where he definitely requires more food.

Underweight. An obviously underweight horse should ideally regain sufficient weight before beginning a fitness programme, otherwise the increase in workload is likely to lead to further weight loss. If work is introduced before then, this should be of low intensity until the required weight is gained by increased calorie intake.

Previous injuries. Such horses may require a specialist plan and advice may be given by a vet. Some types of work may be best avoided (e.g. work on hard or deep surfaces) and exercise may need to be introduced and increased more gradually.

It is important to consider the factors above when exercising horses, as the horse needs to be worked to the required level but should not be over-exerted or made physically uncomfortable. Fitness programmes should be designed so that there is a gradual increase in workload; usually after around 2–3 weeks at one level. It is important to keep this in mind when exercising horses to ensure that the horse is not worked too hard too soon, as this is a very common cause of injury. The following scenario gives an example of too great an increase in exercise:

> You work at a riding school where one of the ponies needs more exercise as he has become difficult for some of the less experienced children to ride. You have been given the pony as a project. You ask if you can take the pony on a local fun ride of 25km (15 miles). Until now, the pony has worked mainly in the school and does approximately two 45-minute group lessons each weekend day and a few lessons through the week. The fun ride would result in a much greater effort for the pony and could increase the risk of injury for the following reasons:
>
> - Rider weight — up until now the pony has been carrying children only.
>
> - Different ground conditions — the pony is unused to varying terrain (uneven ground, softer ground, hard ground).
>
> - Inclines — the pony will not be used to working up and down hills.
>
> - Faster speed — the fun ride is likely to include cantering at a faster speed than the pony has been doing in the school.
>
> - Longer duration — although the pony is working several hours in the school he may not be used to working continually, without a break.

This scenario explains how the factors mentioned earlier can affect the effort required of the horse. The fun ride is a good idea, but some fitness work would be necessary beforehand to ensure that the pony is properly prepared. Hopefully, in a real-life situation, you would have clear instructions from a senior member of staff. However, it is useful to think about these factors when exercising so, if the horse you are riding shows signs of tiring you can adjust what you are doing as required.

Signs that a horse is not coping with the workload

As mentioned, when working a horse you should be aware of signs that he is not coping with the exercise you are doing. The more of these signs a horse shows, the greater the likelihood of tiredness and the need to stop. If a horse shows these signs, either the work should be stopped completely, or the horse given a rest to see if he recovers sufficiently, and the intensity of the work should be reduced if it is continued. The decision depends on how clear the signs are and how many signs of tiredness the horse is showing. Signs of tiredness can include:

Slowing down. This may be most noticeable when out hacking with others. The horse may begin to slow or hang back, or not work as energetically as previously. You may notice that you have to start using your legs a lot more.

Unwillingness or inability to increase speed or change gait. Signs include falling behind, showing a lack of responsiveness to the aids and resistance when asked to increase speed or change gait.

Loss of motivation. A horse who has previously been working up into the bridle may begin to fall back and show little interest in keeping up with others, or move forward less positively between fences.

Reduced coordination. A tired horse may begin to stumble, lose balance or wander. If jumping, the horse may start knocking poles, stumbling or pecking on landing.

Increased brushing or overreaching. These issues can occur as a result of reduced coordination through tiredness. The horse may brush or bang his legs together more than usual, or overreach, especially when cantering and jumping.

Slowing the stride. Becoming laboured in any gait is a sign of tiredness.

Changing the lead in canter and gallop more frequently. Frequently changing lead or becoming disunited can be a sign of tiredness and reduced coordination.

Increased head and neck movement. The horse may start to show an exaggerated rolling head movement.

Increased breathing effort. The horse's breathing will increase and eventually he may begin to blow noticeably. Recovery may take some time afterwards.

Inability or unwillingness to perform a specific movement. This is especially true of jumping where the horse is required to make a large, explosive effort. The horse may begin to refuse or run out.

Summary

- Horses need to be fit for the work they are doing to reduce the risk of injury and ensure they can perform at their best.

- A variety of work helps to maintain soundness and prevents the horse becoming bored.

- The difficulty of the work can be affected by factors that include speed and duration of work, pattern of exercise, ground conditions, hills, weight of the rider and weather conditions.

- Always be aware of signs that a horse might not be coping with the work and seek advice if any occur. Pushing a tired horse to carry on carries a very big risk of injury.

TRAINING TIPS

1. Note the different types of work horses at your yard do on a weekly basis, and note the available variety.

2. When at competitions observe horses after they have competed, especially after cross-country, racing or endurance. Note their breathing, their coordination when walking and how they are handled or cared for. These horses work very hard but it will help you recognise what a horse looks like after strenuous exercise.

3. If you are riding horses to help improve their fitness, try to make note of how they feel at the start of the programme and then when they become fitter; you may notice they begin to find work easier and feel more energetic.

Chapter 7

Horse Walkers

Reason for using a horse walker

Horse clothing and equipment for the horse walker

Using a horse walker

Summary

Horse Walkers

A horse walker, put simply, is a fenced walkway with revolving partitions that allows the horse to exercise without the need for a leader or a rider. Horse walkers are usually circular (but can also be oval) and come in various sizes, catering for four to eight horses at once. The diameter (or oval track) of the walkway will dictate how tightly the horse needs to turn, so a larger diameter is better as it requires a gentler turn. A horse walker can be set to different speeds to suit different horses, and can be set to turn in either direction.

Rubber is commonly used for the flooring as it provides a level, consistent and non-slip surface, is relatively easy to keep clean and can reduce the concussion on the horse's legs. Any all-weather arena surface can also be used, although if the surface is loose (e.g. sand) it may move or become deep over time, and droppings will be trodden into the surface, making it harder to keep clean. Occasionally you may see a walker with a concrete floor. This is not ideal as it can be very slippery, it can cause damage to the horse's shoes as well as sustaining damage to the concrete itself, and there is a high level of concussion on the legs.

The horse walker should ideally be positioned close to the yard, meaning that horses on it can be monitored while other jobs are being done, and the time taken to put horses on and off is minimised.

Although there are many people who see a horse walker as an invaluable piece of equipment on their yard (because of the advantages discussed below), there are others who choose not to use one because of the stress put on the horse's legs by the constant turning. Consider the particular horse and situation when weighing up the pros and cons of using a horse walker.

A five-horse walker.

Reasons for using a horse walker

These vary in relevance for different horses and different situations (e.g. time of year/conditions).

1. As a leg-stretch for stabled horses:

    - Provides additional time out of the stable without the need for extra labour.

    - Movement promotes blood flow and good health.

2. Part of the horse's warming up or cooling down routine:

    - Allows the muscles to warm up and cool down thoroughly, so could help to prevent injury.

    - Saves time when working several horses, as one horse could be warming up on the walker while another is being worked, meaning more horses can be worked in a shorter time.

3. As a variation to ridden exercise:

    - Can be used as part of a work programme.

    - Can be used for exercise if the horse cannot be ridden (e.g. horse has a sore where the saddle or bridle would sit).

    - Can be used to give gentle exercise to several horses at once when there are fewer staff available (e.g. owing to staff illness).

4. To bring a horse back into work after injury or time off:

    - Can be used to introduce gentle exercise.

    - Can build muscle and strength without the weight or interference of a rider.

Although there are various reasons you might use a horse walker, it should not be used as the only form of exercise or as a 'lazy' method of exercising the horse. Its main function for most yards is a supplementary role, alongside turnout and/or ridden or lunge work.

Horse clothing and equipment for the horse walker

Boots

It is a good idea to use front and back brushing boots to protect the horse while on the horse walker. Moving in a constant circle means there is more likelihood of brushing or knocking the legs (as there is when being lunged). Depending on the horse, you may also need to use overreach boots. If the horse is going to be ridden straight afterwards, use the boots needed for riding. Any boots used must be a good fit and secure to avoid them slipping or rubbing.

Rug

Ideally, the less clothing used the better. Some walkers have a roof to keep the horse dry, but a rug may still be needed if it is a very cold day and, if there is no roof and it's a wet day. The drawback with rugs on walkers is that they may rub the shoulders when the horse is moving — and beware of fastenings potentially becoming caught on the fencing. Specialist walker rugs have now been produced, which will keep the horse warm and dry while leaving the shoulders free (reducing the likelihood of rubs), however the fastenings could still potentially get caught. The horse will produce more body heat when moving so unless it is particularly cold or the horse is clipped, he is better off without a rug.

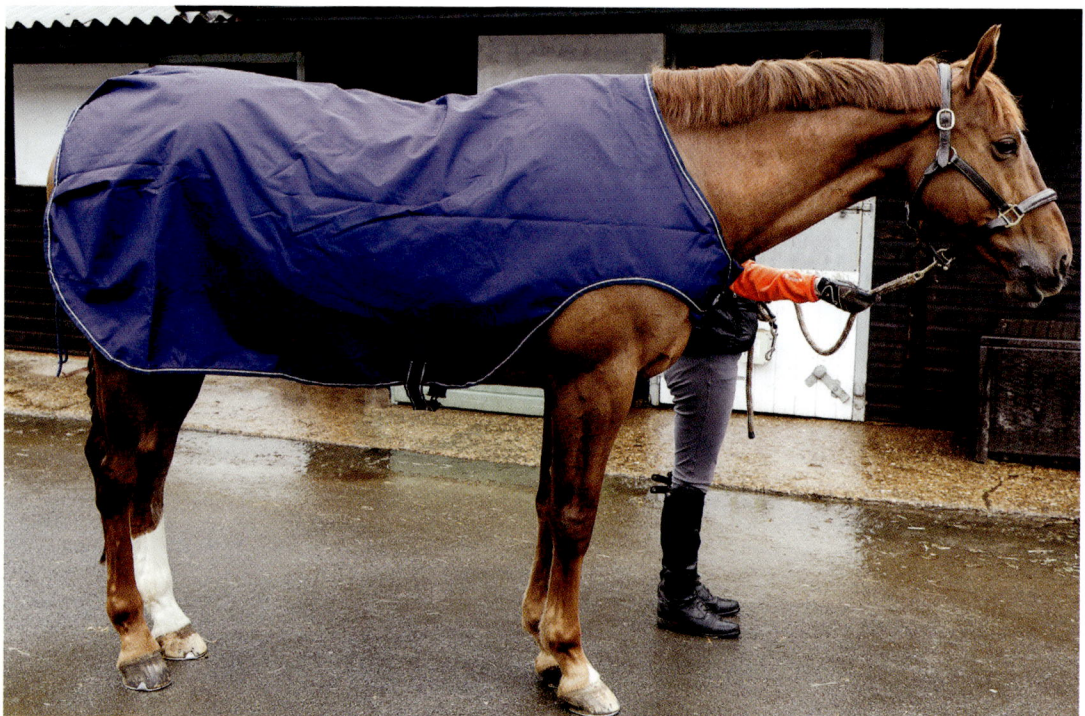

A walker rug covers the majority of the horse, but leaves the shoulders free.

7 | Horse Walkers

Horse walker with a roof fitted.

Using a horse walker

Checks before use

Before the first horse is put on the walker, make sure the power is turned on and check that the walker is working properly. This also enables you to check that the direction and speed are set appropriately, and will in due course let you stop the partition at a place that allows you to put the horse on. It is important for the horses that they go in both directions equally. The best way to do this is by alternating directions on successive days (although this may be difficult to keep track of if different horses use the walker on different days). The walker should be checked on a regular basis for safety, but do a quick visual check before every use of the flooring, partitions and the fencing (see the maintenance section below for more detail). Ideally all these checks should be done before getting the horses ready and bringing them out, particularly if the walker is not used regularly.

Putting horses on the horse walker

Once you have checked the horse walker and the horses are ready, they can be led to it. Horses who are calm and used to the walker may be fine being led in a headcollar, but there are times when you might need a bridle (e.g. a horse known to be strong to lead, or an unknown horse).

The partitions should be stopped in a suitable place to load each horse and allow the leader to exit safely. The gate needs to be opened as wide as possible, like a stable door. It can be useful to have an assistant. Lead the horse through the centre of the gateway into the horse walker, making sure to face him in the correct direction.

Once you have entered, push the gate (but do not secure) to discourage the horse from turning back to it. Release the horse (whether you leave the headcollar on or take it off is down to personal preference; you should follow your yard's policy) and exit the walker, taking care of your positioning and keeping an eye on the horse's body language as you do. Secure the gate and turn the walker on. Observe whether the horse is settled and the walker is moving at an appropriate speed. You should not leave a horse unsupervised while on the walker, but if it is located close to the yard you will be able to keep an eye on it while doing other jobs.

Leading the horse to the horse-walker.

The horse in the walker, ready for the leader to exit.

Taking horses off the horse walker

The length of time the horse is on the walker will vary.

Stop the horse walker with the horse's head level with the gate (the partition needs to be slightly past the gate so that there is room to get the horse out). If the partition stops in the wrong place, send the horse around again rather than pushing the partition backwards. There is usually a slight delay in the partitions stopping, so knowing when to press the stop button is an acquired skill. Enter the horse walker making sure the gate is closed behind you, taking care to position yourself safely. Put the headcollar on or clip on the lead rope ready to lead the horse out. When you are ready, open the gate wide and lead the horse out through the centre. Once all the horses have been removed, remember to turn the power off.

When you are ready, open the gate wide and lead the horse out through the centre.

Day-to-day maintenance

Long-term maintenance (e.g. servicing) should be dealt with by senior staff, but on a day-to-day basis you need to check the flooring, partitions and fencing for signs of wear or damage. The partitions and fencing should be checked for damage or sharp edges appearing (a bent piece of metal can leave a very sharp edge). Any changes to the horse walker or the way it works (e.g. strange noises, rubber flooring lifted, sharp edges on the partitions or fencing) should be reported to senior staff straight away.

You can help to keep the walker running efficiently by removing droppings from the floor after every use. Rubber flooring should be swept if necessary; if an arena surface is used it should be levelled to avoid tracking or unevenness.

Summary

- Key reasons for using a horse walker include: part of the horse's warming up or cooling down; to add variety to ridden exercise; to provide a leg-stretch for stabled horses; can be used when bringing a horse back into work after time off.

- Ideally the horse should wear boots and may need a rug, dependent on the weather.

- The horse walker should be checked before use: you will need to check that the direction and speed have been set appropriately and that the partition has been stopped in suitable place to load the horse.

- To load the horse — open gate wide, lead horse in, ask assistant to close gate to, release horse and exit (keeping safe positioning), close the gate, turn the walker on, check that horse is settled and speed correct.

- Do not leave the horse walker unsupervised when in use.

- To unload the horse — stop the walker when the horse's head is level with the gate, go into the walker (keeping safe positioning), ask assistant to close the gate to behind you, put headcollar on/clip lead rope on, open gate wide, lead horse out, turn power off if horse walker no longer in use.

- Day-to-day maintenance includes checking flooring/partitions/fencing, removing droppings, sweeping or levelling the surface if necessary, reporting any changes to senior staff.

TRAINING TIPS

1. Look at different horse walkers, online or at different yards, and see what options are available. Think about how different features might affect their ease of use.

Chapter 8

Clipping, Plaiting and Shoeing

Clipping

Plaiting

Shoeing

Summary

Clipping

Clipping a horse's hair off during the coldest months of the year might seem a strange thing to do. In fact it is far nicer for the horse not to work in a thick, heavy coat and without it he can cool down and dry off more efficiently.

Clipping the coat from areas such as the neck, where most of the sweat glands are, means he will sweat less and dry off quicker in wet, cold weather, and will look smarter too. A horse with a thick coat will take a long time to dry off, is at risk of catching a chill, and is likely to lose condition.

The first clip is done when the winter coat has fully grown through (generally around the end of September) and the last around the end of January, just before the summer coat starts to regrow. Some horses, such as competition horses with coarse coats or horses with medical conditions that cause their coats to grow thicker than normal, may be clipped out throughout the year to keep them comfortable and looking smart.

There are several types of clip and the one you choose will depend on the amount and type of work the horse is in. Horses in light work or who live out will benefit from having hair left on their back to keep them warm, while horses in hard work will benefit from having more hair removed.

Types of clip

Full clip — *all the hair is clipped off, including head, there may be a saddle patch left on the back.*

Hunter clip — *all the hair is clipped off the body but left on the legs for protection. (There may be a saddle patch left on the back). Half or whole head is removed.*

Blanket clip — *the hair is left on the legs and over the back in the shape of a blanket. Hair removed from neck. Half or whole head.*

8 | Clipping, Plaiting and Shoeing

Trace clip — the hair is left on in the shape of the blanket clip but instead of removing the whole neck a line is taken up to the chin.

Chaser clip — the hair is clipped off from the stifle to the tip of the ears and the head. Leaves the hindquarters covered.

Neck and belly — the underside of the neck and under the belly is clipped.

Preparing to clip

Assembling the clippers

Clippers come in many makes and sizes and can be mains or battery powered. All have two blades that move against each other to cut the hair, attached to the clipper head by a screw. The screws and springs are the most common parts to be lost, so look after them with care.

The following sequence of photos shows how to assemble the clippers:

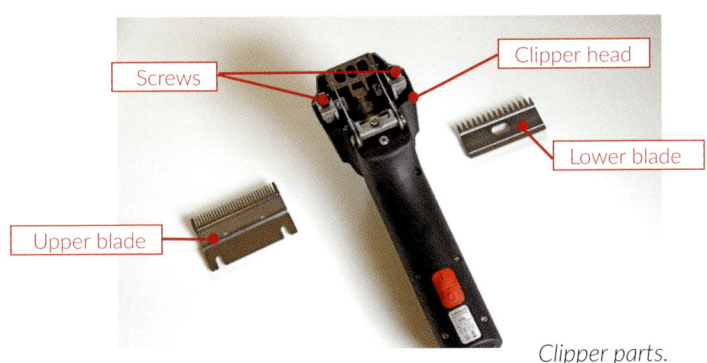

Clipper parts.

i. Loosen the screws, then place the small blade on the clipper head first (make sure it is facing the correct way up).

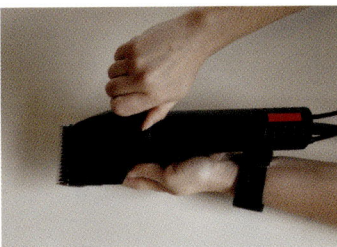

ii. Place the large blade on top.

iii. Tighten the screws to secure the blades.

iv. Turn the clippers over and adjust the tension.

v. Oil the motor and between the blades.

vi. Put the clippers somewhere they cannot be knocked over.

Other items you might need for assisting with clipping

- Overalls to keep the hair off your clothes and suitable PPE for you and the person clipping.

- Ideally, rubber-soled boots to offer protection from shocks/electrocution should there be a problem with the electricity supply.

- Extension lead.

- Circuit-breaker — to cut the electricity if there is a surge or issue with the power supply to reduce the risk of shocks/electrocution. (Some electric sockets may have a circuit-breaker built in.)

- Clipper oil — for oiling the motor and the blades to keep the clippers working efficiently.

- Brush for cleaning hair off the blades and air vents.

- Soft brush for brushing off the horse.

- Suitable rugs to put on the horse afterwards.

- Plaiting bands and tail bandage may be required to keep the mane and tail out of the way.

- Broom and skip for clearing up clipping area.

Preparing the equipment and area

The extension cable should be unwound completely because, coiled up, it in fact constitutes an electrical coil, which could heat up and potentially be a hazard, but is should be positioned where it cannot be stood on or tripped over by the horse, the handler or anyone else. Plug it in (with the circuit-breaker if required) and test the clippers.

Keep the brush and oil nearby as the air vents on the clippers will need regular cleaning and the blades will need oiling throughout the clip.

Ensure that the area in which you plan to clip is free from hazards, is large enough to work in safely and has a safe place to tie up the horse. Ideally the area should have rubber mats. If you are using a stable, remove any water buckets and haynets and bank the bedding up around the sides to make it easier to move around and to sweep the hair up afterwards.

Preparing the horse

The horse must be clean and dry. Clipping over muddy, greasy or wet hair will blunt the blades quickly, and may pull, which is uncomfortable for the horse. The mane can be put into bunches on top of the neck and the tail bandaged to keep it out of the way.

Assisting with clipping

Assisting someone will give you valuable insight into clipping and how horses may react, as well as the potential hazards and how to deal with them. Pay attention to how the person clipping positions themselves around the horse, and to the horse's body language. It is your job to warn the person clipping if the horse becomes uncomfortable or threatens to kick.

You may be asked to hold a foreleg up so the area under the elbow can be clipped safely. This stretches the skin behind the elbow, making it easier to clip.

There are several ways to lift a foreleg but you must make sure you are safe. Stand to the side of the horse, facing his tail, pick the leg up as if you are going to pick out a foot and, when the horse is comfortable, gently extend the leg forwards. You may want to hold the leg just below the knee. Make sure you keep your back straight and bend your knees. If you need to put the leg down, warn the person clipping so they can move the clippers out of the way.

Care of the horse after clipping

After clipping, any loose hairs should be brushed off with a soft brush, to prevent irritation, and the horse should be hot-clothed (see box) and rugged up appropriately.

Hot-clothing

You'll need a cloth and a bucket of hot water. Soak the cloth in the water and wring it out so it is not wet but still hot, and rub it over the horse. The idea is that the cloth's heat lifts grease, dust and hair from the skin without soaking the horse. If the weather is cold, leave a rug folded over the horse's back.

Trimming

Besides clipping, there are other ways to keep a horse tidy, such as pulling the mane to make it shorter, or trimming the untidy long hairs from the heels or under the jaw.

Trimming legs

To trim the hairs from the feathers you will need scissors (ideally blunt-ended, curved ones) and a comb. Using the comb under the scissors gives a more natural outline and provides a barrier between the horse's leg and the scissors. Always tie up the horse and make sure you have enough space to move around him safely. Crouch so you are able to move quickly if the horse moves.

- Make sure the legs are clean and dry.

- Using the mane comb, start at the bottom of the feathers and comb upwards.

- As you comb upwards, trim the long hairs off with the scissors.

- Work your way around the leg.

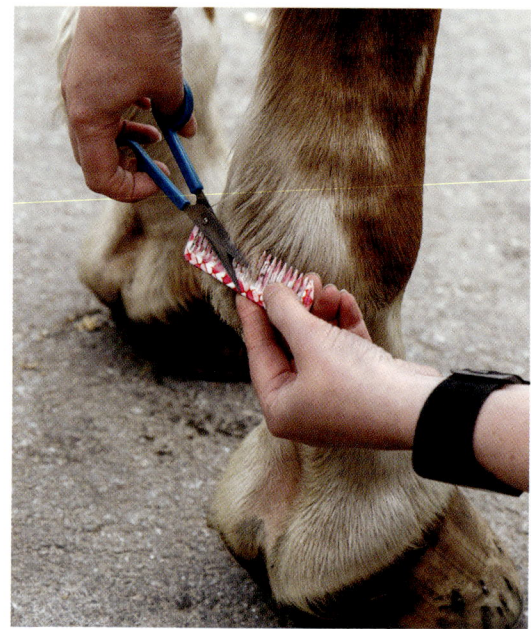

Trimming around the feathers, blunt-ended scissors are recommended.

Trimming ears

Trimming the ears is a delicate task. You should only trim the long hairs that stick out of the ear and not the hairs inside as these helps protect the inner ear. Put a headcollar on the horse and ideally ask someone to hold him for you, or untie the lead rope and leave it loose through the string. Some horses are very sensitive around their ears and may throw their heads up or pull back when you try to touch them. Gently push the edges of the ears together and carefully trim the long hairs sticking out.

Tidying the mane

You may need to tidy a horse's mane to make it shorter and easier to plait. If you are going to 'pull' the mane, ideally this should be done straight after exercise when the horse is warm and the pores are open so the hairs should come out more easily, making the experience slightly less uncomfortable for the horse.

8 | Clipping, Plaiting and Shoeing

- Tie up the horse or ask someone to hold him for you.

- If the horse is tall you might need something secure to stand on.

- Using a mane comb, comb the mane to remove tangles.

- Ideally the mane should lie on the right-hand side of the neck.

- Starting at either the poll or the withers, lightly take hold of a small piece of mane and, holding the ends back, comb the hair towards the crest until you are left with the long hairs on the underside of the mane.

- Pull these hairs out either by wrapping them around the comb and pulling down, or using your fingers. Using your fingers is a good way to make sure you are not pulling too much hair out at a time and causing discomfort to the horse. If pulling out the mane hurts your fingers, it is likely that you are hurting the horse.

- Repeat the process, moving along the whole length of the mane until it is at the length you require.

Horses can be more sensitive at their withers and their poll, so take your time, and if the horse really objects, it may be better to pull the mane gradually over several days.

An alternative to pulling the mane is to shorten it using a specially designed comb that cuts the mane in a feathered manner. It is preferable to use one of these if a horse dislikes having his mane pulled.

Native breeds of horses and ponies often do not have their manes pulled or feathers trimmed; if they are being shown in breed classes they are shown in their natural state.

Backcomb the mane until you are left with the long hairs from the underside of the mane.

Tidying the tail

Tail pulling is a method of tidying the top of the tail. When viewed from behind, the tail should look symmetrical. You are in a vulnerable position standing behind the horse pulling a tail

Complete Horsemanship Volume 2

so make sure you have someone to hold him and stand slightly to the side of the quarters rather than directly behind. If the horse is new to having his tail pulled, or starts to show signs of discomfort, it may be better to spread it over several sessions. A razor can be used as an alternative to pulling to save any discomfort.

- Stand to the side of the horse's quarters and brush out the tail thoroughly. An unwashed tail is easier to hold on to than one that is freshly washed. You could wear rubber gloves for extra grip.

- Starting at the top of the tail, take a few strands of hair from the underside and pull them out.

- Alternate sides, taking a few strands of hair at a time. You may want to take a few hairs from the front of the tail to reduce the thickness. Be careful not to leave any bald patches.

- Check that the tail looks symmetrical.

- Once the tail has been pulled, it can be dampened and a tail bandage put on to lay the hairs flat.

To finish the look, the tail should be trimmed so it is level. Ask a helper to put their arm under the dock to raise the tail as if the horse is moving, then trim using scissors.

Trimming the tail with the help of an assistant.

Plaiting

Plaiting the mane

Plaiting a horse's mane enhances the look of the neck by showing off the topline, and is used for competitions, hunting and showing, although some native breeds are shown unplaited or even with specialist plaits.

Traditionally an odd number of plaits were put down the horse's neck, as an even number may create a midpoint that 'splits' the neck into two sections. The number of plaits will depend on the length and thickness of the mane and the size of the plaits you require.

Items required for plaiting:

- Bands or needles and thread
- Plaiting comb
- Water brush
- Bucket of water
- Step or box to stand on

The mane should be clean but ideally not freshly washed as this can make it difficult to keep hold of. You can dampen it down with a water brush to help keep the hairs in place and make it slightly easier to grip. There are products available specifically designed to make plaiting easier and quicker, such as plaiting spray.

The basic process is shown in the accompanying pictures.

i. Starting at the poll, split the mane into equal-sized sections using a plaiting comb and secure loosely with a band. Plait the first bunch and secure at the end with a band.

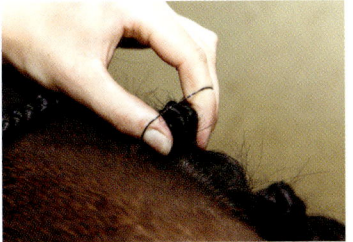

ii. Fold or roll the plait under itself to create a ball shape and secure with a band. Repeat for all bunches.

iii. The forelock is plaited in a French plait and finished by rolling it under itself.

iv. A plaited mane.

Plaiting with thread

Plaiting with thread is best done out of the stable where the needle won't be lost in bedding if it is dropped.

- Thread several needles and secure them somewhere safe.

- Dampen the mane.

- Split the mane into sections.

- Starting at the poll, plait the first section. When at the end, secure with the thread using a figure of eight shape (bring the needle up through the middle of the plait, going left, under, back up and through the plait, then the same to the right and repeat until the plait is secure).

- Fold the plait in half and push the needle through the centre of the plait by the crest to hold the plait in place.

- Fold the plait in half again and repeat until the plait is secure.

- Once secure, bring the needle back down through the plait and cut the thread at the underside.

- Repeat for all sections.

Specialised plaits

Horses and ponies with long manes that do not lend themselves to traditional hunter plaits can be plaited with a running or a crest plait. A running plait is a loose plait that starts from the poll and runs along the ends of the mane in one long plait. A crest plait is similar but is tighter and sits along the crest of the neck rather than the bottom of the mane. In either case, the forelock tends to be left loose.

Plaiting the tail

The top of an unpulled tail may be plaited to tidy it up for showing or competition. Plaiting tails neatly takes practice and patience to find out what works for a particular horse, and you. The trick is to make sure all the pieces taken from the sides are the same size and the plait is kept pulled tight in the centre of the dock as each piece crosses over. Crossing the pieces over the top of each other will create a flat plait, while crossing them under each other will create a raised one. As you are working at the back of the horse, make sure the horse is secured and that you are positioned safely.

- Dampen the top of the tail to make it easier to hold on to.

- Take a small piece of hair from either side at the top of the dock and cross the pieces over each other.

- Take another small piece from one side and start the plait.

- Continue down the dock.

- The length of the plait will depend on the horse's conformation — some suit a longer plait and others a shorter one. Once you have reached the desired length, plait the loose ends of hair and secure with a band.

- Fold the end of the plait under itself and secure with a band.

i. Cross the hairs over to start the plait.

ii. Work your way down the tail taking small pieces of hair from each side.

Shoeing

There is a lot of truth in the saying 'no foot, no horse'.

A horse's hoof grows at a rate of approximately 6–10mm (¼–⅜in) per month, which means the whole hoof is regrown approximately every twelve months. Although the growth is continual, the rate can be affected by things such as nutrition or the time of year (hooves tend to grow faster in the summer months). As the hoof grows, the edges can become misshapen and crack or flake off. To keep the feet in good condition the horse should ideally be shod or trimmed every four to six weeks by a registered farrier.

All farriers should be registered with the Farriers Registration Council, or the Irish Farriery Authority in the Republic of Ireland.

Some horses will manage perfectly well unshod, but others require the extra support and protection a shoe provides. As the forelegs tend to take more weight than the hind legs it is quite common to see horses shod in front but not behind.

In the wild, a horse naturally wears the hoof wall away as he moves about, allowing the hoof to shape itself. Ridden horses wear their hooves down faster than they can regrow. Shoes provide a barrier between the foot and the floor and help prevent excessive wear to the hoof wall.

Reasons for shoeing:

- To prevent excessive wear on the hoof wall.

- To provide a cushion between the sole and the ground to protect the hoof from bruising.

- To help correct or compensate for conformational defects.

- To provide extra grip on tarmac/concrete — road studs or nails can be used.

- Stud holes can be added for studs to be screwed into to provide extra grip on grass.

Removing a shoe

In an ideal world the farrier would be the only person required to take off a shoe. However, taking a shoe off is a good skill to learn in case you find yourself with a partially attached shoe that your horse has trodden on and twisted.

If you need to remove a shoe, ideally put on a pair of long chaps (farrier chaps if you have them) to protect your legs because if the horse pulls away suddenly it can hurt.

Although other common farrier's tools are shown in the photo opposite, the tools you will need for removing a shoe are: a buffer, a hammer and pincers.

Ideally have someone hold the horse, or tie him where you have space to work. If you are doing this in a stable, put the bedding up in case a nail drops into it.

If it is a fore shoe that is loose, pick up the horse's leg and place the foot between your legs just above your knees to leave both hands free. If the loose shoe is on a hind foot, pick up the foot normally, then gently stretch it back (keep a bend in the hock) and rest it over your thigh. Throughout the removal process, illustrated in the accompanying pictures, keep your knees bent so you take the weight through your legs and not your back.

8 | Clipping, Plaiting and Shoeing

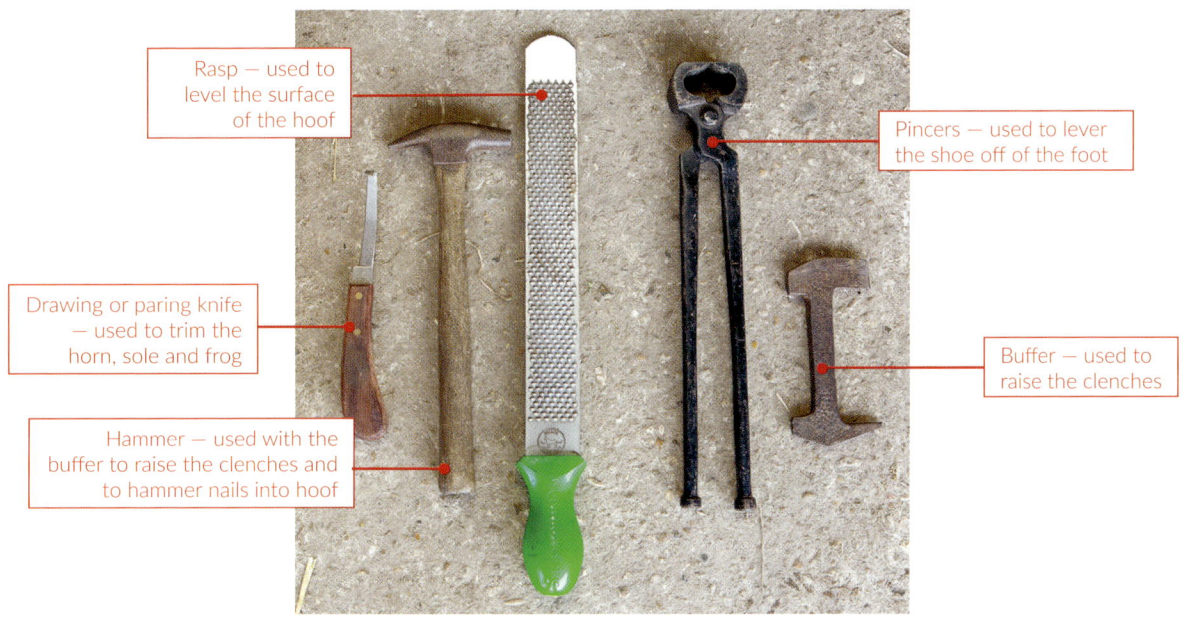

- Rasp — used to level the surface of the hoof
- Drawing or paring knife — used to trim the horn, sole and frog
- Hammer — used with the buffer to raise the clenches and to hammer nails into hoof
- Pincers — used to lever the shoe off of the foot
- Buffer — used to raise the clenches

Basic farriery tools

Using the buffer and hammer, knock up the clenches, it might be possible to remove the nails one by one, using the pincers to pull them out of the shoe, once the clenches have been knocked up.

Place the pincers at one side of the heel and pull inwards to lift the shoe off the heel, repeat at the other heel and then work your way down, alternating sides, until the shoe is off. Make sure any dropped nails are picked up and that all nails are removed from the foot.

113

Summary

- Clipping is carried out mainly during the winter months to remove the thick winter coat. This enables the horse to work comfortably, dry off quicker (which prevents chills), and look smart.

- The type of clip needed will depend on the amount and type of work the horse is doing.

- Plaiting a mane and tail helps to show off the horse's conformation.

- A horse should be trimmed or shod every four to six weeks by a registered farrier.

- Shoeing helps to prevent excessive wear to the hoof wall.

TRAINING TIPS

1. Practise plaiting at every opportunity and experiment with different techniques. There are many online tutorials offering hints and tips.

2. Offer to assist with clipping by holding the horse or ask to observe as much as possible.

3. Watch the farrier at work. Some may let you take a shoe off under their supervision.

Chapter 9

Transporting Horses

Travel equipment for a horse

Loading and unloading

Summary

Complete Horsemanship Volume 2

Transporting Horses

Taking a horse out in a lorry or trailer can be an exciting experience for the horse, especially if he associates the travel equipment or vehicle with something such as a competition. As such, some horses can become excited or nervous when the travel equipment is put on and can fidget or become strong to lead if they have to wait around, so it is a good idea to check and prepare the vehicle first so that the horse can be dressed and loaded straight away without having to wait.

Travel equipment for a horse

As a horse stands in a moving vehicle, he may lose his balance at times (just as we might do when standing on a train or bus). Therefore we need to dress the horse for protection and safety.

Travel boots and bandages

Protective travel boots come in many shapes, sizes and colours. The areas that are most at risk of injury and require protection are the horse's knees, hocks, coronet bands and heels. Many travel boots are shaped to fit the horse's legs, but you can also buy unshaped ones that can sometimes feel less restrictive to the horse. The important thing is that they fit so that they give maximum protection and comfort. The boot should come high enough to cover the knee or hock and low enough to cover the coronet and heel, and the shaped parts (if there are any) should sit snugly around the corresponding joint. The width should allow the boot to sit comfortably around the horse's leg without leaving a gap or needing a lot of overlap. If too wide, it will most likely slip down while loading or travelling and perhaps get caught around the foot, which could cause the horse to panic and also damage the boot.

Some people use travel bandages instead of boots. These are put on the same way as stable bandages (see Chapter 3) but the padding and bandaging are longer to cover and protect the

A front travel boot, which is protecting the knee, coronet and heel.

knee, hock, coronet band and heel. Occasionally you may see overreach boots worn with bandages to make sure the coronet and heel areas are protected. Similarly, knee or hock boots are sometimes fitted for extra protection.

Bandages can often provide more support than travel boots, as they fit more snugly and evenly, which would be particularly useful to a tired horse after competition. However, if put on badly, a bandage could cause injury (e.g. pressure sores). If too loose it may slip, become caught around the feet and cause the horse to panic. Nevertheless, bandages can offer a better fit than travel boots (particularly for a horse with odd proportions) as they can be tailored to the individual, whereas travel boots come in fixed pony, cob and full sizes (although there may be slight variation between brands). Some horses prefer bandages because they are less bulky and interfere less with their movement. On the other hand, travel boots are quicker and easier to put on and off than bandages. Horses sometimes get a little excited when they get to a show or event, and removing bandages from a dancing horse is quite difficult. There is a place for both travel bandages and boots; which you choose depends on personal preference and the situation.

Tail protection

The tail, or more specifically the dock, needs to be protected when the horse is travelling, as the dock is often very close to the side of the horsebox or breech bar of the trailer. Occasionally the horse will lean back on to these areas to balance, and this can damage the tail if unprotected.

A tail bandage, used to cover the dock area of the tail, is usually made of elasticated material, whereas a stable bandage would typically be made of non-elasticated fleece or wool. As with a leg bandage, the tail bandage needs to be applied with even pressure, tight enough to stop it slipping down the tail and becoming tangled round the horse's legs, but not so tight that it will cause damage. A tail bandage applied too tightly or with uneven pressure will affect the blood supply to the tail, which could cause the hair to fall out.

Putting on a tail bandage

Before starting, stand slightly to one side so that you are not directly behind the hind legs and the horse can see you. Lifting the tail with one hand, place the end of the tail bandage under the dock at the top. Some horses dislike this and may try to clamp their tail down. If this happens, gently ease the tail away until you can start to apply the bandage. The bandage needs to be as high up the tail as you can get it, to offer the most protection. Leave a small length of the bandage showing above the top of the tail.

Complete Horsemanship Volume 2

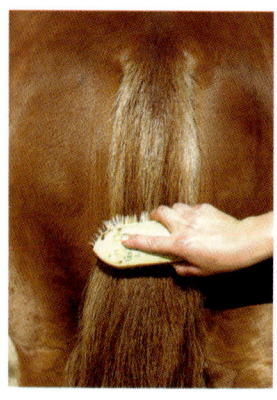

i. Wet the tail so the hair is lying flat.

ii. Try to make sure that you remove any wrinkles from the bandage and it is as high as possible.

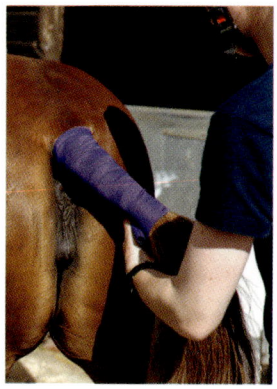

iii. Continue the bandage working your way down the tail using even pressure, with each wrap overlapping the previous by roughly half.

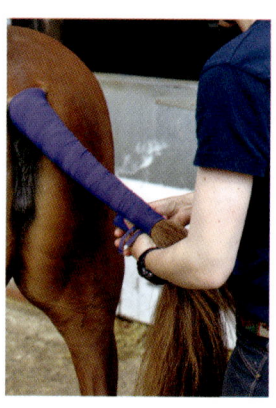

iv. The bandage should cover the end of the dock before you start to work your way back up.

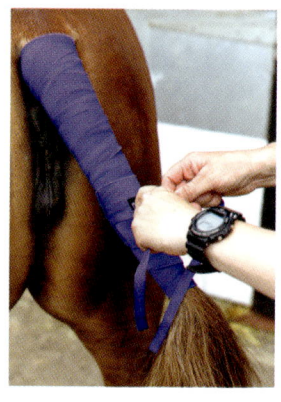

v. Work your way back up the tail until you get to the end of the bandage, which is usually about a third of the way back up.

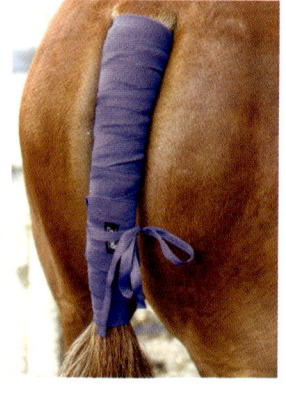

vi. Wrap the tapes around the tail in opposite directions before tying them together like you tie a shoelace, making sure the knot sits to one side of the tail to avoid a pressure point.

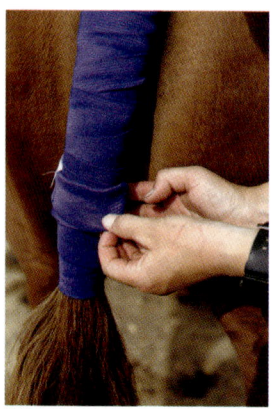

vii. Fold the bandage down over the tapes to avoid the tapes being rubbed undone.

Putting on a tail bandage.

Removing a tail bandage

It is best not to leave a tail bandage on for more than two to three hours as it will affect the blood supply to the tail. If your journey is longer than this, use a tail guard (see below) instead.

To remove a tail bandage, untie the tapes then, holding the tail bandage at the top of the tail, slide the whole thing downwards and off the end of the tail.

Re-rolling a tail bandage

Once a tail bandage has been removed, unravel it and if it is clean enough, roll it back up straight away so it's ready to use again. Start rolling the bandage from the end with the tapes attached, and with the tapes on the inside.

Continue rolling the bandage, keeping it as tight as you can, otherwise it will be hard to put back on a tail. Some people find it easiest to roll the bandage against their leg; others prefer to put the excess bandage over their shoulder and roll the bandage towards them. Whichever method you prefer, keep it off ground so it doesn't get dirty or trip you up.

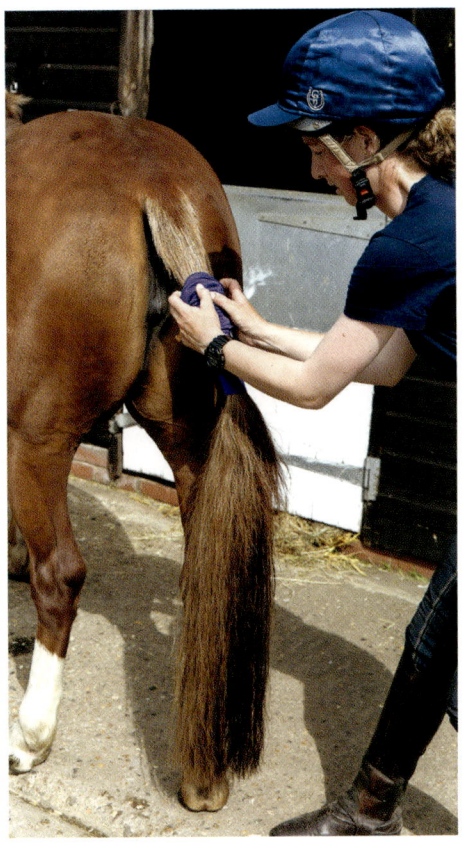

After remembering to untie the tapes, remove the tail bandage all in one go from the top.

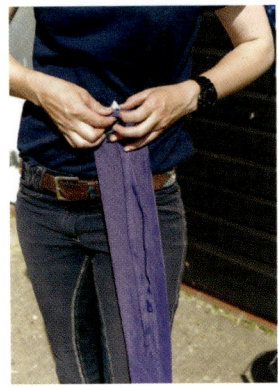

Roll the bandage from the tapes end with the tapes on the inside.

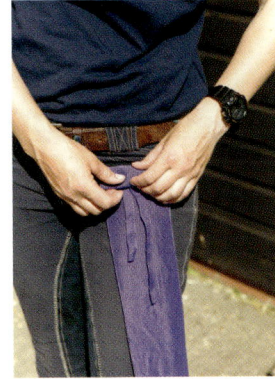

If you roll the bandage against your leg, you need to keep the end of the bandage off the floor.

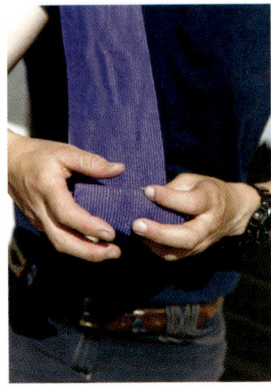

If you roll the bandage towards you, the excess can be placed over your shoulder to keep it off the floor.

Tail guard

As mentioned above, a tail guard can be used instead of, or in conjunction with, a tail bandage. Tail guards are made of various materials, including neoprene and padded cotton, and is secured by Velcro straps. It is used as an alternative to a tail bandage to protect the dock, as it can be quicker and easier to put on, and can quite often provide more protection. It can also be worn on longer journeys than a tail bandage, without causing problems to the blood supply. The tail guard should extend to the end of the dock for protection, but if it is slightly short you could consider using a tail bandage as well.

To put on the tail guard, stand to one side of the horse's quarters and place the guard as high up the tail as it will go. Secure it in place with the Velcro straps, tight enough that it does not move when you pull on it gently, so it will stay on for the duration of the journey. To remove it, simply unfasten the straps and slide the guard off.

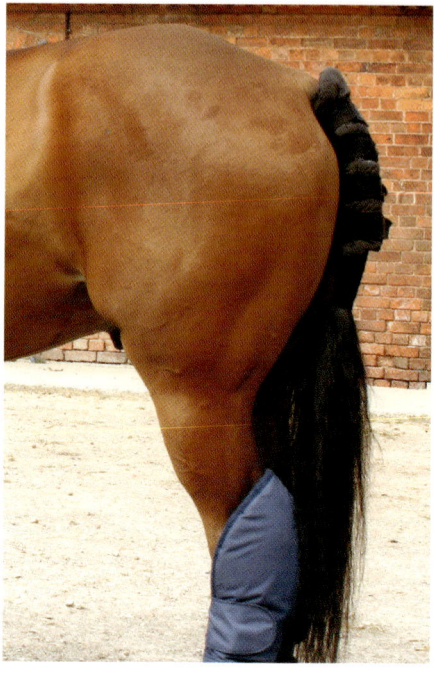

This padded tail guard is a little too short so a tail bandage has also been used to give the horse more protection.

Headcollar

It is a good idea to use a leather headcollar while travelling, as leather will break under stress but nylon will not. The headcollar needs to be fastened properly (straps tucked in rather than left dangling) and should fit the horse's head without rubbing on the bony areas. The noseband should be above the fleshy part of the nostrils with enough room to fit three fingers all the way around.

If you do not know the horse, it is always best to load in a bridle to give you more control. This can be fitted over the top of the headcollar and removed once the horse is secured in the horsebox/trailer. The reins can be used to lead, or the lead rope could be clipped to a coupling to make sure that pressure is placed on both sides of the bit. If not leading with the reins, they should be twisted and secured in the throatlash.

A well-fitting leather headcollar.

Rug

A rug can give the horse's body a certain amount of protection while travelling, particularly if he tends to lean on the walls or partitions, as well as helping to maintain his body temperature. Which one you use, if any, will depend on the weather and the horse. If it is warm, you may use a thin cotton sheet, a thin cooler rug, or travel the horse without a rug to prevent overheating. If it is colder, you would want to use a warmer/thicker cooler rug. In very cold weather, you may need to consider using more than one cooler rug or even a breathable stable rug over a cooler rug. How the horse travels will also influence the decision. Bad travellers who get upset will quite often sweat more than good travellers. Also bear in mind that although a horse is not moving around much when travelling, he is using his muscles to balance and thus gets warmer than he would standing in the stable. On a longer journey when the weather may be changing, the horse should be checked at every rest stop and the rugs changed or removed if necessary.

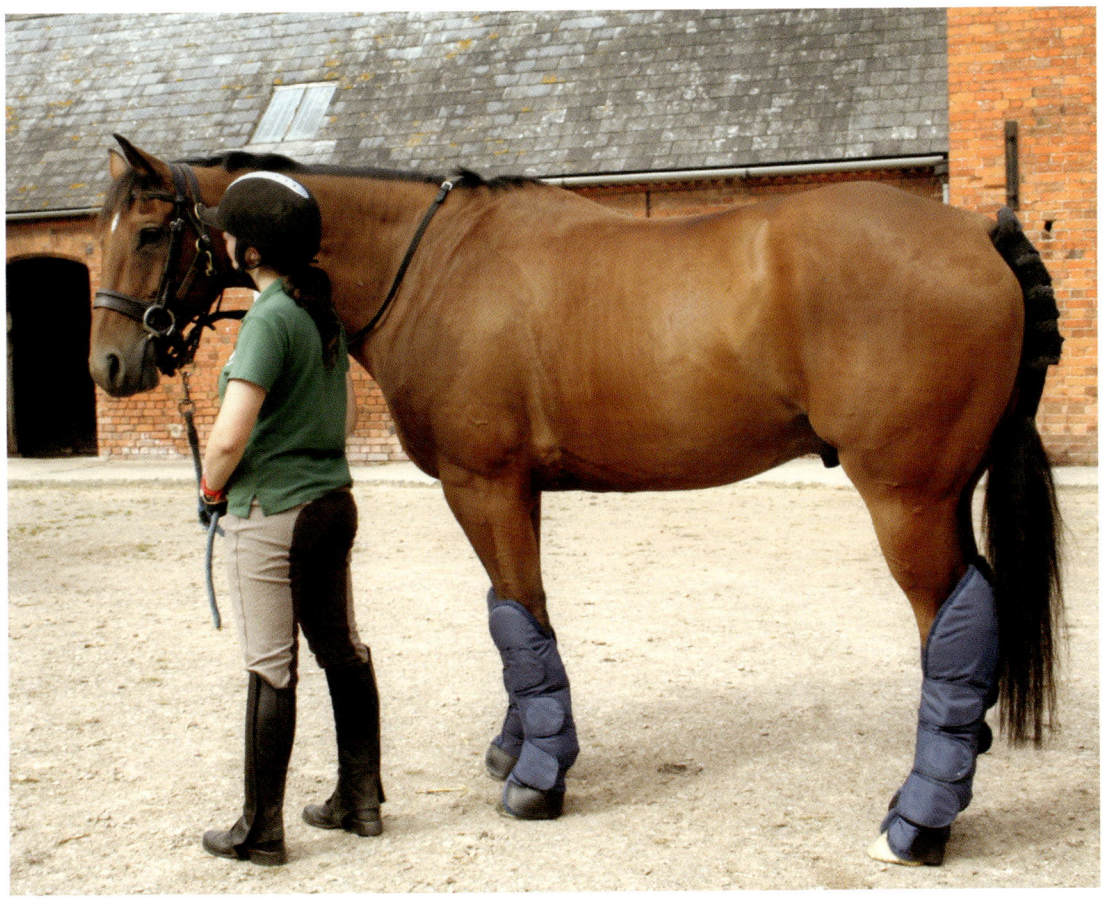

Horse dressed to travel on a warm day.

Loading and unloading

When loading and unloading it is always best to have someone there to help you move partitions or put the breech bars and the ramp up or down. You need to communicate effectively with each other so that you both know what is happening all the time, to help keep you, the assistant and the horse safe. Both you and your assistant should wear a hat, gloves and suitable sturdy footwear.

Final checks before loading

The horsebox or trailer should already have been checked for general safety and suitability, but you need to carry out some other quick checks before loading the horse. Your loading area needs to be free of anything that could cause a potential hazard to the horse or to the person leading and there should be plenty of room to lower the ramp. There should be a straight route up to the bottom of the ramp so the horse can approach and walk straight up it, rather than having to turn on to it. The surface where the vehicle is parked should not be slippery or stony to minimise any risk of injury from the horse slipping. If the journey is a long one and you think the horse will need hay and water, make sure you load these.

Lowering the ramp

If the loading area is safe the ramp can be lowered. If it is heavy or not well sprung, you will need someone to help you. If you are unsure of the weight, check with someone more senior first so that you do not risk injuring yourself. If in doubt, ask for help; it is no good realising the ramp is too heavy when it is halfway down. Once you have undone the ramp fastenings, stand to one side to lower it; don't risk severe injury by standing directly underneath it, where it could fall on you. Once lowered, the ramp should touch the ground at both sides, so that it will not move when the horse stands on it. A ramp that moves as the horse walks up it could worry the horse and make him reluctant to load. Levelling the ramp will also prevent it from becoming twisted or damaged.

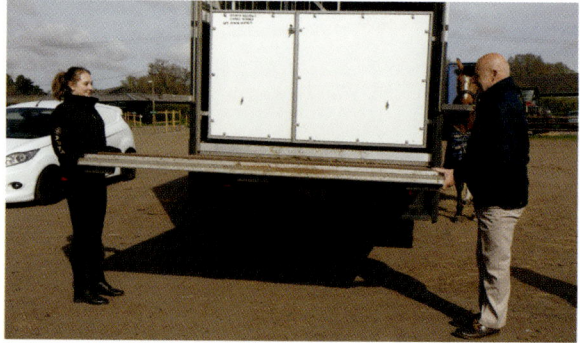

Keep safe by lowering the ramp from one side.

Opening partitions

When loading into a horsebox, you will need to open the appropriate partitions and secure them back out of the way. If there is only one horse being loaded, he should travel furthest forward for the smoothest ride. The partitions need to be opened as far as they will go, to give the horse plenty of room as he loads. Make sure there is nothing sticking out from the partitions that could catch him. If loading into a trailer, open both front and back ramps and, if possible, move the back section of the partition to make the trailer look more open and inviting, although not all partitions allow this. If there is only one horse travelling he should be loaded into the right-hand side (furthest from the kerb) to give the smoothest ride. This also makes the trailer more balanced, as the camber of the road often tilts the trailer slightly left.

Once the partitions are secured back, step back and double-check that everything is ready for you to load; it is better to realise sooner rather than later if you have forgotten something. Now is also a good time to check that there is string to tie the horse to, attached to an appropriate, safe place (e.g. a tie ring, rather than to the window bars or the partition). With a trailer, have the jockey door unfastened but shut to, so that you can get out once the horse is loaded.

Loading

When ready to load, first make sure your helper is not standing too close to the ramp (which could put the horse off) but is close enough to help when needed. Walk the horse positively towards the centre of the ramp, making sure you are positioned just in front of the horse's shoulder. If you amble uncertainly towards the ramp, the horse will pick up on this and may think there is something to worry about. Approach the ramp from far enough back that the horse walks freely forwards in a straight line before you get to the ramp. Approaching on an angle or turning could cause the horse to trip up the ramp or encourage him to stop or veer past it instead.

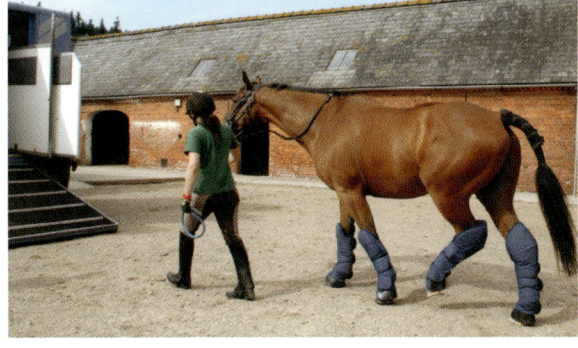

The horse should be walking freely forwards towards the ramp in a straight line.

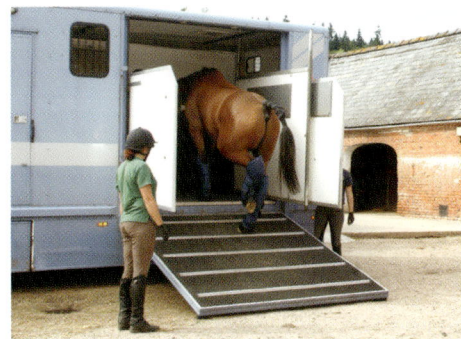

Walk positively straight up the ramp and in.

Once the horse is in the vehicle, you may need to move him into position (moving him over if necessary as you would in a stable). Then you can ask your assistant to move the partition (or breech bar in a trailer) into place. If you are loading into a trailer, you need to be in front of the breast bar before the breech bar is put up so that you do not get squashed. It is important that the horse knows where the assistant is so he is not shocked by any sudden movement. The assistant simply saying something like 'Breech bar going up now, or 'Partition coming round now' will let the horse — and you — know where they are. As the partition or breech bar is moved into place, try to keep the horse still. Keep a gentle contact on the lead rope or reins, talk quietly to him, and be ready to stop him if he tries to move. The partition should allow space between the walls and the forelegs and hind legs, as well as either side of him. The horse should not appear 'wedged in'.

Once the partition or breech bar is in place, the bridle (if used) can be removed and the horse's lead rope can be tied to the string with a quick-release knot. The partition or bar should always be secured before the horse is tied up; this prevents him from shooting backwards down the ramp at speed if he panics and pulls back.

With the partitions/bar and horse secured, the ramp can be put up ready for the journey. With your assistant's help, stand either side of the ramp, and lift it (remembering to bend your knees rather than your back). After fastening it securely, the horse and vehicle are ready for the journey. Check that all ramps and jockey doors are shut securely before setting off.

Unloading

On arrival at your destination, park where the ramp can be lowered on to a non-slippery surface with plenty of room for the horse to be unloaded safely. With your helper on the opposite side of the ramp from you, lower it gently to the floor. Try not to let it bang as this may scare the horse or damage the ramp. You can then untie the horse ready to unload. Unless you know the horse very well and he is quiet and easy to unload, it is recommended that you use a bridle over the headcollar to give you more control. The horse should be untied and you should be in position to unload before the partition or breast bar is moved. Ask your assistant to open and secure the partition as far back as it will go, before they move down the ramp and out of the way. Once they are well out of the way, turn the horse to face the ramp and ask him to walk slowly down the centre of it. It is best to keep a contact on the lead rope or reins to discourage him from running or jumping down, and be aware of where his feet are so you do not get trodden on. Keep the horse straight as he descends and steps away from the ramp, so he doesn't trip or slip.

Remember, if you are at a competition or another exciting place the horse may be more keyed-up than normal, so be prepared for this.

Once back home, the horse should be taken back his stable, undressed, groomed and rugged up as necessary. Once he's comfortable, clean the vehicle ready for the next journey. All

9 | Transporting Horses

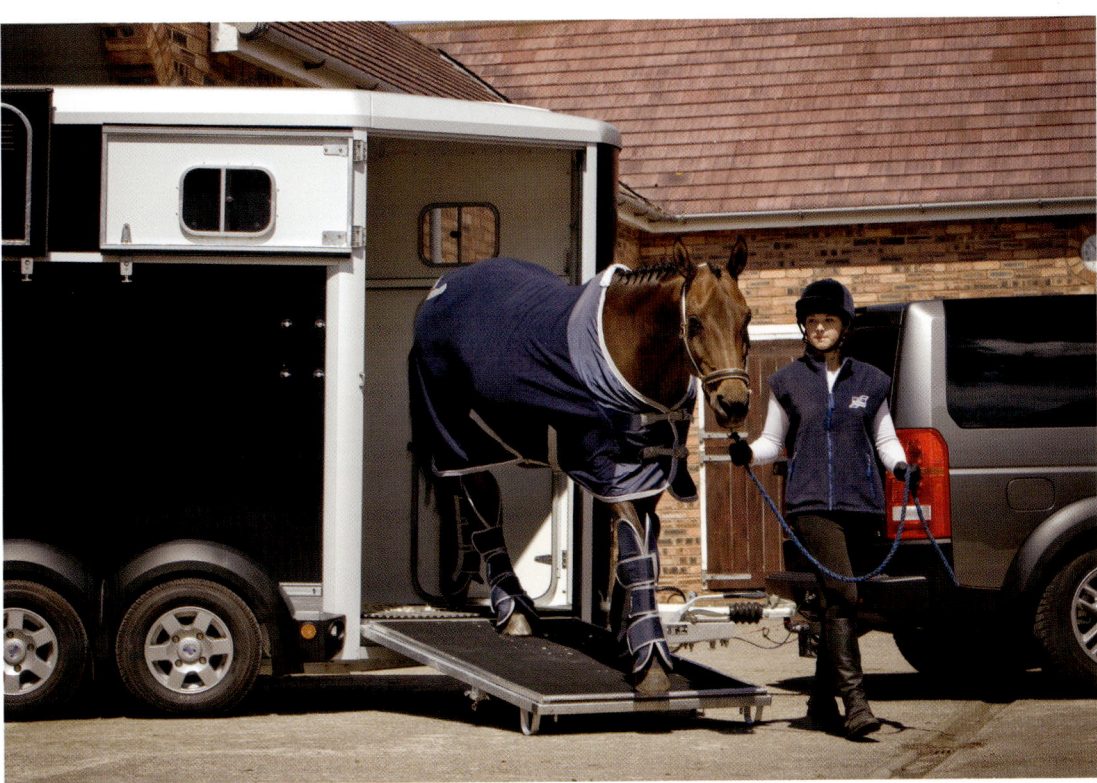

Keep the horse steady and central going down the ramp.

droppings and any damp bedding should be removed and the floor swept so that it can dry out where necessary. The partitions can be replaced and the ramp put up, ready for the vehicle to be parked up.

Summary

- Prepare the vehicle for travelling before dressing the horse.

- Add everything you are likely to need, such as appropriate tack and hay or water if necessary.

- The horse should be dressed in travel boots or bandages, a tail guard or bandage, a leather headcollar and a suitable rug, if necessary.

- Make sure the vehicle is parked on a non-slip surface, with plenty of space for the ramp to be lowered.

- When lowering the ramp, make sure you stand to one side — not directly underneath the ramp. You may need an assistant if the ramp is heavy.

- The partitions should be open fully and secured before loading the horse.

- When loading a horse into a lorry or trailer you should walk positively in a straight line towards and up the centre of the ramp.

- When unloading, lead the horse straight down the centre of the ramp and straight off the bottom.

TRAINING TIPS

1. Look at different types of lorry and trailer and how the partitions and fastenings vary.

2. Visit a tack shop or look online to see the equipment available for travelling.

3. Visit a show/event to see how horses are dressed for travelling and the types of vehicles available.

4. Ask if you can observe or assist someone experienced in loading or unloading their horse.

Chapter 10
Stable Design

Size of stables

Construction pros and cons

Some key considerations

Summary

Stable Design

Domesticated horses and ponies must often spend time in stables as well as in a field. Part of the responsibility of owning or looking after a horse is to ensure that he has a suitable living environment.

Size of stables

A stable's size and shape will vary depending on whether it's been purpose-built or converted from an existing building, but it should be of a suitable size for the horse, with enough room for him to move around, lie down and get up comfortably. As a general guide, a stable measuring 3.66 x 3.66m (12ft x 12ft) would be the minimum required for an average horse (an 18hh horse would need something bigger) and a pony requires a minimum of 3.05m x 3.05m (10ft x 10ft). The eaves of the roof should be high enough (approx. 3.66m/12ft) that the horse will not hit his head and the doorway should be wide enough (about 137cm/4ft 6in) for the horse to pass through without banging his hips on the frame. The stable doors should open outwards so they do not swing into the horse. Some indoor barns have sliding doors that save space as they do not block the central passageway when opened. They can have different types of locking mechanisms, but most click when shut properly.

Construction pros and cons

Each type of yard has its good and bad points and although you can't change the position of a stable, it helps to be aware of these points so you can make the most of the facilities you have.

An indoor stable yard with sliding stable doors with integrated-weave grilles. The rotating feed bowls are a labour-saving feature. Note the drain in the centre of the passageway, which can make it difficult to lead horses safely out of reach of stabled horses. The clear panels in the roof provide some natural light.

Types of stable

Stable type	Considerations	Pros	Cons
Indoor stable yard	• Must have good ventilation • If there are doors at either end they can create a wind tunnel	• Offers protection from weather • Can have everything under one roof • Can see all horses (especially if bars separate stables)	• Horses may not like being close to one another • Narrow passageways can making leading difficult • Easier spread of disease between horses • If no windows looking out, not much visual stimulation for horses • Can have poor ventilation
Outside stable yard	• Should face away from prevailing wind • An overhang will help protect the stables from the weather	• Good ventilation • More difficult for disease to spread	• Exposed to weather • Can be difficult to observe horses because of design of stable

A purpose-built outdoor courtyard. Note the overhang to provide protection from the weather. Light switches and plugs are positioned out of reach of the horses. The top doors are secured back.

Wall and roofing materials

Materials	Pros	Cons
Wood	• Cheap • Quick and easy to construct • Can replace individual boards	• Horses can chew or kick through boards • Requires annual maintenance • Can be a fire hazard • Requires waterproofing if used outside • Warm in summer • Cold in winter • Can be dark
Brick	• Long-lasting • Warm in winter • Cool in summer • Fireproof • Horse won't chew them or kick through	• Expensive and time-consuming to construct
Breeze block	• Relatively cheap • Fireproof • Easy to construct • Horse won't chew or kick through	• Can be cold if not insulated
Felt	• Economic • Can cover wooden roof • Easy to replace	• Can rip in wind • Can make stables dark
Onduline	• Light weight • Flexible • Can have clear plastic inserts to provide natural light	• Can cause condensation if unlined
Slate or tile	• Long lasting • Warm • Can replace single tiles/slates	• Heavy — needs solid supporting structure • Expensive

Some key considerations

Ventilation

Good natural ventilation is essential to help maintain horses' health. Windows, louvre boards, ridge vents or chimneys all encourage fresh air to be sucked in and stale air to be pushed out of a stable.

Windows should ideally be situated where they will not cause a draught across the stable and they should open inwards to stop rain or snow getting in, as should any slats. Any glass should have a grille over it to reduce the risk of breakage.

Louvre boards are usually positioned in the eaves on the end walls of stable blocks. They have gaps in between them and are usually angled upwards to prevent rain or snow entering.

Barns typically have vents or 'chimneys' situated along the ridge to draw the stale air up and out, allowing the cooler air in.

A window with a louvre board design.

Flooring

Stable and yard flooring should be even and non-slip. Concrete is probably the most common flooring as it is reasonably cheap and long-lasting. Ideally, it should be brushed to make it less slippery.

Rubber matting can add a layer of protection and makes the floor a bit warmer. If the mats are not sealed they should be lifted regularly and the floor beneath cleaned.

All stables should be free draining, ideally towards the back of the box, so urine is carried away from the front where the horse tends to spend most of his time, and away from any forage fed from the floor. Drainage channels inside or outside the stable should be kept clear.

Some older stable yards may be paved with cobbles or bricks, which can make for an uneven floor as they start to wear away and cause urine to pool, besides being difficult to sweep.

Lighting

Ideally the stable should have lots of natural light. But for safety, all light fittings should be encased in plastic and positioned high enough in the roof that the horse will not hit his head on them or break them. Light switches should be positioned outside the stable, out of the horse's reach, and should be weatherproof. All wiring should be encased in plastic to protect it from the elements and from vermin.

Stable door

Stable doors should have horse-proof top bolts and kick bolts at the bottom, to minimise the risk of horses opening the bolt themselves and escaping. A metal strip at the top of the stable door protects it from chewing. These can be extended partway down the door to protect the front of the door from teeth.

If there is a top door it should be secured back so it doesn't blow closed in the wind.

Stable doors should have horse proof top bolts and kick bolts at the bottom, to reduce the risk of horses opening the bolt and escaping. The metal strip over the top part of the door protects it from being chewed.

Fixtures and fittings

Stable fixtures and fittings should ideally be kept to a minimum and should be assessed for practicality and necessity. The fewer fixtures and fittings, the less there is for the horse to hurt himself on, or to damage.

Tie-ring

A tie-up ring (with string attached) on the same wall as the door is a necessity for tying up the horse and haynets, and allows the handler to go in and out of the stable without having to walk behind the horse. The haynet ring should be high enough up to keep the horse from getting his feet tangled in an empty net.

Haybar/rack

A haybar or hayrack may be used as an alternative to a net. Hayracks tend to be fitted fairly high and can take up a lot of space. There is a small risk of the horse getting a hoof stuck in between the bars, and hay seeds or dust can drop out and get in the horse's eyes. Some have hatches that open outside the stable, which is time-saving but if you fill them using loose hay rather than sections it can be messy.

Haybars in the corner of the stable provide a more natural feeding position for the horse. They are easier to fill, but should be checked regularly for signs of damage such as chewed edges or the attachments coming undone.

Removable corner feed manger.

Corner hay manger.

Water supply

Water can be supplied by buckets or an automatic water drinker. Buckets should be made of plastic or heavy rubber and ideally placed in the corner of the stable, with the handles against the wall, to prevent them from being knocked over by the horse. They can be placed in a tyre to reduce the risk of them being knocked over, but this takes up a lot of room and can be dangerous if the horse gets a foot stuck between the tyre and the bucket. Buckets are useful to monitor how much a horse is drinking daily but are labour-intensive as they require regular checking and refilling.

Automatic drinkers are labour-saving as they consistently provide fresh water, but they can be difficult to clean and (unless costly individual water meters are installed) it is not possible to monitor how much water the horse is drinking They must be maintained regularly and checked for signs of damage, and the pipes lagged sufficiently to prevent freezing in the winter.

Automatic water drinker.

Rug racks

Rug racks are a common feature inside or outside the stable. They too should be fixed high enough that there is no risk of the horse catching a leg in the straps, and to prevent the rugs from touching the floor where they can soak up the damp. If you hang rugs inside the stable, make sure they are not where they can be chewed or pulled on to the floor for the horse's entertainment!

Rug rack.

Extras

Any extras such as toys or salt licks should be checked regularly for safety and ideally removed if not being used. Some salt lick holders have sharp edges and can rust over time when they lose their plastic coating.

Summary

- Stables should be a suitable size for the horse.
- Indoor and outdoor stables each have pros and cons.
- There are a variety of materials that can be used for constructing stable yards.
- Fixtures and fittings should be kept to a minimum.

TRAINING TIPS

1. When possible, have a look around different types of yards and at the types of stables and the fixtures and fittings.

2. Speak to people on the yard about what they like or dislike about a yard's layout.

3. Some big equine events have stabling manufacturers' stands or displays — look at the latest designs and consider how they would work on your yard.

Chapter 11

Care of Horses at Grass

Water supply

Shelter

Field boundaries

Hazards

Summary

Care of Horses at Grass

For horses to stay healthy and safe in a field environment they have various needs that must be met, such as a constant supply of water, shelter from the elements and a safe boundary to contain them.

Water supply

The horse must have continuous access to a fresh, clean water supply. The way in which this is achieved will vary from yard to yard and will depend on preference, availability and practicality.

Troughs

A trough is the most efficient way of supplying water to field-kept horses. Water troughs come in different shapes and sizes, and must be checked for safety to ensure there are no sharp edges that a horse could cut himself on. It should be large enough to supply the number of horses in the field. Depending on the design one trough can supply two fields sharing a fence line, making it more economical.

An automatic trough is the most time-efficient system as it refills itself every time it is used. These troughs are supplied from water pipes, which can be expensive to lay if the trough is a long way from the water supply, but the cost is offset against the labour of manually filling troughs or buckets in a field.

All troughs will need regular cleaning, although in a smaller trough the water is refreshed more often, which results in a slower deposit of dirt than in larger ones where the horses will drink only a small proportion of the water at a time. Some troughs have a plug in the bottom, to assist with emptying the water out to clean them, although they may also be vulnerable to leaks. They should be checked daily for debris such as leaves that may have fallen in, and for ice forming in the winter. In winter, there is a danger of the pipes freezing in very cold weather if they are not lagged sufficiently, or the ballcock being jammed. If this happens another method of providing water will have to be used.

Troughs can be quite labour-intensive if they need to be refilled by hand, particularly at times when the horse drinks more, e.g. summer months and very dry, cold weather. Such troughs are most suitable for fields or paddocks near to the yard so that water does not have to be carried long distances. Using a hosepipe may be easier and quicker than carrying water containers or buckets, although the location sometimes makes using a hosepipe impossible. There is, however, an advantage of refilling manually, which is that you can monitor how much the horse is drinking, although if there are several horses in the same field it is very difficult to monitor who is drinking what.

Stream

A running stream can provides a constant supply of water and is less likely to freeze than static water sources. However, it can be difficult to know if the water has been polluted further upstream, and the stream may carry debris. The stream bed could also cause problems; if it is sandy, sand or silt may build up in the horse's stomach, which could lead to colic.

If a stream is used as a water supply it must be easily accessible by the horses, with no steep, slippery banks, boggy ground or drop into the water. Depending on water levels the suitability may vary. In very wet weather it may run too high to be safe to use and during very dry months the flow may be very low or may even stop. The questions about pollution and access quite often mean that a stream is not a viable water source and it may need to be permanently fenced off to avoid problems and another water source used instead.

Shelter

Horses should have shelter available all year round from the sun, wind, rain and snow and also from flies and other insects that can annoy them. There may be some natural shelter already growing in or around the field, but shelter may also need to be man-made.

Natural shelter

Natural shelter comes in the form of hedges or trees in or around the field. A good, solid hedge can provide excellent protection from wind, driving rain and low sun, but may not be as effective for flies and midday sun (where the sun is directly overhead). Regular checks also need to be made for poisonous plants such as foxgloves. If the hedge is also the fence line, it must be checked regularly to make sure that no gaps appear that a horse could push through (particularly in winter, when it will have fewer leaves and gaps become more obvious).

Hedges and trees provide natural shelter.

Trees (as long as they are not poisonous to horses — see Hazards, later this chapter) can provide good shelter from rain, snow, sun and flies, but may not be as effective against wind. Check the trees regularly for damage to the trunk or fallen branches that may present a hazard, particularly after stormy weather. Low-hanging branches may also injure the horse or damage rugs if they catch on them.

The natural landscape in and around the field, such as undulations or hillsides, may provide a limited amount of shelter from wind and driving rain, but this is not ideal as the only form of shelter.

A bank offering a limited amount of shelter.

Man-made shelters

Field shelter

This is a stable-like structure, often made of wood. It can offer good shelter in all weathers, but is not ideal in a field with a lot of horses as it may not provide enough space and one horse may become penned in (and even hurt) by another. It is a good idea for the shelter to have only three sides so that there is a large entrance/exit, hopefully minimising the risk of a horse becoming trapped. The size of shelter needed will depend on the number of horses in the field; it may be that more than one is required, and the open side should always face away from the prevailing weather.

The field shelter needs to be facing away from the prevailing weather to provide maximum shelter for the horse.

Mobile field shelters, built on skids, are designed so they can be moved if the ground in or around them becomes poached, or from paddock to paddock if you are separating one large field into smaller paddocks and rotating the grazing. The shelter can be moved by using a four-wheel drive vehicle or a tractor by means of a hitch at the side of the shelter. When not in use the hitch should be safely secured against the side of the shelter, to prevent a horse injuring himself on it, or it becoming damaged. These shelters are less expensive than building a shelter in each field and may not require the same planning permission as a fixed structure; as they do not sit on a permanent base such as concrete or hard core – but advice should always be sought from the area planning authority before erecting any type of field shelter. A barn or an open-sided barn could also be used as a field shelter.

Walls

Drystone walls are not commonly found across the UK, but can still be seen in Scotland, Ireland and upland areas of England. If they are kept in good repair, they can provide some shelter against wind and driving rain. However, they are not as effective against sun and flies, only offering shade when the sun is low.

Rugs

Rugs can be classed as a form of shelter as they protect the horse too. Modern turnout rugs are lightweight, breathable, windproof and waterproof, and come in a variety of thicknesses, which can be interchanged depending on the weather. Fly rugs will protect the horse from both flies and sunlight. Fly masks protect the horse's eyes, ears and face from flies, and fly-repellent will also help. Rugs can be very individual to both the horse and the weather, but they also move with the horse, providing protection wherever he goes. However, there is the potential that they may slip or become damaged, and they do not cover every part of the horse.

> Quite often using more than one type of shelter gives the horse the best all-round protection.

Field boundaries

Post and rail fencing

A post and rail fence is commonly made of wooden posts and rails, but can also be made using heavy-duty plastic.

Although a wooden fence is expensive to install, it can have a very long life expectancy if well maintained. It needs to be treated each year with a wood preservative to prevent it from rotting and this can take quite a long time depending on the length of the fence. The fence can also be damaged by horses chewing, rubbing or leaning against it. Any broken or damaged parts should be repaired or replaced quickly, as split wood or stray nails can cause injury.

Wooden post and rail fencing is pleasing on the eye but can be expensive to install and maintain.

This type of fence will commonly have two rails, but the number can vary depending on their use, e.g. a field with foals in it may need more rails, closer together to prevent foals from slipping under or through. Over time, the posts may start to lean, especially if the ground is often wet, but if the posts are erected into concrete the risk of this is minimised.

The use of plastic rather than wood is still expensive to install but can drastically reduce the maintenance required, making it more economical than the wooden post and rail. The plastic does not need regular treatment and, as it does not absorb moisture, it will not rot. It is very durable and has a long life expectancy, even with minimal maintenance.

Hedges

A hedge can be a very good option for a field boundary since, as mentioned earlier, it also provides shelter. However, it must be high enough that the horse cannot jump it, and solid/thick enough that he can't get through it. A hedge is often used in conjunction with another type of fence, such as post and rail, so horses can benefit from its advantages (e.g. shelter) while it is also more secure. As mentioned earlier, the hedge should be checked regularly for poisonous plants, e.g. foxglove or deadly nightshade, and should trimmed to encourage it to grow from the bottom. A pre-existing hedge obviously does not cost anything to install, and maintenance costs should be relatively low.

Electric fencing

Electric fencing can take a few different forms. The posts may be temporary ones, stuck into the ground via a metal spike, or more permanent wooden ones that have been hammered into the ground. Temporary posts can be moved as and when required very easily, but can be easily knocked over by horses. The permanent posts give a more secure fence but cannot be moved. The electric strands can either be rope, tape or wire. Wire is often only used as cattle fencing, and is not suitable for horses because it is very difficult to see. Rope and tape are more appropriate for horses but it is best to have at least two strands to make it more visible and a more effective barrier.

Electric fencing is relatively cheap and easy to install but can need a lot of day-to-day maintenance, especially when used with temporary posts, as these often start to lean, with the tape or rope becoming slack or broken. The important thing to remember about electric fencing is that it is only truly effective if the electric current is working well. It is necessary to check frequently that there is a constant power supply, and if this comes from a battery it will need regular recharging. The fence also needs checking for things that may break the circuit and short the electricity (e.g. overgrown grass or weeds).

An electric fence with a good power supply can be very effective as horses will not want to touch it, so will not chew or lean on it. However, some horses, particularly smaller ones, will still push through the fence regardless of the electric shocks, so it is not always effective. For

A well-maintained electric fence can be very effective.

security and safety, an electric fence is not advised as the only boundary fencing, and its best use may be to split a larger field into smaller paddocks. It can be used alongside another form of fencing, e.g. post and rail fencing, to make a more secure and effective barrier. Used either on the inside of the other fence or as the top rail, it can protect the other fence from horses leaning or chewing on it.

Gates

Gates and gateways should allow enough room for you and your horse to pass through them safely and comfortably. They must fasten securely and ideally situated in an area of good drainage. If the gateway becomes wet and muddy it may be necessary to ask for hardcore to be laid down. Gates leading on to a road should be padlocked.

Hazards

Fields should regularly assessed for hazards. Remove them if possible, or fence them off to avoid horses becoming ill or injured.

Some hazards are easily removed, e.g. fallen branches and litter, but some may be permanent and more of a problem. Footpaths run across the countryside all over the UK, and will sometimes run across a field that you want to use for turnout. Anyone can use a public footpath, and this can be a hazard in itself. Some people walk their dogs along footpaths, and it's a good idea to put signs up asking for them to be kept on leads. Often it is best to fence the horses away from the footpath to avoid problems.

You may find holes made by rabbits or badgers appearing in your field. These can be catastrophic if a horse accidentally puts a foot down them, so check the field regularly for holes, and fill in or fence off any that you find.

A pond or area of stagnant water is another potential hazard, which could give a horse colic if he drank from it. This should also be fenced off.

Poisonous plants

It is important to be able to recognise common poisonous plants and trees to minimise any risk to grazing horses. Some common ones poisonous to horses are shown below:

Ragwort at the rosette stage (above left) and at the flowering stage (above centre). Ragwort is a resilient plant that can grow anywhere. When digging up ragwort, make sure you get the roots as well.

Foxglove — a plant most commonly found in shady areas such as woodland, hedgerows or moorland.

The sycamore tree has distinctive leaves and seeds. The seeds from the sycamore have been linked to atypical or seasonal myopathy.

Laburnum is a highly poisonous deciduous tree, and all of its parts are toxic. It has distinctive yellow pea-flowers that hang in long, drooping clusters. Its leaves grow in threes (a little like clover) and black seeds grow inside pea-like pods. Laburnum is a popular garden tree, so any fields close to housing should be checked, and fenced off if necessary.

Yew's distinctive needle-like leaves and red seed coverings. Yew is highly poisonous to horses. Any fields abutting churchyards, in particular, should be checked for proximity of yew and fenced off if necessary.

The oak tree's leaves and acorns — green acorns from oak trees can be toxic to horses.

Deadly nightshade is a poisonous plant that can be recognised by its bell-shaped purple flowers and shiny berries, which will range from green through to black when ripened. The leaves are oval-shaped with pointed ends. It can usually be found in woodlands, field margins and hedgerows, but also grows in open pasture or any disturbed land. It is not normally very palatable to horses but they may eat it if food is sparse or it has been accidentally made in with hay. Remove any deadly nightshade that you find in your grazing land.

Summary

- When living in a field environment, horses require constant access to clear fresh water, shelter from the elements and safe boundary fencing.

- Shelter can be provided by trees, hedges, purpose-built structure and rugs.

- All fencing should be well maintained.

- Any hazards that cannot be removed may need to be fenced off.

- All poisonous plants and trees should be removed or fenced off where possible.

TRAINING TIPS

1. Take note of different types of water supply, shelter and fencing you see around local fields and whether it would be suitable for horses.

2. Have a look at the variety of fencing/water troughs, etc. available in farming shops, how they work, and what kind of maintenance they would require.

3. Go for a walk and try to identify any poisonous plants along the way.

Chapter 12

Tack and Equipment

Adjusting the fit of a bridle

Checking the fit of a saddle

Caring for equipment

Summary

Tack and Equipment

For the horse to be able to work comfortably it is important that the tack he wears fits correctly and is suitable for the job the horse is doing. It is easy to overlook gradual changes to the fit, especially if you are putting the same tack on the same horse daily. It is good practice to make assessing the fit of the horse's tack part of your routine checks to ensure the comfort of the horse.

Adjusting the fit of a bridle

Making adjustments to a bridle is relatively straightforward if you know the bridle already fits that horse but might need some minor adjusting because it was put back together incorrectly after strip cleaning for example, or the bit needs to be changed back after a cross-country session.

Start by checking the tack over for safety as you would normally. Check the stitching for signs of rotting and the leather and buckles or billets for signs of wearing or splitting. Any missing keepers or signs of wear and tear should be reported to your supervisor.

Put a headcollar on the horse and tie him up. Before putting the bridle on it is useful to check the length against the horse's head to avoid trying to put on a bridle that is too short or too long.

Undo the lead rope and either leave the end threaded through the string or hold it in your hand. Some horses might react to the bridle being held by their head; by holding the rope or leaving it through the string it may stop the horse feeling restricted and reduce the risk of him pulling back. Carefully hold the bridle up to the side of the horse's face to assess whether it is long enough. The headpiece should be level with the poll and the bit rings level with the mouth. If you find the bit is hanging beneath the horse's mouth, the cheekpieces should be shortened. Likewise if the bit is sitting above the horse's mouth the cheekpieces should be lengthened before the bridle is put it on.

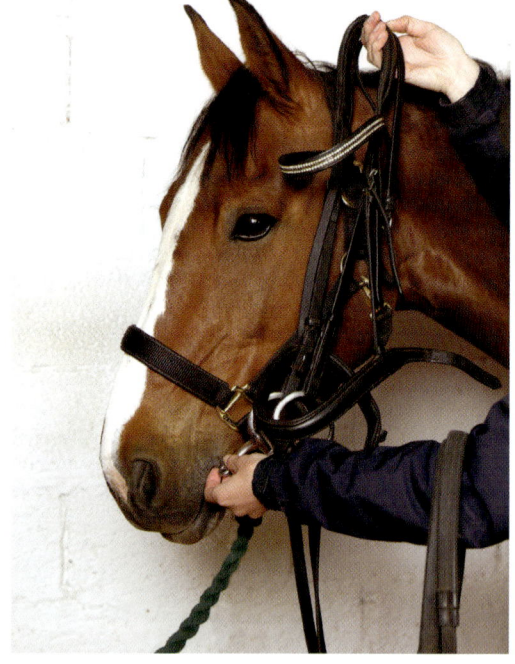

Hold the bridle up against the horse's head so you can measure the length and adjust the bit to an approximate height before putting the bridle on.

12 | Tack and Equipment

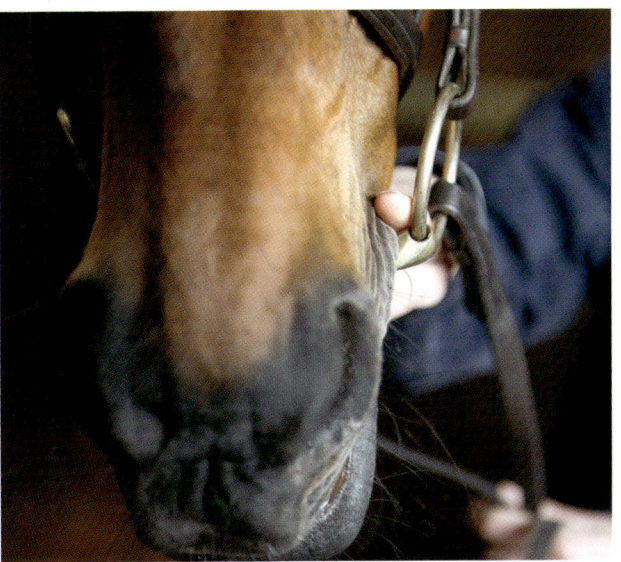

There should be room to fit a finger between the horse's mouth and the bit ring to prevent the bit pinching the lips.

A correctly fitted bridle.

Take the runners and keepers out from the cheekpieces and leave them out in case you need to make a quick adjustment to the cheekpieces once the bridle is on and then put the bridle on the horse.

The bit should be adjusted first as it will cause the most discomfort to the horse if it is not in the correct place. If it is too high it will pull the corners of the lips back and if it is too low it can bang on the horse's teeth.

The bit should sit level across the horse's mouth and be fitted so it creates a wrinkle in the each corner of the horse's mouth. There should be enough room to fit a finger either side between the bit ring and the lips to prevent rubbing. Once you have adjusted the bit, do up the throatlash and noseband and then recheck the fit of the bridle.

Noseband

Check the noseband for fit. All nosebands should sit level across the horse's face when viewed from the front, and be positioned so they are not rubbing on the bony projections of the horse's face. They should not sit on the fleshy part of the horse's nose, which could damage the nasal cartilage and interfere with the horse's breathing. You should always be able to fit a minimum of one finger between the straps of a noseband and the horse's face so the horse has room to open his mouth slightly and relax his jaw. The headpiece of the noseband will pass over or under the main bridle headpiece, depending on the design of the bridle. Make sure these straps are not twisted or placing pressure on the poll or ears.

A cavesson noseband should sit two fingers below the projecting cheekbone and be fastened so you can fit two fingers all the way between the horse's nose and the strap.

A flash noseband sits slightly higher than a cavesson (one finger below the projecting cheekbone) and is fastened slightly tighter to prevent it from being pulled down the nose by the lower strap. The lower strap should sit on the bony part of the nose and not restrict the horse's breathing. Both parts should be fastened so that you can fit one finger between them and the horse's face. The buckle should fasten on the soft part of the nose behind the nostril.

A drop noseband should fit approximately four fingers width above the top of the nostrils so it sits over the bony part of the nose just above the fleshy part, to avoid damaging the softer cartilage below or interfering with the horse's breathing. The lower strap lies in front of the bit rings and fastens in the chin groove. The noseband should be fastened with room for two fingers to fit between the strap and the nose.

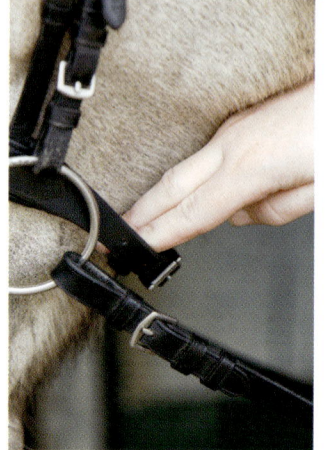
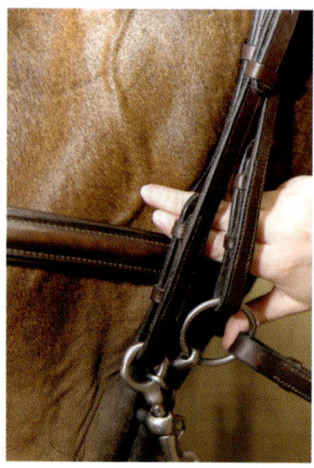

There should be room for two fingers to fit around the noseband. The noseband should sit approximately two fingers below the protruding cheekbone.

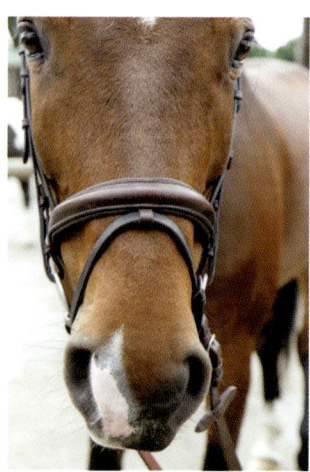
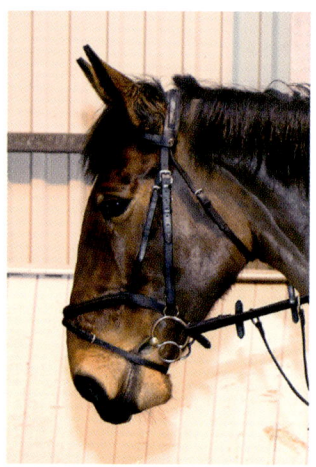
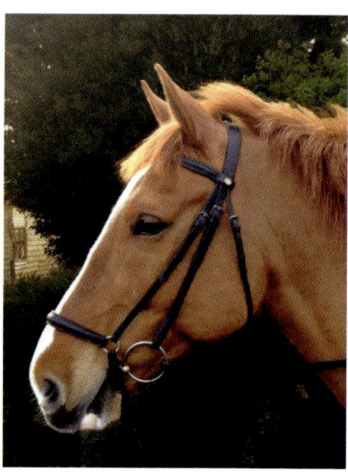

The picture on the left shows a correctly fitted flash noseband. In the picture on the right the bottom strap has pulled the cavesson part of the noseband down, which could potentially interfere with the horse's breathing.

A correctly fitted drop noseband.

With a grackle noseband the top straps sit under the cheekpieces, fastening under the cheekbones, and the lower strap sits in front of the bit and fastens in the chin groove. The crossover point should sit on the centre of the nose and there should be one to two fingers clearance between the horse's head and the straps. If the grackle has rings these should not interfere with the projecting cheekbones.

Padding lifts the noseband off of the nose, preventing rubbing. The rings of the Mexican grackle should sit clear of the projecting cheekbones.

Checking the fit of a saddle

Saddle fit will alter as the horse gains or loses condition throughout the year and although you will require a qualified saddler fitter to make any adjustments to the saddle, you should be aware of how to check the basic fit of a saddle so you can potentially pick up any changes early and avoid causing the horse undue discomfort. Prolonged use of an ill-fitting saddle can cause uneven muscle development, rubbing, hair loss or broken skin and can affect the horse's movement.

Before putting the saddle on the horse's back take the time to look at the panels and check if they are even. Lumps along the panels can be a sign of uneven flocking, which can create pressure points along the horse's back and can be an indication that the saddle requires re-flocking. Check the stitching for signs of rotting and the leather and girth straps for signs of wear and tear, such as the holes stretching.

When checking the fit of the saddle on the horse, tie up the horse in a safe place, preferably on flat ground. Try to keep the horse standing as square as possible throughout your checks. Gently place the saddle on the horse's back without a numnah underneath. This allows you to see how the saddle sits along the horse's back. You can check the basic fit of a saddle either with or without a girth attached; if you are not using a girth make sure you keep hold of the saddle at all times to prevent it falling off the horse's back if he moves.

Check that the saddle is not pressing down on the withers or pinching at the sides. There should be two to three fingers clearance (although it does depend on the individual saddle and horse) in between the pommel and the top of the withers and one finger at either side of the withers. Some close-contact saddles may fit closer to the withers than this but no saddle should be sitting on the withers. A saddle that is too wide will sit close to or on the withers and one that is too narrow will sit high up off the withers with no room at the side.

The panels should sit flat and level and should not sit up off the horse's back. When viewed from the side the saddle should sit level so as not to tip the rider forwards or back. Daylight should be visible through the gullet and there should be enough clearance to be able to fit three fingers between the gullet and the spine. If the saddle is too wide the gullet might touch the spine; if it is too narrow the panels may pinch on the spine.

There should be no tight spots between the front of the saddle and the horse's shoulder. You should be able to run a flat hand smoothly down between the front panel and the shoulder on each side. Any tight areas will reduce the movement of the shoulder-blade.

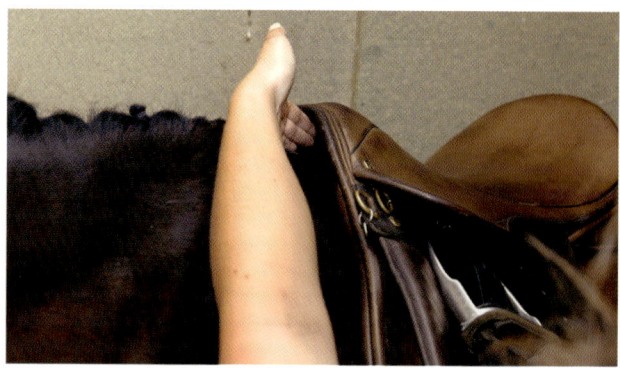

There should be two to three fingers' clearance over the withers at the front of the saddle.

The saddle should sit level when viewed from the side and the back.

Checking for tightness. Start by the withers and run a flat hand down the length of the saddle.

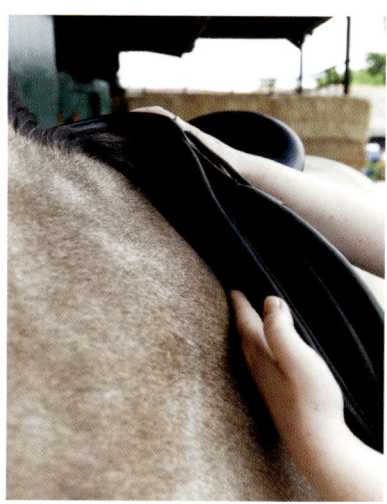

If the saddle appears to fit well on the horse's back, with no uneven pressure, put on the numnah and pull it up into the gullet to ensure it doesn't place pressure across the withers or spine, and then recheck the fit of the saddle.

Caring for equipment

It is important to keep tack and equipment clean. Horse tack and equipment is expensive but if well looked after it will last a long time. Cleaning and correct storage of equipment will help keep it in good condition as well as making it easy to find when you need it. Regular and thorough cleaning of tack and washing of items such as boots, numnahs and girths is also important in preventing the potential spread of disease, especially if horses are sharing tack.

All leather items that are not kept soft and supple will dry, harden and crack, making them more likely to break, compromising safety. Regular cleaning and oiling of all leather items will help keep them supple. (This includes any leather items such as a leather lunge cavesson, leather attachments on rollers or rugs, leather boots and headcollars, not just basic tack.) If you are storing tack that is not in use, thoroughly clean and oil it first then store it in a warm, dry area to help prevent mildew forming. Items such as cheekpieces, stirrup leathers or irons should be stored in their pairs.

Ideally, tack should be wiped over after every use to prevent grease building up. The bit should be thoroughly rinsed after every use and all remnants of saliva or chewed food removed. Tack should ideally be stored in a well-ventilated, warm and dry room, away from direct sunlight, which can damage the leather. Bridles should be hung from the headpiece and saddles stored on suitable stands or racks. You may want to put padding underneath the saddle to prevent the saddle rack leaving a mark. Placing a saddle cover over the saddle will help to protect it from accidental scratches and prevent dust and hair from collecting on top of it.

Brushing numnahs and girths off after each use will prevent a build-up of hair and, if they are damp, they can be hung upside down over a saddle rack to dry off. Regular washing will prevent a build-up of grease and hair on the underside, which can irritate and rub the horse's back.

Saddles stored neatly in a tack room.

Get into the habit of brushing off items such as boots and bandages before storing them in pairs or sets. Bandages should be rolled up correctly with the Velcro done up on the inside so they are ready for use when required. Correct storage will help to prolong the life of boots and bandages by protecting them from rodents and moths. It also reduces the risk of rubbing on the horses' legs, which can cause irritation and could cause sores. Velcro fastenings should be cleaned regularly with a Velcro brush to keep them free from hair and dirt, which will compromise the adhesion of the Velcro.

Before storing rugs, check, repair and wash them. Storing them neatly folded in bags saves space and keeps them clean. Clearly labelling the bags will make it easier to locate the rug you require without having to open the bags. Rugs can also be hung up on rug racks in a well-ventilated warm environment that allows the air to circulate. If using a rug rack make sure both front buckles of the rug are fastened to prevent the fastenings stretching.

Rugs stored neatly on rug racks.

Summary

- It is good practice to check the fit of your tack every time you tack up a horse.

- The changing condition of the horse throughout the year can affect the fit of the saddle.

- Keep tack clean and in good condition for safety, disease control and long life.

- Wash bandages, numnahs and boots regularly.

- Clean and repair tack before it is stored in a rodent-free, warm, dry environment.

TRAINING TIPS

1. Observe a saddle fitting session and ask questions about what you see.

2. Check the fit of one saddle on several different horses (with permission from the saddle's owner). See how the fit differs between horses.

3. For more information contact The Society of Master Saddlers or visit their website www.mastersaddlers.co.uk.

Chapter 13
Lungeing

Reasons for lungeing

Safety while lungeing

Fitting tack for lungeing

Handling and use of equipment

Aids and body language

The lungeing process

Problems that may occur when lungeing

Summary

Lungeing is a valuable skill but learning to do it proficiently takes time. As well as being used in the horse's initial training, it is an alternative form of exercise to ridden work. However, lungeing involves risks for both handler and horse, so safe procedures must be followed, with both wearing protective equipment. Lungeing provides an opportunity for you to hone communication skills with your horse. It is a great feeling to see a horse respond to your aids from the ground.

Besides developing clear communication, you must learn to handle lungeing equipment safely, with the eventual aim that you can do so almost automatically so your full focus can be on the horse.

Reasons for lungeing

- As a rough guide, 30 minutes of lungeing provides the same amount of exercise as riding for one hour in the school. Thus it is a very useful exercise method, especially in commercial yards where there are lots of horses to work. However, 15 to 25 minutes of work on the lunge is sufficient exercise for most horses. As it requires horses to work actively on a continuous circle, working them for too long can be demanding on their joints, muscles, tendons and ligaments.

- It provides variation to your horse's exercise routine. Horses, like people, can become bored with the same routine every day.

- In some situations horses can be lunged for exercise when they cannot be ridden. This enables them to be kept fit or at least given some exercise, especially if they are stabled with no turnout.

- Sometimes a horse may be lunged prior to being ridden, for example as a warm-up or to settle him down if he is fresh.

- Lungeing is used throughout the horse's training. A horse being backed learns to respond to voice aids, which the rider can use later to help him understand leg, rein and seat aids. In later training it helps work and strengthen the horse without interference from a rider.

Safety while lungeing

As mentioned, there are risks associated with lungeing, especially with fresh, young or inexperienced horses, although all horses can be unpredictable. You should therefore wear a riding hat that meets current safety standards, and suitable footwear. Well-fitting gloves will make it easier to handle the lunge line and whip as well as provide protection from rope-burn if the horse suddenly pulls the lunge line through your hands.

Ideally, you should lunge in an enclosed area such as an arena or a lunge pen with an all-weather surface, with the door or gate shut. If the horse gets loose, he will be contained and less likely to injure himself or others. The surface should not be slippery, too hard or too deep to minimise the risk of injury to the horse. The area should be free from hazards such as whips, jump cups, coffee mugs and drinks cans. Jump poles stacked on kicking boards can be unsafe, as can jumping equipment left in a pile in the arena. If other horses are being lunged in the arena at the same time, place poles with gaps between them across the arena to separate them. Be aware of what other people are doing and also how their horses' behaviour might affect your horse, especially if the horse is fresh. When leaving the arena always ask permission to avoid upsetting the other horses.

It is not a good idea to lunge in the same arena as others are riding in. If the lunge horse were to get loose and gallop around with the lunge line trailing, it would be a significant and scary hazard.

Be aware of your surroundings and remain alert. If horses grazing nearby become spooked and start galloping about, the horse you are lungeing is likely to react. Horses are often sharper in cold or windy weather and thus more likely to spook, buck or shoot off, especially if you are lungeing in a field — we don't all have access to outdoor or indoor arenas. If using a field, it may be helpful to mark out a lungeing area using safe hedges or fence lines, barrels or markers. Select the best going available, but vary the area where you lunge to avoid the ground becoming muddy or poached in wet conditions.

Fitting tack for lungeing

The tack needed for lungeing includes a bridle (with noseband removed), lunge cavesson, side-reins, saddle or roller, brushing boots (front and back) and possibly overreach boots. It is important to check that the equipment is safe (e.g. the stitching and condition of the leather) and fits correctly so it is comfortable.

Lungeing from a cavesson provides a point of contact with the horse without interfering with the contact between the bit and side-reins. It also means you do not have to unclip the lunge line from the bit each time you change the rein. The cavesson can be put on under or over the bridle, depending on the type

A horse suitably tacked for lungeing, with handler wearing hat, gloves and suitable footwear.

of cavesson and how best it will fit with the bridle. You might choose to put it on over the bridle if the horse is going to be ridden after being lunged. Before putting on the bridle and cavesson, remove the bridle's noseband to reduce bulk. The cavesson should be fitted so that the noseband sits one to two fingers below the horse's projecting cheekbone. The straps need to be done up firmly, so it does not move across the horse's head and catch the outside eye if he pulls to the outside on the circle. Once the cavesson and bridle are fitted, twist the reins and thread the throatlash through them to stop them falling over the horse's head if he puts it down.

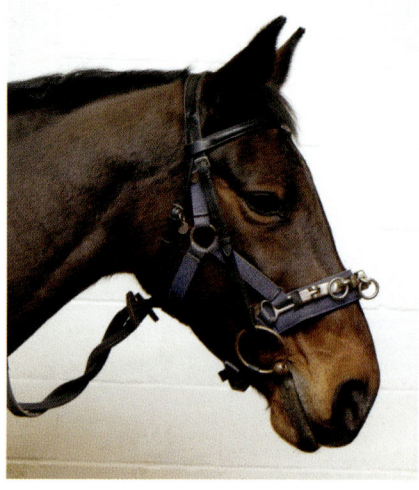

If putting the cavesson on under the bridle, simply put it on and secure the straps, then put the bridle on over the top. Make sure the reins are securely twisted.

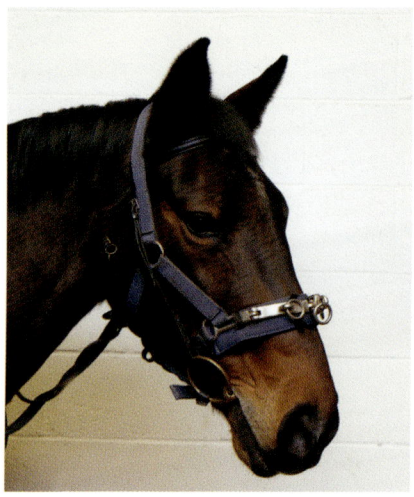

If putting the cavesson over the bridle, do up the noseband strap under the cheekpieces after putting the cavesson on. The other straps can either be done up over or under the cheek pieces according to which looks most comfortable for the horse.

Saddle or roller and side-reins

Saddle and side-reins

Put on the saddle as usual but twist the stirrup leathers to stop the stirrups falling down and banging against the horse's elbows and sides while you lunge.

Thread the side-reins under the first girth strap and attach them to the second or third strap. Attaching side-reins this way will prevent them from pulling the girth straps forwards.

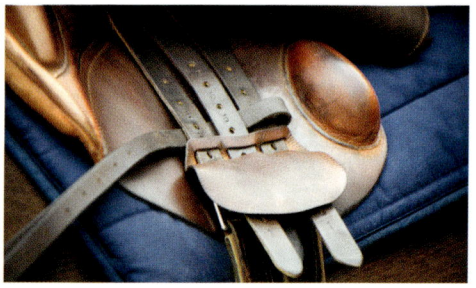

Side-reins attached to the girth straps above the girth guard to prevent them slipping down.

13 | Lungeing

Two different methods of securing stirrups for lungeing.

Side-reins also need adjusting to make them roughly the right length for the horse. Start by attaching them to the girth then with the horse's head and neck straight in front of him, take them forwards and upwards until they reach the horse's poll or forwards towards the bit as shown in the picture. Once adjusted, the side-reins can be clipped to the D-rings of the saddle so they are secured while you warm up the horse.

When the side-reins are fastened and the horse is working, the horse's head should not fall behind a vertical line from browband to ground. It is better to make them longer rather than shorter as they can always be adjusted once you start lungeing.

Measuring the approximate length of the side-reins with a fist between the end of the side-rein and the bit. The horse's head should be straight and in a relaxed position when doing this.

Roller and side-reins

A roller is often used instead of a saddle, if a horse is not going to be ridden. The roller should sit where the girth would lie if using a saddle. It should have a padded underside to prevent pressure on the horse's back but extra padding may be necessary for comfort. The roller should be done up firmly and you should just be able to slide the flat of your hand comfortably between the horse and the roller's girth. The roller may have several rings for attaching the side-reins. You will usually attach them to the lower rings to encourage the horse to work long and low and stretch across his back. The higher rings may be used with horses working in a more advanced outline.

Brushing boots

Ideally the horse should wear front and back brushing boots to protect his legs. Working on a constant circle, there is a higher chance of brushing or knocking the legs, which may also happen if the horse becomes excited and bucks or shoots forward. A horse who is known to be excitable on the lunge or is prone to overreaching may even need overreach boots to protect the bulbs of the front heels.

Handling and use of equipment

In addition to the tack described you will also need a lunge line and lunge whip. It takes practice to handle these correctly and you may feel you have a lot in your hands, especially when unclipping the side-reins while holding the lunge whip and line. It is easy to tangle or drop the line, but the aim is to handle the equipment almost without thinking, so your full attention can be on the horse. Practise if possible with an experienced horse.

Lunge line

The lunge line should be neatly coiled and ready to feed out when the horse needs it. If looped, each loop should be smaller than the previous one to allow the line to unravel freely. Never wrap the lunge line around your hand, as you could be hurt or dragged if the horse pulls away suddenly.

If handed a lunge line by someone else, it is best to roll it yourself to ensure that it is done correctly. If you are going to lunge on the left rein, hold the line at the clip end with your left hand and roll it into neat loops with the right. The loops should not be too large in case you trip on them. Ideally, coil the lunge line ready before attaching it to the horse. However, if you need to re-coil a lunge line while holding the horse, you should place it on the ground and stand between the line and the horse. Try to ensure that the horse stands still and does not stand on the lunge line.

Ideally, roll up the lunge line ready for lungeing before attaching it. However, if handed a horse it is best to re-coil the line.

It will take practise to coil up the lunge line and let it out avoiding tangles or twists. When learning to lunge you can practise doing this with the lunge line clipped to a wall or fence. Practise coiling it up, walking away and letting it out through your hand, then walking back in and coiling it up into your opposite hand.

When lungeing, keep a contact with the horse via the lunge line. It should be straight and should not sag down to the ground. As a guide, the line should never sag lower than the level of the horse's knee; if it drops too low there is a danger that the horse may stand on it or get a leg entangled in it.

A person practising coiling up the lunge line.

An example of a good contact.

This lunge line is dropping too low and could be a hazard.

While lungeing, you can either hold the lunge line in one hand or in both. Try both methods and see which works better for you. The arm holding the line coming from the cavesson should be bent at the elbow, and held at normal riding height to provide a steady and consistent contact.

When lungeing the lunge line should be wound up and held in either one or both hands. It should be tidy and it should not be wrapped around your hands, to prevent your hands getting caught and the risk you may get dragged.

Whip

When leading the horse, the whip can be held under your left arm so you have both hands free. When leading the horse to and from the arena, avoid dragging the end of the whip on the floor. However, once lungeing, there is no need to pick the end up each time you change the rein, so long as you are aware where it is. While lungeing, avoid startling the horse with the whip — take it behind you when swapping it between hands so it does not point at the horse. It is not a good idea to crack the whip if there are other horses nearby being handled or ridden, as it may unsettle them.

A horse being led with the lunge whip held under the handler's arm.

13 | Lungeing

As this horse is being sent out on the circle, the handler is reaching behind their back to take the whip.

Aids and body language

Voice aids

The horse will respond to your tone of voice. To make an upward transition or ask the horse to go more forwards, use a higher tone of voice. Try to make it vibrant, enthusiastic and clear. Most horses will understand the familiar commands 'walk on', 'ter-rott' and 'canter'.

To make a downward transition or ask the horse to go slower, use a lower tone and speak a little more slowly. Sometimes it can help to add a drawn-out sounding 'and' before the command, e.g. 'and wa-alk'.

When lungeing, as with ridden work, the aim is to have the horse obedient to your aids. Only speak when you want the horse to respond to your voice. Use your voice clearly and back up your aids with the whip if required for upward transitions, by flicking it towards the horse's quarters, always in conjunction with a voice aid. If there's no response you can gently flick the quarters with the whip, again with a voice aid, but you may need to make the circle smaller in order to reach the horse. The whip can be also used very effectively as a 'pointer' not only towards the hindquarters to encourage the horse to move forward, but also pointed towards the inside shoulder of a horse who is tending to 'fall in'.

Positioning when lungeing

This section deals with the general principles of positioning and body language once the horse has been started on the lunge. The overall lungeing process in discussed in the section that follows.

Your positioning and body language help you communicate as you lunge. Generally, you want to stand tall, square on to the horse, confident in your manner and clear in your commands. From this basis, you can adapt your position in relation to the horse to encourage him forwards or steady him. On a circle, think of yourself as the apex of a triangle, with the horse as the base and the lunge whip and lunge line as the sides. In this way, the horse is kept 'between whip and lunge line', the lungeing equivalent of keeping the ridden horse 'between leg and hand'.

To send the horse forwards, position yourself in line with the horse's hips, slightly behind your standard position for lungeing. Face further inwards (turning your right shoulder further towards the horse, for example, if on the left rein). If the horse is not responding you may need to shorten your lunge line as you move slightly closer to him, but not so close that you are in danger of being kicked. Be mindful that, even though this manoeuvre may be necessary in order to establish closer communication with the horse, it will make the circle smaller, which will make it harder for him to go forwards. You will need to walk a small circle with the horse to enable you to keep the contact without the circle becoming too small. Once the horse is more responsive, stand still and send him back out on to a larger circle again.

If you are lungeing a lively horse and want to steady him, position yourself slightly further forwards. Face further inwards towards the horse (your left shoulder turned towards the horse on the left rein). However, take care that the horse does not turn in to face you. Your voice is often the best way to steady the horse, and lowering the height of the whip may also help.

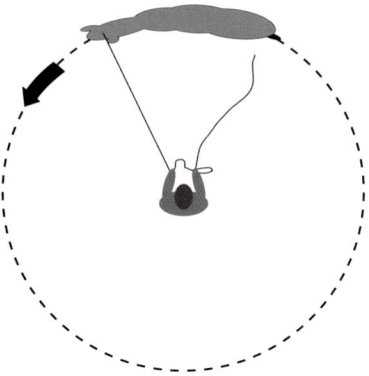

The desired position when lungeing.

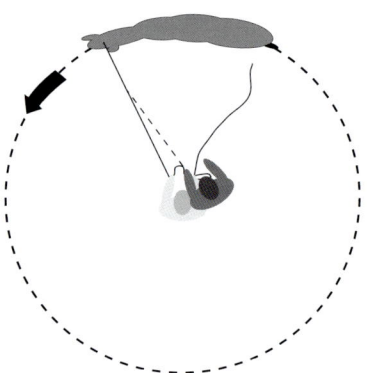

Person Lungeing positioned slightly further back in relation to the horse to encourage the horse to go forwards.

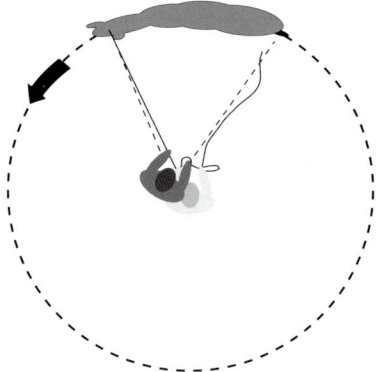

The person lungeing is positioned slightly further forward to encourage the horse to steady.

The lungeing process

Learning to lunge is best done with an experienced, calm horse, who will be more forgiving if you make a mistake or take a while to organise your equipment. It also prevents both you and a less experienced horse learning bad habits.

Starting and warming up

First warm up the horse, without the side-reins attached if he is sensible.

Most horses are easier to lunge on the left rein because we tend to lead them on the left, so it is usual to start on this rein. Lead the horse forwards in walk in a small circle, with the whip under your left arm. Begin turning your body to face the horse to send him away from you. Reach behind your back with your right arm to take the whip, quietly pointing it towards the horse's shoulder. At this point you should be able to stand still and the horse should move away from you.

As the horse walks forwards and away, feed the lunge line gradually through your hand. Try not to walk backwards, away from the horse, but use your body language to move the horse away from you. Ask him to walk on and point the whip towards his shoulders, and the horse should walk positively forwards on a large circle of 18–20m if the length of the lunge line permits. If the horse is quite eager, use your voice and body language to keep him steady, and lower the whip. The horse should walk actively and ideally be overtracking, however some horses may need to warm up before they are able to do this.

> **Some terms used in this section**
>
> ***Overtracking*** *is where the hind feet step over and in front of the prints the forefeet have made. In most horses, this is an indication of an active walk.*
>
> ***Tracking up*** *means that the horse's hind feet are stepping in line with the prints the forefeet have made. In most horses, this is an indication of an active working trot.*
>
> ***Consistent rhythm*** *means clear, regular footfalls of the horse.*

Start to warm up the horse by walking then trotting on both reins. (Changing the rein is explained in the next section.) Stay in trot if the horse is likely to become excited in canter. If a horse is very excited at the start of the lunge session, attach the side-reins for greater control. Spend a little longer without side-reins with an older, stiffer horse who needs to loosen up, or one who is not going properly forwards.

Working in side-reins

After about five minutes with some work on each rein most horses should have warmed up sufficiently for the side-reins to be attached. Indications that the horse has warmed up include 'carrying' the tail; the tail swinging with the movement; tracking up; relaxed, active, fluent movement; stretching and lowering of the neck.

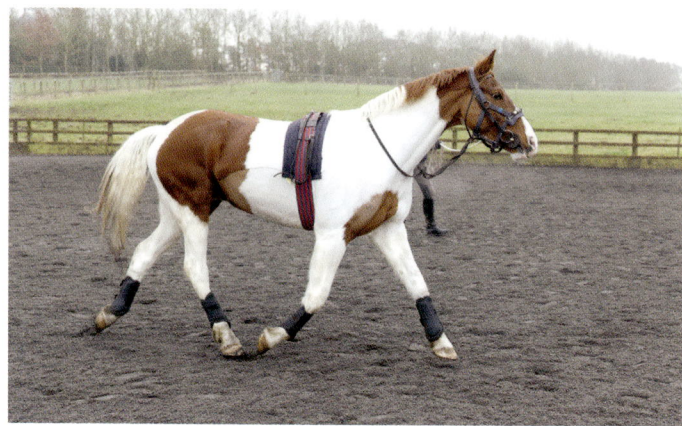

A horse warming up without side-reins, in an active trot, tracking up.

Once the horse is warmed up, the side-reins should be clipped to the bit below the reins with the clip facing outwards, away from the horse. Clip the furthest side-rein on first to avoid having to walk around the front of the horse afterwards. Side-reins are used to provide a consistent contact and help the handler to maintain control.

The side-reins should be clipped to the bit with the clip facing outwards, below the reins.

Once you have asked the horse to trot, he should work actively, with his hind feet tracking up into the imprints of the forefeet in a regular rhythm. His head should be on or slightly in front of the vertical. If the side-reins are too loose or too tight, adjust them.

A horse working actively on the lunge, tracking up with their head slightly in front of the vertical.

13 | Lungeing

In this picture the horse is not trotting actively enough and the head has fallen behind the vertical.

Changing the rein

In the example, we will change the rein from left to right.

Step 1.   Ask the horse to walk and then stand. If he does not stand, quietly begin to walk towards him while repeating the command.

Step 2.   Having brought the horse to a halt (and prior to walking towards him), put the whip under your left arm.

Step 3.   Swap the lunge line into your right hand. As you walk towards the horse, roll the lunge line up, maintaining the contact with the horse so it is ready to be used for the new rein.

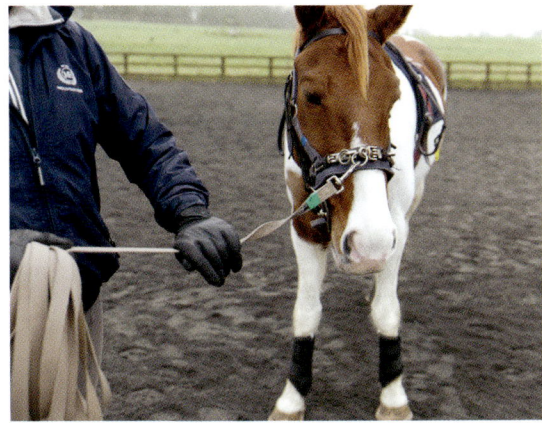 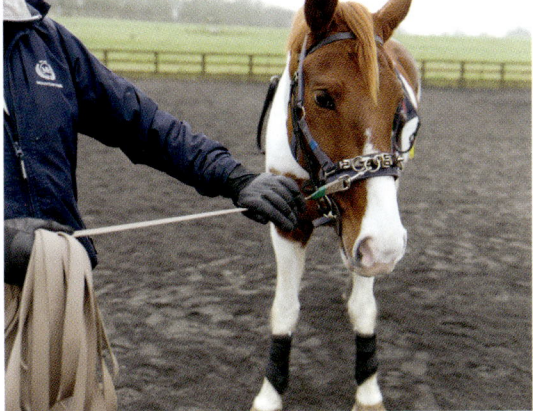

If there are any twists in the lunge line, remove them by pushing them towards the horse (the lunge line clip can twist where it is attached to the cavesson and the line should straighten).

Step 4.   Move around the front of the horse to the other side. Your whip can stay under your arm.

Step 5.   Lead the horse forwards, then on to the right rein.

Step 6.   Send the horse out on to the circle as described earlier, reaching behind your back to take the whip.

Transitions

During the lunge session you can work the horse in trot and include transitions forwards to walk for a few strides before trotting again. Transitions help the horse to work from behind and remain attentive. Vary the size of the circle to help with bend, suppleness and obedience. If the horse is calm, include some transitions between trot and canter, but don't persist if the horse becomes excited or the canter is rushed and unbalanced. Work the horse evenly on both reins.

Cooling down

In all, 20 minutes should be sufficient exercise, including warming up and cooling down without side-reins. When cooling down, ask the horse to walk actively to encourage overtracking, with his head and neck lowered to stretch the back.

A horse cooling down after a lunge session.

Problems that may occur when lungeing

The most common problem is the horse turning in, which may occur if you position yourself too far forwards, or if the horse is confused about what you are asking him to do. Some horses, especially ponies, learn to do this to avoid working on the lunge. They can become exasperatingly quick at it! If this happens, approach them at their shoulder and send them back out on to the circle using the same method as when you started. Position yourself a little behind the horse, ready to send him forwards if he tries to turn in.

The horse you are lungeing may become excited, charge about and buck, risking injury. In this situation keep the circle large to minimise that risk. Use your voice to steady the horse and position yourself further forward in relation to the horse. Horses often show initial excitement but usually settle. If they are excited, put the side-reins on sooner rather than later to control the speed, channel the horse's energy and focus him on you and on working.

Remember that the overall aim is a horse going forwards willingly and calmly, staying out on the circle, working with a supple bend, responding readily to your aids in transitions.

Summary

- Lungeing is a valuable alternative to ridden work.

- Wear correct protective equipment to reduce injury risk.

- Lunge in a safe area.

- Take care to fit lungeing tack correctly.

- Become proficient at handling the lunge line and whip without the horse before attempting to lunge a quiet, experienced horse.

- Learn how to position your body to activate or steady the horse.

- Warm up without the side-reins unless the horse is excited.

- If lungeing is the only work for the horse that day, make sure he is well exercised.

- Ensure that the horse is cooled down after the main work by walking actively to stretch his neck and back.

TRAINING TIPS

1. Learn to handle the line and whip confidently before attempting to lunge a suitable horse.

2. Try to maintain the triangle of horse, whip and line when out on the circle.

3. Make the circle temporarily smaller to encourage an inactive horse to go forwards with the whip.

4. Use transitions for variety and to maintain the horse's attention.

5. Watch other experienced people lungeing to pick up tips, including positioning in relation to the horse and the use of voice aids.

Chapter 14

Flatwork

Riding in a balanced position

The aids

The scale of training

Riding in the school

Riding outside

Dealing with problems

Summary

Riding in a balanced position

Once you have mastered a good basic position in walk, trot and canter, you can start to turn your focus to improving your depth of seat and to refining your aids. This will enable you to begin to influence the way in which the horse goes. You should start to develop and improve your 'feel' through your seat.

Becoming more secure in the saddle, with greater stability and better body control, will make it easier to apply aids with more precision. This will give you more control and increase your influence over the different horses you ride.

As you become more independent you will:

- Work with increasing effect and be able to ride horses with sufficient active forward movement when riding in a group, open order or individually.

- Ride more accurate school figures including circles, loops and serpentines using effective aids to encourage the horse to bend the correct way.

- Demonstrate better transitions by riding forward from your leg into a steady contact, often referred to as riding between leg and hand.

- Develop your feel and knowledge for how the horse is working.

- Work consistently to improve your riding without stirrups in walk, trot and canter.

- Develop a more secure and effective riding position.

What makes a balanced position?

Work on improving the depth of your seat and core stability will continue throughout your riding career. The following are all contributory factors when working on the development of your position.

This rider is sitting in a balanced position.

Sit in the lowest part of the saddle

If you sit on the back of the saddle, your lower leg is likely to slip forward, putting you out of balance and behind the movement of the horse. Remember that when your horse is in motion you have to absorb movement through your joints and muscles. To do this you need to work at your suppleness and core stability, particularly when it comes to sitting trot. This may take time and perseverance.

Upper body position

Your upper body should be supple and upright, with your shoulders open and level, vertical to the horse's back, with your seat bones equally placed either side of the centre of the saddle. Think of your neck being an upright column so that it is vertical and not dropping forward. Look and think ahead. If you lean to left or right, your weight is not evenly distributed and the horse has to adjust how he moves to carry you. If uncorrected over time this is likely to result in uneven muscle development (asymmetry) for both you and the horse. It is important, therefore, to have someone check your position from behind and to note how straight you are. If you have mirrors in the school use these to check your position when riding by yourself.

Leg position

A stable, controlled leg position is really important for maintaining your position and applying effective leg aids. If your lower leg is uncontrolled and constantly swinging against the horse's side, you cannot expect him to listen to your aids. The stirrup leather should be in a straight line vertical to the ground, with the widest part of your inner lower leg lightly in contact with the horse's side, the thigh flat and with the heel down just behind the girth. Your stirrup should be on the ball of your foot. The whole idea of a correct leg position is that you should not have to move your leg to use it to regulate forward movement — you simply increase or decrease the pressure — although it is sometimes necessary to adjust your leg position to give various other aids. If the horse does not listen to the leg aid then you need to consider whether you are using it correctly and reapply the aid. If the horse is not responding to your leg aid you may need to back your leg up with the whip.

Whenever using the whip it should always be in conjunction with the leg aid, and should not be used randomly.

The pelvis, knee and ankle joints should be supple and elastic to absorb your horse's movement. Supple knee and ankle joints also help to maintain a consistent position and to keep your seat in the saddle. If your lower leg is positioned too far back, it will tip you forward in front of the movement. Conversely, if your lower leg is too far forward, it will affect your ability to follow the movement of the horse and use your legs effectively.

Arms, hands and contact

It is important to link the action of your hands and seat. The ideal is a light, consistent contact with the horse's mouth, but if your seat is unsteady and your back is not supple then your hands will also move. Therefore, the more secure your seat is, the stiller the contact can be. Your upper arm should lie lightly by your side with the elbow bent and positioned slightly in front of your upper body, with your hands about 10cm (4in) apart just above the horse's withers. Hold your hands with the thumb on top so that your elbows don't turn out. The rein should be between your third and little finger and under the thumb. By keeping your thumb down on the rein, it will slip less, allowing you to keep a more consistent contact.

Summary of riding position

It is easy to look good posing for a picture at the halt. However, it is more difficult to maintain a good position on the move. If your body conforms to a straight line from your shoulder through your pelvis to your heel, you will be in balance over your horse's back. However, the shape and design of the saddle you are using can influence this, and also the most suitable length of stirrup leathers for you to adopt.

In walk, the seat should swing lightly in harmony with the movement of the horse's back and the contact, while maintained lightly, mirrors the movement of the horse's head and neck. In trot the hands will remain still as the horse's head and neck move much less than in walk and canter. Rising to the trot from the knees can have a stiffening effect on your back, as can rising by standing in the stirrups, which almost inevitably puts the rider out of balance with the horse. Instead, when rising, move the pelvis forward and back softly to make the rise easier. In canter your seat should remain in the saddle and not move up and down out of the saddle. In order to achieve this your pelvis needs to stay relaxed, with your back remaining elastic and supple. Your upper body should remain upright and not rock forward and back as this makes it more difficult for your horse to maintain balance.

Before you ride a transition, turn or school figure always do a quick check of your position and make sure you are sitting in the best balance you can. This will allow you to apply clear aids, maintain your position throughout the movement and stay in harmony with your horse.

Working without stirrups

Working without stirrups will help to develop your balance and depth of seat and lengthen your leg position. Sit up tall without tensing and try to relax your hips and let your legs hang down so your thighs are straight, making sure your lower legs do not move too far back. Remember the line from ear, shoulder, hip to heel. Think about keeping your feet horizontal and not letting your toes drop down. You will be able to feel the movement of the horse through your seat and, as your seat develops, you should be able to feel which hind leg is moving forward under the horse.

When working without stirrups it is best to try to absorb the horse's movement through your lower back, seat and legs and allow the horse to move you. If you consciously try to move yourself you may end up out of sync with the horse. In trot and canter you will need to engage your core muscles to keep yourself secure while absorbing the horse's movement. You may find it easier to sit to the canter than the trot — however, always be prepared in the downward transition from canter to trot. If the horse has started to move more energetically forward in the canter the trot is likely to feel bouncier, so make sure that you steady the horse as you return to trot. After even a short time working without stirrups you should feel that you are sitting deeper in the saddle. Your stirrup leathers should feel short when you take your stirrups back; you can lengthen them, but it is best to only go down only one or two holes. Longer leathers may feel comfortable in walk, but you will lose your balance in trot and canter if they are too long.

A rider in a balanced position in trot with no stirrups.

The aids

Basic principles

Leg and rein aids should always be used in conjunction with each other, but each rein and leg can be applied slightly differently to refine your aids and increase your control over the horse.

It is a very basic principle that the legs are used together to ask the horse to go forward, and the reins are used together to ask the horse to slow down or stop. There is another principle, of riding 'leg into hand', whereby the rider's legs encourage the horse to step forward into the hands so that, for example, the horse steps forward into halt, rather than being 'pulled back' into it. So, we can say that the rider's legs work in conjunction with the hands. However, in order to develop your skills and gain more influence over the horse's way of going, it is necessary to learn to use each aid to some extent independently of the others — that is to say both legs, or both hands, do not always do exactly the same thing as each other. Some simple examples of this are as follows.

The inside leg is used next to the girth to require forward movement or impulsion and to bend the horse around a turn or circle.

The outside leg is used slightly behind the girth to control the quarters and to keep the horse straight (see Straightness later this chapter).

The reins help to control the direction and speed of the horse, help to balance the horse and contain the impulsion requested by the legs. The hands should be carried as a pair, with an equal feeling on both sides, and contact should be soft and flexible and you should be able to feel the horse's movement down the reins.

The inside rein is used to guide the direction of the horse and ask for flexion.

The outside rein is used to control the outside shoulder, the speed of the horse and to re-balance the horse.

Your weight should be even on both seat bones on straight lines and your body should mirror the direction of the horse around turns or circles, meaning that slightly more weight will be in your inside seat bone when turning.

Flexion and bend

Flexion occurs between the poll and withers and is a preparation for bend. Bend occurs through the horse's body: the horse should appear to be bent uniformly around turns and circles.

To bend the horse, the inside rein is used to guide him around the turn. It should not be pulled back, but it can be taken slightly away from the horse's neck, just enough for the horse to follow if required. The outside rein stays on the outside of the withers and is used to control the amount of bend around the turn and to balance the horse. This can be done by quietly increasing the pressure down the rein and then relaxing it again.

The inside leg is applied beside the girth to produce impulsion and bend and the outside leg is placed slightly behind the girth to prevent the quarters from swinging out, so the horse bends around the turn.

14 | Flatwork

This horse is bending around the rider's inside leg.

The Scale of Training

The Scale of Training is used as a foundation for the training of horses; it is based on six building blocks that are interlinked with each other. By developing your position to become balanced and independent in your seat and improving your feel you can begin to consider the Scale of Training at a basic level and apply it to your own riding.

The building blocks are as follows.

1. Rhythm

Rhythm is the regularity of the gait. The gait should not be too hurried or too laboured and the rhythm should be correct for the gait. Walk has four beats to a stride, the trot two beats and canter three beats. The tempo is the speed of the rhythm and you are aiming to keep this consistent in each pace through everything you do, for example riding school figures or changes of rein.

2. Suppleness

Lateral suppleness is the horse's ability to maintain the required bend and change it easily. A supple horse who responds willingly to your bending aids will be capable of better quality work and will be more comfortable to ride than one who does not. Many horses are stiffer on one rein (their stiff side) than the other (their soft side). They will find bending round your inside leg more difficult on the stiff side and may try to fall in against your inside leg and cut across corners or circles to make it easier for themselves. As you start to make circles and turns smaller the horse may try to fall out and make the circle bigger if they are stiff and find it difficult. It is important to be able to recognise on which rein the horse is more supple.

3. Contact

The contact is what you feel down the rein: ideally the contact should be soft, even and responsive. You may notice that some horses feel heavy in your hands, with the horse leaning on the bit in downward transitions. Others may hollow and lift their head and neck to evade your rein aids, while some horses may be harder and more unresponsive on one rein. Think about the contact you offer the horse. As you develop a more independent seat your rein contact will become stiller. Try to always maintain a steady, soft rein contact and work with your coach when riding different horses to use exercises that will improve the feel you have down the rein.

4. Impulsion

Impulsion is the energy within a gait. It should not be confused with speed. The horse should move forward willingly away from your leg aids without running. You will eventually be able to contain this energy through your seat and reins to help to develop impulsion as the horse uses his hind legs to push himself forwards.

5. Straightness

This means that the horse's hind legs step into the tracks of the forelegs both on straight lines and circles. Learn to feel whether the quarters are moving out to one side or another. A supple, active horse will find it easier to remain straight.

On a curved line, a straight horse will look to be following the line of the curve with his whole body.

6. Collection

Collection is a higher-level concept; it happens when the horse lowers his hindquarters, flexes his hocks well underneath him and takes more weight behind. This makes the horse lighter on the forehand. You will start to work to achieve this once your riding has advanced and you begin to ride horses training at a higher level.

14 | Flatwork

Riding in the school

Consideration for the horse and other riders

The better you ride, the better your horse will go. Therefore, when things go wrong — and they will — don't blame the horse but think about your own riding, the way you have applied the aids and what you could do differently. Show respect for your horse with a sympathetic, considerate approach. The ideal to keep in mind is that of your horse working willingly forward into a steady but elastic contact within his capabilities.

Extend this consideration to other riders in the school, especially when working in open order (i.e. not 'as a ride'). Pass left to left and allowing plenty of room between horses. If a rider and horse are jammed between the wall of the school and another horse, injury can result. It is sensible to ride your transitions away from the track so as not to interfere with the work of other riders. Be observant and make sure you are looking where you are going. If you are in

Give way to riders in a faster gait than you by riding on the inside track.

walk stay on an inside track and allow riders working in a faster gait to pass you on the track. If you are working in a warm-up arena or with a group of unknown riders be prepared to alter your movement quickly, or ride a quick transition to avoid a crash, as not everyone will be observant or aware of the school rules.

Correct trot diagonals and canter leads

Trot diagonals

It is important for the horse's balance that you ride on the correct diagonal in trot. This is known as the outside diagonal. You will be rising as the outside shoulder goes forward and sitting when the shoulder is back. If you are on the incorrect diagonal aim to change it smoothly by sitting for an extra beat. When changing the diagonal it is up to you to decide where to change it so that your horse's rhythm and fluency are not disturbed. Therefore, when changing the rein try to pick a point where the horse is straight before changing to the new direction, so you are in balance for the turn.

When you make a transition into trot take up rising within the first stride or two and try to feel whether you have picked up the correct diagonal (it should feel smooth and balanced) before glancing down to check it if you need to.

When out hacking, make sure you change your diagonal from time to time and are not always on the same one. Prolonged rising on the same diagonal can create muscle imbalances for both horse and rider over a period of time.

Canter leads

As your canter work progresses you should recognise incorrect canter leads quickly and be able to change the lead smoothly and quietly. As you pick up canter try to feel what is happening underneath you. If the lead is incorrect, you will not feel the inside foreleg reaching further forward than the outside one: the canter will probably feel unbalanced and the horse may try to fall in across the school. A correct lead should feel balanced and smooth — however, you may still need to glance down to check that the lead is correct form time to time.

The horse can strike off on the incorrect canter lead for many reasons such as a lack of preparation or an incorrect or unclear aid from the rider, insufficient forward movement in the trot, or resistance. To correct a canter lead, return the horse smoothly to trot and rebalance him if required. Make sure the trot is active before asking for canter again in a suitable place. Ask for canter in a corner or on a curved line, as the natural direction of the curve will make it easier for the horse to pick up the correct lead. Make sure you apply the aids clearly, trying not to lean forward in the transition, which can disturb your horse's balance.

Riding school figures and exercises

School figures offer variety in your work and include:

- 10, 15 and 20m circles.

- Turns across the width of the school.

- Turns on to and off the centre line.

- Long (e.g. F to H) and short (e.g. H to B) diagonals.

- Three- and four-loop serpentines.

- Shallow loops (5m).

- Tear drops (half-circles and inclining back to the track).

To progress your riding of school figures your focus should now be on:

- Developing your accuracy throughout the movements and recognising when the horse is drifting off the line or finding it difficult to bend.

- Maintaining a good rhythm and tempo throughout and recognising when the rhythm has changed.

- Improving the suppleness of the horse.

By riding accurately you will be developing the efficiency of the aids you apply and develop your feel as you recognise when the horse is drifting off the line of the movement. It will also help to improve your coordination and timing of when to apply the aids. Knowing the size of the arena you are riding in will help you establish how big to make the figures; arenas are rarely exactly 20 x 40m.

When changing from one bend to another in a movement such as a serpentine, aim to ride straight for one to two horses' lengths while you change your aids and the bend. This helps to make the change of bend smoother and more fluent, with less risk of the horse falling on to the inside shoulder into the new bend. In training, it is useful to have poles to ride between for straightness and accuracy.

To ride accurate school figures, it is important to give yourself markers or tangent points. These will give you something to aim towards and also help you see if the horse is drifting off the line, falling in or falling out.

Circles and turns

You will be familiar with how to ride a circle shape and can now start to focus on how the horse is moving around the turn. A horse who is supple and finds it easy to bend should be relatively easy to keep on the line of a circle and to keep in a rhythm around the turn. A horse who is stiffer may try to fall out by pushing out through his outside shoulder and making the shape bigger. This can also happen if you just use your inside rein to turn the horse and don't use your outside aids to help keep the horse straight. To correct this you need avoid pulling on your inside rein and use your outside rein to straighten the horse's neck and control the outside shoulder and your outside leg to encourage the horse's hindquarters to follow the tracks of the forelegs so the horse bends around the curve throughout his body. You should be looking around the circle and focusing on where you want to go. Your body position should mirror the position of the horse's, with the outside leg positioned to 'hold' the quarters if they attempt to drift out and your shoulder moving forward to mirror the outside of the horse around the turn.

The opposite of falling out is falling in, where the horse turns his neck to the outside and pushes his inside shoulder in towards the middle of the curve instead of bending around your inside leg. To correct this you need to make sure the horse's head and neck stay directly in front of him and use your inside leg firmly to bend the horse around the curve and your inside rein to encourage the horse to look around the turn. These issues may not show up until you start to work the horse in a faster gait or start to make the circles and turns smaller.

Four-loop serpentine

With a four-loop serpentine, each loop will go to the side of the arena. The loops should be of equal size and split the arena into four equal sections. The edge of the second loop will be ridden across the centre of the arena (between E and B) cutting it in half. The half-circles are smaller than for a three-loop serpentine and therefore you will be asking for a greater amount of bend, increasing the difficulty of the movement. As you work the horse on both reins through a serpentine you will be able to compare how easy the horse finds turning one way compared with the other. Aim to keep the loops equal-sized and to ride straight for a few strides each time you cross the centre line. You should also be focusing on maintaining a good rhythm throughout the serpentine.

Loops

Loops are useful for learning to change the horse from one bend to another smoothly, to improve the horse's suppleness and the coordination of your aids. When you are riding a shallow loop think about riding a smooth curve. The loop should take up the length of the long side and be symmetrical, with a clear change of bend. If the loop is 5m wide it will touch on the three-quarter line and a 10m wide loop will touch the centre line in a 20m wide arena. The widest part of the loop should be at E or B. The incline away from and back towards the track

Riders on the first loop of a serpentine.

should be ridden at the same angle. You may find some horses are reluctant to leave the track and eager to head back towards it — making the second part of the loop shorter and the incline steeper. You need to make sure that you ride a clear change of bend and don't let the horse fall back towards the track and also ensure you ride into the corners before and after the loop.

Change of canter lead through trot

This exercise can be ridden as a figure of eight or by changing canter leads through trot across the diagonal (e.g. M to K). Either way, prepare early enough for the canter to trot transition by lifting your sternum and opening your shoulder-blades as you ride forward in a balanced canter before asking for the downward transition with a clear aid. Rebalance the horse in trot and change the bend then ask for the new canter lead; ideally you should stay in sitting trot to make the transition fluent.

With a responsive horse, you would ride two strides of sitting trot changing the aids and bend before asking for the strike-off on the new canter lead. With a less responsive horse, it is better to stay in trot for more strides until the horse is positioned correctly, balanced and ready to be asked for the new canter lead.

Riding transitions

Transitions from one gait to another should be smooth and flowing. To achieve this, prepare in plenty of time before asking for any transition. Preparation may mean using your inside leg to request more activity, or steadying your horse if he is too strong by sitting up and balancing him by using the outside rein.

When asking for any transition the principle is 'leg before hand' to keep the horse's hind legs stepping under his body and his back swinging to maintain balance and correct weight distribution. You should now also be able to start to influence the horse with your seat. When you want the horse to be more active, try to stay soft and 'allow' more freely with your seat. When you want to steady the horse, try restricting the movement through your body; this will send a message to the horse to steady. When you want the horse to stop you should stop the movement through your body; this aid can be used momentarily when asking for a downward transition, before allowing free movement in the next gait. In downward transitions, ride your horse forwards into a steady contact in order to flow forward smoothly. In a downward transition if the hand only is used without the leg, the transition is more likely to be abrupt and jerky. The key to a smooth transition is a balance between leg and hand.

Riding with the reins in one hand

Riding with the reins in one hand will help you develop an independent seat, as you have to rely more on your body position and leg aids to control the horse. It will also take practice. When riding in the school it is usual to ride with the reins held in the outside hand. This will allow you to turn your body more easily in the direction of travel.

The following sequence of photos shows how to put the reins in one hand.

i. From holding your reins normally.

ii. Turn your hands over so that your knuckles are on top.

iii. Place one hand on top of the other and take hold of the bottom rein with the top hand.

iv. Let your free hand drop down by your side.

This method separates the two reins, allowing for independent action with each.

The whip should be held in the outside hand, but positioned on the inside or outside of the horse. The inside hand should hang down by your side behind your thigh. The reins are swapped into the new outside hand when the rein is changed.

Riding with the reins in one hand will help you to develop your seat and leg aids.

The aim of this exercise is to encourage you to start riding more with your legs and seat to control the horse. Practise riding turns and transitions.

Carrying and using a schooling whip

Use of a long or schooling whip allows you to keep both hands on the reins while using it, making it easier for you to maintain a consistent, steady contact. It is important to remember that the whip is not used as a punishment, but to support your leg aids in creating a willing response from the horse to your aids. Hold the whip with the top close to your thumb and with the whip lying over your thigh. Generally it is held in the inside hand to support your inside leg in requesting energy and bend, and so as not to scrape against the wall of the school. However, it can if necessary be used to support your outside leg. Use the whip lightly just behind your leg, in conjunction with your leg aid. The process should be that, if after first applying a leg aid, you feel you need to use the whip, apply the leg aid again and use the whip at the same time. Then apply just the leg again and you should get a better response from the horse.

Don't use the whip on the flank as the horse is more likely to object or buck if you do so. When riding it is important that you can control a long whip and that it is not flicking your horse's barrel distractingly or held out to the side and likely to upset other horses as they pass you.

Learn how to change the whip from one hand to the other quickly and quietly to support whichever leg your horse is not responding to willingly, or when changing the rein. It will take time and practice to do this quickly and quietly without accidently hitting the horse. Don't change the whip from one hand to another if it is likely to unsettle your horse or disrupt the fluency of a movement. Sometimes it is a good idea to walk or halt before changing the whip from one hand to another.

i. Put both reins into the hand holding the whip. Your other hand can then reach over and take hold of the whip below the holding hand.

ii. Pass the whip over the withers.

iii. Lay the whip against your thigh and retake the reins in each hand.

Assessing and describing a horse's way of going

A big part of progressing in your riding is to ride lots of different horses and compare how they go and whether you find them easy or difficult. A horse's type and temperament may influence his way of going, as will his conformation and level of training. Some horses will be more balanced than others. You will find some horses more comfortable and straightforward to ride but you need to practise riding all types of horses to develop your skills.

When getting on any horse, whether it is for the first time or one you have ridden many times, it is a good idea to have a plan of transitions and movements you are going to ride so that you can assess the horse and how he reacts.

Make sure you work evenly on both reins and in all three gaits. Start by warming up the horse and don't forget to cool down at the end of a session.

Some areas to consider when assessing a horse are outlined below. Always try to be positive about the horse you are riding — every horse can teach you something.

You can use the first few steps of the Scale of Training as a basis for your assessment.

1. *Rhythm* — does the horse maintain a steady rhythm in all three gaits?

2. *Suppleness* — does the horse find it easier to bend on one rein compared to the other? Are you able to ride accurate school figures?

3. *Contact* — consider how the horse you are riding responds to the rein aids. Does the horse feel even in both reins?

4. *Impulsion* — when you apply your leg does the horse move forward willingly? Is there energy in the gait without the horse running?

5. *Straightness* — does the horse carry his head and neck straight in front of him and do the hindquarters follow the prints of the forefeet?

6. *Collection* — collection is a higher-level concept, it happens when the horse lowers his hindquarters, flexes his hocks well underneath him and takes more weight

Try to have a plan of work when riding so you can start to assess the horse's response to your aids and identify whether the horse has a stiffer side.

behind. This makes the horse lighter on the forehand. You will start to work to achieve this once your riding has advanced and you begin to ride horses training at a higher level.

Evaluating your own performance

Evaluating your own riding critically, and considering carefully how the horse responds to your aids will help to improve your riding, master new skills and make progress. For instance, if a horse doesn't canter when you ask him to do so was this because you didn't make the trot active enough beforehand, were your aids were unclear or did you lean forward and unbalance the horse? Even the most experienced riders have areas of weakness in their position that they constantly have to work on to improve. Being honest with yourself and being aware of your weak areas and working on them every time you ride will help you progress. By evaluating your riding and finding the cause of the problem, it can be corrected.

Through this approach you will begin to recognise why things are happening, such as a poor transition caused by lack of preparation and the horse not being forward enough, and what you can do to prevent it happening again.

The better your horse performs for you, the more likely you are to enjoy riding and find it rewarding and satisfying.

Discuss your performance with your coach at the end of each session.

Riding outside

A group of riders in an open field.

Riding outside in a field is an opportunity to test the skills learnt in the arena and to apply them outdoors. It is the horse's natural environment, provides variety in his work, encourages him to go forward more willingly and offers you more space to develop your confidence and control in canter work, cementing your partnership with the horse. Riding up and down slopes develops agility and balance. When outside, the horses you ride may become distracted by the sights and sounds they will not see or hear indoors, for example heavy traffic, other livestock or movement in the distance. If the field you are riding in is bordered by hedges, watch out for anything on the other side that might startle your horse. Strong winds may upset a horse and he may try to turn his hindquarters into the rain. When anything of this nature happens, it is important to use your leg and hand aids to refocus the horse's attention on you.

While walking in the field take note of the ground conditions. This may include muddy or slippery patches, or holes that need to be avoided when trotting and cantering. After walking to warm up, and checking the terrain, start your work in trot by asking for a forward-going, active gait. Move the horse around the area by using changes of rein, school figures and transitions to focus his attention on you, just as you would in the arena. The horse should still be obedient and bending round your inside leg. Be aware of other riders and horses and follow the rules of the school, as you would in an arena.

If riding downhill, aim to keep your horse steady by using your leg and rein aids so that he doesn't rush or become 'long' and unbalanced. A useful guideline is that your upper body should remain at a right angle to the slope on which you are riding and your lower legs should remain in position. If your legs slip forward, this will put you behind the movement and out of balance. Leaning forward will put more weight on to the horse's forehand and unbalance him.

When riding uphill, encourage the horse with your legs to use his hindquarters actively. Adopt a forward light seat to free your horse's back, maintaining a steady, consistent contact to help the horse maintain his balance.

Riding uphill in an open field.

The forward light seat

Riding outside is a good time for you to start developing a forward light seat. The aims of a forward light seat are:

1. To take the weight off the horse's back, making it easier for him to use his back and hind legs. This is helpful to both horse and rider when you begin to ride onward-bound canter or gallop in the open, whether in a competition, on some kind of sponsored ride, or simply when it's time for you and the horse to have fun.

2. To help the rider develop strength, balance and security. These factors are useful in themselves, but will be particularly helpful when you progress to cross-country jumping.

To ride in a forward light seat the stirrup leathers are shortened one or two holes from flatwork length, depending on the horse and the saddle. The shorter stirrup leathers close the angles of your ankle, knee and hip joints and also make it easier for the upper body to incline forward from the hip, making it easier for you to go with the movement of the horse over a jump.

How far forward the upper body is inclined will vary, depending on the build of the rider. Some riders have shorter backs and longer thighs and it might not be comfortable for them to adopt the same forward position as a rider with a long back and shorter thighs. What is important is that you are balanced, stable and secure when riding in your forward light seat. When your upper body inclines forward, the stability of your lower leg is crucial in maintaining your position.

A rider in a forward light seat.

For a secure forward light seat, the following points apply:

- Stirrup leathers will be at right angles to the ground and at a shorter length than when riding on the flat.

- Heels down.

- Lower legs in light contact with the horse's barrel.

- Knees and ankles elastic to absorb the horse's movement.

- Avoid gripping up with the knees.

- Back flat.

- Upper body inclined forward slightly from the hips.

- Elbows bent.

- Contact even and steady.

- Head up — looking where you are going.

As you develop your light seat your aim will be to become more secure in your position with steadier and more controlled lower legs. Your aids will combine the action of leg and hand more effectively. It can sometimes be useful to use a light seat between fences to take the weight of the horse's back, then sit up as you approach each fence. Riding over fences is discussed further in the next chapter.

Dealing with problems

Horses are herd animals and have a strong flight instinct. These natural instincts can predispose the horse to behaving in a certain way when frightened or lacking in confidence.

When asked to leave a group of horses you might find you need to ride forward positively if the horse you are on tries to nap back towards the others and is reluctant to leave them. This type of behaviour can sometimes be seen in group situations when the riders are lined up and one rider tries to take their horse out of the line.

You might find that a horse takes a dislike to a particular area in the arena and refuses to go near it or tries to run past it. First of all, look for a possible reason — has something changed such as new jumps being stored there, a flapping banner or has something that has always been there been moved? Horses who are ridden in the same environment daily, such as riding school horses, can become unsettled when something familiar to them changes.

In such situations you need to focus the horse's attention back on to you. Move the horse away from the area in question and ride transitions or school figures until you have the his attention, then gradually move your way up the arena towards the problem area by gradually making the space you work in bigger, until you are able to pass the area without incident. Turn the horse's head away from what he is scared of and use your inside leg to bend him around and keep him moving forwards. It may several attempts before you are able to settle the horse. Stay calm and positive in your riding; if you become tense or upset the horse will pick up on it and, in his perception, you are reinforcing the need to be scared. You can also use your voice to encourage the horse and reward him. If there is another sensible horse in the arena it may be possible to take a lead past the problem area until your horse has settled.

Out hacking you may encounter all sorts of objects that provoke a reaction from the horse. He could be frightened by and refuse to go near flapping polythene, water, a stationary digger or roadworks. The air brakes of a passing lorry hissing suddenly, an air balloon or a helicopter low overhead may all frighten a horse. Horses' reactions to such things may vary. Some horses may shy/spook, some may nap and others plant or refuse to move. Other horses may have a reverse reaction and try to gallop away from whatever is worrying them, shooting backwards, whipping around and trying to gallop back home to other horses. This is an example of the horse's instinct to be back with the herd for security. All these reactions are a result of symptomatic lack of confidence or fear in the horse.

Bucking can occur for a variety of reasons, such as a saddle pinching, back pain, disobedience, freshness, excitement or simply feeling good. If the horse is fresh, with excess energy, bucking is an outlet for that energy. Your horse might be excited by others galloping in a field and want to join in the fun with his friends, in which case the bucking is symptomatic of the fun and excitement.

Sometimes horses resist simply because they cannot cope with what is being asked of them and are stressed. This might be because they are faced with a fence that is too high to jump, too wide or scary for them. Another example might be an inexperienced horse at a show environment that is unfamiliar and frightening to them.

When experiencing any of these situations it is important to ride positively forwards. If a horse lacks confidence he needs to be able to look to the rider for support. It is also important to consider *why* the horse may be reacting in a certain way; some work may need to be done to improve the horse's confidence. In such a situation you should look to your supervisor or coach for guidance.

Summary

- Improving the depth of your seat will allow you to ride with a greater stability and apply clear, more precise aids.

- Learning to use your aids independently will give you greater influence over your horse.

- The Scale of Training is used as a foundation for training horses.

- Think about the horse's rhythm and suppleness when riding school figures.

- Ride accurate school figures with correct bend.

- Ride downward transitions forwards from the leg into a steady rein contact.

- Practise transitions and changes of direction while riding with the reins in one hand.

- Recognise whether a horse is forward, rhythmic, supple, responsive to the rein and straight.

- Practise riding at all the gaits in the open, and up and down hills, always being mindful of ground conditions. Practise riding in a forward light seat at canter.

- Turn your horse's head away from objects that frighten them and use positive leg aids to ride them past.

- Assess constantly how well you feel you are riding and how the horses you ride are responding to your aids in order to improve and progress.

TRAINING TIPS

1. Riding lots of different horses will help you to develop your riding.

2. If possible, in between lessons, try and ride on your own so that you learn to recognise and think through some problems by yourself.

3. Working in walk, trot and canter without stirrups will help you to develop a deeper more secure seat.

4. Lunge lessons are an excellent way to work on your seat without worrying about controlling the horse.

5. Practise assessing the horses you ride and evaluating your own performance.

Chapter 15

Jumping

Skills to progress and develop

Introduction to jumping

Riding a course of fences

Summary

Jumping

If you have been working over poles and are confident cantering in a forward, light seat you should now be ready to progress to jumping.

Skills to progress and develop

All the skills listed below will contribute towards safe and effective riding over obstacles.

- Working sensibly and confidently when trotting and cantering with other riders in an open, undulating field.

- Recognising different types of going and precautions to take when riding on them, for example, hard or soft ground.

- Developing security and balance in your forward light seat.

- Control of speed, gait and the ability to create an active, forward jumping canter.

- Being able to ride a good track around and over fences with balanced turns, straight approaches and controlled landings.

- Demonstrating a secure posture and supple folding over fences up to 80cm (2ft 6in).

- Jump grids and courses including doubles up to 80cm (2ft 6in) confidently.

- Dealing with refusals and run-outs.

- Reflecting objectively on your own and your horse's performance.

Introduction to jumping

Warming up for jumping

As with flatwork, warm up by walking actively first, then trotting, riding changes of direction, school figures (whether in the school or not) and transitions to make the horse forward and supple. Use transitions to establish the best canter you can and ensure that the horse is responsive to your aids. An energetic jumping canter will be more open, with greater ground cover, than a working canter in an arena. An open field is a good place to work on this, because you can ride bigger circles and longer straight lines than in an arena. Asking the horse to go forward in canter and then to steady him tests your 'accelerators and brakes' as the horse needs to be obedient when jumping. You want the horse to go forward willingly when you ask for this with your leg aids and to steady his speed promptly without fighting against the contact.

The phases of a jump

There are five phases to a jump: approach, take-off, flight, landing and getaway.

The approach should be straight and active, at a right angle to the centre of the fence.

When taking off, the horse lifts his forehand and folds his forelegs. During this phase the rider starts to fold forward to go with the horse's movement.

During the flight phase, the horse stretches over the fence, using his back and neck and folding his hind legs. The rider's upper body should fold forward, going with the movement of the horse, allowing with the hands so that the horse can stretch his head and neck. The rider's lower legs should remain in position, with the heels down just behind the girth.

In landing the horse lifts his head and neck and unfolds his forelegs while the hind legs are still clearing the fence. Here, the rider's upper body should start to unfold, otherwise the rider is likely to be too far forward and unbalanced on landing.

In the getaway phase, the horse is moving away from the fence and his balance here influences how he will approach and jump the next fence. The rider should not be in front of or behind the movement, as this will affect the horse's balance. The rider should be looking ahead and riding the line planned.

With smaller fences the movements of the horse during these phases will be less pronounced, but the rider should be staying in balance and harmony with the horse.

i. Approach.

ii. Take off.

iii. Flight.

iv. Landing.

v. Getaway.

The phases of a jump.

Pole work

Pole work can be used to help develop jumping as well as for warming up. If you have not ridden the horse before it is can be a good idea to start by trotting him over a single pole on the ground, to assess how he is going to react. Your aim is to maintain a good trot rhythm as you approach, trot over and ride away from the pole. Plan your turns just as you would on the flat and aim for the centre of the pole, crossing it at a right angle. The horse should bend his joints and swing through his back over the pole. If the horse runs and becomes unbalanced over the pole you may need to alter your approach to make it slightly shorter and work on transitions away from the pole to make sure you can stay in control. Once you are happy trotting over a single pole, approach it in canter and practise maintaining the canter rhythm over the pole.

Practise cantering over single poles. Have an experienced helper on the ground to replace any poles your horse may knock out of place.

Once you are happy over a single pole, introduce a line of three or more trot poles approximately 2.74m (9ft) between each depending on the length of your horse's stride. You are still aiming to maintain the rhythm and straightness over the poles. With this exercise, look up and don't allow the horse to speed up over the poles.

As well as lines of poles you can practise riding a course of poles on the ground in trot and canter. This allows you to develop the skills of riding lines between obstacles, maintaining a regular rhythm throughout and riding accurate approaches, turns and getaways without having to jump.

Single fences

When you are ready to move on from pole work, the next step is to have a small cross-pole behind a single ground-pole as an introductory jumping exercise out of trot. The pole 2.74m (9ft) in front of the cross-pole is to encourage your horse to remain calm and steady, rather than rushing at the cross-pole, and to take off in the right place. Complete your turn so that you are at a right angle to the cross-pole and aim for the centre of it. It is your job to get the horse to the fence in a good balance and rhythm.

The placing pole helps the horse take off in the correct spot.

Keep the weight in your heels and your leg aids on. Sit up on landing and ride forward away from the fence in a straight line, in either trot or canter.

Once you are comfortable jumping from trot you can progress to jumping out of canter. Take the placing pole away and aim to keep the horse in a forward-going, rhythmical canter. You will feel whether you fold and stay in harmony with your horse correctly. If you feel you are not going with your horse, it is important not to brace yourself against the movement, tightening your muscles.

Develop your confidence by jumping single fences. Little and often is the key! Include small spreads and fillers when you feel ready. From this, continue to progress by riding sequences of three or four fences, looking ahead to ride good lines between them.

Basic gridwork

The initial stages of gridwork.

A grid is a line of fences and poles, and is a useful exercise for developing suppleness in the rider and horse. When working through a grid you will need to move smoothly in and out of your jumping position maintaining balance over your legs as you ride over a line of fences. It is also very important to be straight and active on the approach to a grid. You may start with two fences and then the grid can gradually be built up to include more. Grids with four or more elements are great for quickening your reactions, making your folding over the fence more supple and developing confidence.

You can also practise riding doubles. A double is two fences in a straight line with either one or two non-jumping strides between them. Start with a cross-pole and then an upright fence one non-jumping stride after it. Approach the cross-pole in an active canter and focus on the middle of the second fence to help you ride straight between the two fences. Sit up as you land after the cross-pole to remain in position between the two fences. Your legs need to stay in position to channel the horse into an even rein contact and remain forward and straight. With practice your folding will become more supple and your reactions quicker.

i. A rider going over the first part of a double.

ii. Sitting up on landing.

iii. Maintaining an upright position between the fences.

iv. Folding over the last fence.

A rider going through a double.

Dealing with run-outs and refusals

There are many reasons why your horse may run out or refuse a fence. If this happens, consider why it happened — was the horse going forward with sufficient impulsion, was the approach straight, were you committed to jumping the fence?

If your horse runs out to the left, he has evaded the right rein and ignored the left leg. Turn, therefore, to the right before re-presenting the horse to the fence from a short, active approach, with a positive lower left leg and a strong right rein and the whip in your left hand. Consider whether to aim slightly to the right of centre of the fence. Should this happen at the second element of a double, it is customary to jump both elements of the double again, and this is required in showjumping competitions.

If the horse refuses at a fence, again re-present him from a short, active approach with positive use of your lower leg, but keep your shoulders back and seat in the saddle, looking ahead so that a sudden refusal does not unseat you.

Use of the whip

If you need to use your short whip jumping, hold the horse straight with the reins in one hand and apply the whip immediately behind your heel to support your leg. If the whip is used down the horse's neck with the reins in both hands, there is the danger that, if the hand is unsteady, you are saying 'stop and go' at the same time. The aim of using the whip behind your heel is to deliver a clear message that says 'go!'

Riding a course of fences

Walking the course

The next goal is to jump a course of fences up to 80cm (2ft 6in) high, with changes of direction, spreads, uprights, fillers and related distances (that is, three to five strides between two fences).

Before doing this, walk the course on foot. The aim of walking the course is to learn the sequence of fences and then to plan your ideal turns and lines of approach. You should also pay attention to the ground conditions and be aware of anything that may distract your horse. It is also useful to decide which canter lead to start on, which may be influenced by the layout of the first part of the course. Aim to ride smooth, flowing turns that allow space for you to turn your horse straight in the approaches. If the horse lands after a fence on the incorrect lead before a turn, correct this quickly and smoothly if you possibly can by trotting, and asking for a strike-off on the correct lead.

A course of fences.

Walking the distance between fences.

Work out the number of strides between fences by striding out the distance between the elements of the double and any related distances. There is a table of jump distances in the coaching chapter of this book. It will take practice to do this accurately. Four of your own normal strides should be the equivalent of one canter stride. The related distances note at the foot of the table explains how to relate your own strides to that of the horse.

Riding the course

Approach the first fence in a positive, active, forward canter. It is your task to dictate and maintain the quality of the canter. Remember that, as with flatwork, the first principle of jumping is to ride forwards. Check through turns that the horse is 'in front of your leg' before turning into a fence. In the air over a fence be looking ahead to the next fence. Try to bend the horse around your inside leg to discourage him from falling in through the turns.

Try to maintain the correct rhythm around the course, using your aids to return to it if it is lost after a fence. Don't allow a keen horse to speed up or a lazy horse to lose impulsion after each fence.

A rider riding over a variety of fences within a course and each time looking ahead to the next fence.

If you or your horse makes a mistake, put it behind you and focus ahead on the rest of the course. Remember to breathe evenly and calmly to avoid becoming breathless.

If your horse overshoots a turn or you lose control of the canter, it is better to circle, improve the quality of the canter and then approach the fence, rather than attempting it with an unbalanced canter.

If you can jump a course like this confidently in a consistent rhythm with a secure position, straight approaches, balanced turns and landings, you have made a good start to your jumping and have a promising foundation upon which to build further progress.

Summary

- Riding in a forward light seat takes the weight off your horse's back and can be useful between the fences when riding a course.

- Start warming up for jumping by trotting over a single pole.

- Follow this by trotting over the pole with a cross-pole behind it.

- Jump the cross-pole in canter without the pole in front of it.

- Develop your confidence by jumping lots of single fences.

- Introduce spreads and fillers when you feel ready.

- Jump small sequences to learn to ride good lines between fences.

- Introduce combinations and grids to develop your jumping technique.

- You should go with the horse's movement in the five phases of the jump.

- Before jumping a course, walk it on foot carefully to help you ride it better.

- Ride forward on the course, focusing on rhythm, looking ahead, riding smooth turns, approaches and landings.

- If a horse runs out to the left, turn right before re-approaching the fence.

15 | Jumping

TRAINING TIPS

1. Watch professional riders showjump or ride across country and take note of how they adapt their positions to stay in balance with the horse.

2. If you hack out, use this as an opportunity to practise riding in light seat in all three gaits and strengthen your lower leg position.

3. Offer to pole-pick during jumping lessons and use the opportunity to practise striding out distances that an experienced instructor has set up and watch how different horses jump through them.

Introduction

The definition of a coach includes the words 'teach, instruct, train, inform, impart knowledge, prepare and give guidance'. Historically, equestrian training evolved from a military background where frequently the participants were instructed what to do. There was little feedback, riders doing as they were told without necessarily understanding why, and therefore they took little responsibility for developing their skills with real empathy for the horse.

The horse should be the centre of all learning: once the basic skills of a rider are established the training of the horse should be paramount. Riders should be encouraged to understand the basic principles of training the horse along with the influence that their position and core stability will have over the control of the horse.

A 'teacher or instructor' imparts knowledge and experience, giving guidance to help develop new skills. They should have good observation and listening skills, with a real desire to help improve practical ability and understanding.

The words 'coach' or 'trainer' envelope all of the above, but include in addition the development of providing the rider with the ability to take responsibility for their own learning, development of skills and success.

A high-performance coach tends to be regarded as someone who has competed successfully and trains competition riders at the highest level. However, a coach who has worked in the riding industry training children, riders with disabilities, or examination candidates, may well have developed their coaching skills to a technically much higher level in their area of expertise, and such a person should be recognised as a high-performing coach.

As a coach you need to develop your own coaching philosophy, which contains your own values and beliefs. The most important principles should always be the welfare of the horse, your moral, ethical and social values, along with the safety of horse and rider. You should also work within the British Horse Society's Accredited Professional Coach Code of Conduct. This is available on the BHS website.

After the session you should always self-reflect on what went well and where you might need to develop your coaching skills further. It is a good idea to keep a logbook of what you do with each of your clients or groups, and you can reflect on what helped them in the construction of your session, effectiveness of the language you used, which learning style was most productive, etc. This self-reflection will help you decide if there is any training you would like to undertake to support your work as a coach — often known as 'continuing professional development' (CPD). It could be watching more experienced coaches, maybe getting someone to mentor you, attending a coaching seminar or conference, going to a competition and watching the working-in, writing for a dressage judge or helping a course-builder for the day by putting up fences and also picking their brains. Self-help can be free if you are prepared to give the time. If you recognise your weaknesses and work on them you should be able to develop into an inspirational coach and give yourself great satisfaction as you see your riders develop.

Hopefully, you will be enabled to take yourself and your clients along an exciting and stimulating journey to many successful, even life-changing, outcomes.

Chapter 16

Coaching Concepts

Welfare considerations

Coaching theory

Summary

Coaching Concepts

This chapter discusses some important theories and concepts that lie at the heart of successful coaching and looks, in principle, at how these should be applied to the coaching of riding.

Welfare considerations

Any coach in any field should have the physical and mental well-being of their clients in mind, and this is especially true of riding coaches, who work in a high-risk sport and whose clients may include children and vulnerable adults, and also clients with various medical conditions. Therefore, it is essential that anyone working in this field is familiar with procedures and practices intended to maximise the welfare of those being coached.

Safeguarding and protecting children and adults at risk

As mentioned, when teaching riding it is very likely that some of your clients will be children. The protection of children, young people and adults at risk while participating in equestrian sport is of the highest importance, as people who ride should be able to take part in an enjoyable, safe environment and be protected from harm.

Health and safety — provision of a suitable coaching environment

Since riding is a high-risk sport, it is extremely important to take measures to ensure that all parties involved are as safe as possible — this includes the coach, the rider(s) and the horse(s). When planning a lesson it is important to take note of anything that could potentially cause an accident — a process known as risk assessment. By reviewing risks you will be able to put relevant actions in place to reduce the risk of accidents. We mentally assess risk all the time throughout everything we are doing. However, it is a good idea to have risk assessments written down. For example, if you work at a yard it is likely that there will already be written risk assessments for various activities and areas of the yard.

Completing a risk assessment is easy to do (see sample extract on the following page). First, you need to identify the hazards and who is at risk from them, and then state the procedures that are in place to control the risks. If there are any further actions required these should also be stated on the form.

RISK ASSESSMENT

Organisation Name:_____

Area/Activity (Hazard)	People at Risk	Control measures in place	Action by whom and when
Jump equipment	Rider could be injured if they fall on equipment. Horses could stand on jump cups causing injury	Jump equipment is stored outside of the school when not required. If in the school it is positioned or stored so there is sufficient space for riders to move around. Jump cups should be removed from wings when not in use and stored in a storage container.	Daily checks by all coaches, that jumping equipment is stored correctly
Teaching groups of riders	There is a risk that horses may kick each other or other riders if horses get too close	Clear instructions are given to riders to maintain a sufficient distance and follow school rules. Consideration is paid to the order that horses are put in when working in ride order.	Manager to keep horse information up-to-date, so any horses known to kick can be identified; monthly updates
Repair work being carried out to neighbouring stables	Noise from the work may startle horses; riders may be at risk of falling off	Communication with construction workers so times of work are identified. When teaching lessons can be taught at the far end of the school to minimise risk of horses spooking. Nervous horses will be used in the indoor school.	Regular communication with construction workers, weekly or daily if necessary while work is being carried out

Example of a risk assessment.

The provision of a suitable coaching environment clearly includes such things as the physical location in which a coaching session takes place, but the term 'environment' as used here also includes other factors that could have an impact on welfare. These include the following.

Coaching area

It is likely that most of the time you will be teaching lessons in an enclosed arena. This is the ideal situation as, in the eventuality that a rider falls off, the horse is contained in one area. This, therefore, is the most suitable place for beginner and novice riders as they are less likely to be fully in control of the horse. However, even in this environment, there is potential for something to go wrong. As a coach it is essential to develop your awareness so you can anticipate problems and take the relevant measures to prevent them.

There may also be situations where you might be teaching in a field or other open area — in such cases, put out some markers or cones to define the arena space. Also, from the safety aspect, make sure that all gates are shut.

Other aspects of the coaching area that require attention are:

Surface. Attention should always be paid to the ground conditions; there are risks to both riders and horses if the ground is too deep, hard or slippery. In many circumstances you will be teaching on an all-weather surface, however these surfaces can vary depending on how well-maintained they are. Be prepared to alter your ground plan (e.g. placement of jumping grids; marking off a boggy patch) in the case of a deep spot or uneven footing.

Fencing or barriers. The fencing of the arena, or any barriers used to divide a teaching space, should be checked for suitability and security. Anything such as sharp edges or broken rails, that could be hazardous to horse or rider should be avoided.

Equipment storage. When not in use, jump-building equipment should be stored outside the school. However, at busy riding schools lessons may alternate between jumping and flatwork and it is not always practical to remove equipment between lessons. In these circumstances it is best to store wings and poles together in the centre of the arena. The jump cups should be removed from the wings and stored in a container. If left on the wings there is a risk that a rider or horse might catch themselves on the cup, potentially causing an injury.

External hazards. Even when a lesson takes place in a secure arena there might be hazards outside the arena that could affect the safety of the riders. Horses turned out in fields bordering the arena can distract those in the arena if they start to gallop around. In such circumstances, you may need to bring the horses used in the lesson to walk and make sure you have control of the ride until the horses in the field settle. Other factors you may need to be aware of include things such as any type of building work near the arena, children or animals running alongside the arena or birds flying out of hedges.

Jumps stored neatly outside the arena when not in use.

Horses

There is always a risk of injury when handling or riding horses. All horses are unpredictable — even laid-back experienced ones. They will shy away from anything they perceive as dangerous, and this can cause them to shoot forwards or jump to the side unexpectedly or, in a worst-case scenario, buck, rear or bolt. Even if a horse is not reacting particularly violently, it is easy for an inexperienced person to be injured as they may not be able to read the horse's behaviour and may not move out of the way if, for instance, one horse reacts to another horse. For these reasons it is important always to try to manage activities between participants and horses in a way that makes the situation as safe as possible.

When working in groups, horses will need to be kept at least a horse's distance away from each other, so that if one did kick out he would be less likely to connect with another horse or person. This advice includes when horses are lined up in the school before and after riding, and when they are tied up on a yard. As a coach it will be your responsibility to be aware of the horses in your group and their behaviour, as well as factors that may cause them to react. You should then be able to diffuse situations before an incident occurs.

Tack

It is vitally important to check that tack is safe for use. Ideally, tack should be checked on a regular basis and it can be most convenient to do this thoroughly while it is being cleaned. However, as a coach you should make a general check of the tack before your lessons begin, while helping riders to adjust their stirrup leathers and girth, or while a rider is adjusting their own tack. The main areas to check are the stirrup leathers, girth straps, reins and cheekpieces.

It is also important to be aware of the fit of the tack; horses may change shape through the seasons, or may have lost or gained weight for other reasons, and younger horses will change shape as they grow and develop more muscle. So it is important to note any signs that the tack is not comfortable for the horse; this may include not only physical signs relating to how the tack is sitting, e.g. space between withers and pommel, but also signs from the horse when ridden. If you notice any changes to the horse's way of going, or the rider mentions any changes, it could be an indication that the tack is causing discomfort. Signs might include the horse being unwilling to go forwards, tension, tail-swishing, grinding teeth or bucking. If a horse displays any behaviour that may suggest discomfort you should always report this to a senior staff member at the centre or, if the client is riding their own horse, you should advise them to take the appropriate action — e.g. have their saddle checked by a qualified saddle fitter, or have the horse's teeth or back checked.

The weight of a rider can also affect the fit of tack. This is of particular importance in a riding school situation, where the horse will be ridden by a variety of riders, so it should be taken into consideration when the tack is fitted, especially if the horse is likely to be carrying a larger rider, to make sure that the horse is comfortable.

As well as the fit of the saddle you should check that the tack has been put on correctly; this should include the bridle and the numnah. Make sure the numnah is big enough, that the front has been pulled up into the pommel to prevent pressure over the withers and, if it has attachments to secure it to the saddle, that they are fastened correctly. If numnahs are not fitted correctly, in addition to causing discomfort to the horse, they may slip back during the lesson, causing disruption if the rider has to dismount for this to be corrected.

Rider's safety equipment

Hats. All riders should wear a hat that is approved to the current safety standards. Riding school insurance will dictate this, so it is essential that all client's hats are checked. There are several different standards that are acceptable — for details of these you can refer to the British Equestrian Trade Association's (BETA) guidance.

All hats approved to current standards will have a retaining harness that can be fastened securely. If you notice that a client is wearing a hat that looks old, worn or does not have a secure fastening, it may not be approved to current standards, so make sure you check. When teaching private clients, if you notice that their hat is not up to the current standard you should advise them about this and emphasise the importance of wearing a suitable hat.

As well as being to the correct standard, it is important that the hat fits the rider. Obvious signs that a hat does not fit include excessive movement, slipping down over the rider's eyes, or the rider saying that the hat feels tight and uncomfortable. In these situations at a commercial school the rider should borrow a suitable hat from the centre.

Riders should always be advised to purchase their own riding hat from a reputable tack shop and have the new hat fitted by a suitably qualified person. It is not advisable to purchase second-hand hats as their history is unknown, and the protection offered by a hat will diminish if it receives a knock, e.g. from a rider having a fall or from being repeatedly dropped on the floor.

Body protectors. Some people prefer to ride in body protectors, especially for jumping. If you are teaching a cross-country session riders should always wear body protectors. Similarly to riding hats, it is important that a rider has a correctly fitting body protector, which should be fitted at the time of purchase. Signs that a body protector does not fit include the bottom of it hitting the saddle, which can also cause the shoulders and top of the body protector to rise up. If the body protector restricts the rider and they are not able to sit in an upright position it is not suitable. If you think a body protector does not fit you should advise the rider gets this checked by someone who has had appropriate BETA training.

Footwear. Ideally, clients should wear riding boots when riding as these have been designed specifically to reduce the risk of the rider's foot becoming caught in the stirrup. However, even if the rider is wearing riding boots the size of the stirrup irons should always be taken into consideration as there is a risk that the rider's foot could become caught if they are not big enough. New riders may not have riding boots and often wait until they have decided that they would like to continue riding before making an investment to buy all the correct gear. In these

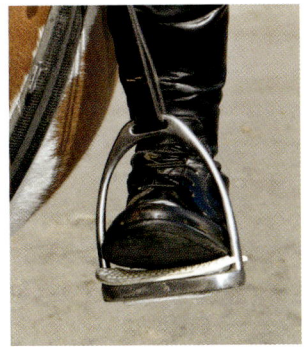
Stirrup too small.

Stirrup too big.

This stirrup is the correct size, although the foot is not quite central in the stirrup.

circumstances the rider should be advised to wear shoes with flat, smooth soles and small heels. Trainers are not suitable as they have no heel and can slip on the stirrup iron if the sole is wet — and they often have a raised lip that can get caught in the stirrup.

Clothing. It is important that the rider is comfortable and able to move. Any type of clothing that restricts movement or has a thick seam down the inside of the leg is not suitable, e.g. tight jeans. It is best that clothing is not too baggy or so loose that it may flap and startle the horse or get in the way. Riders should be advised against wearing jewellery as it can become caught and cause injury.

General welfare of participating parties

Throughout all training sessions the welfare of all parties is of paramount importance.

Horse

Fitness and workload. When teaching a client on their own horse, it is likely that the lesson will be the horse's only session of the day — although, this does not exempt you from pointing out any concerns you might have about the horses' welfare. However, when teaching at a riding school the horses may be required to do further lessons or hacks later in the day. It is important that such horses' working hours are divided as appropriate between beginners, lunge lessons, private lessons, group lessons and hacking. Varying the horse's work will go some way to avoiding boredom and staleness. The most popular horse is always in danger of being overused, while the less genuine individual stays in his stable and eats hay! Allocating horses appropriately on a rotational basis is fair for clients and horses.

Within an individual session, the amount of work done should take into account the horse's overall workload, and horses should be given sufficient rest breaks to ensure that they are able to recover from work done. There are a variety of exercises whereby you can work the riders without overstressing the horses. These include stretching exercises, lateral work in walk and work without stirrups.

It is important to pay close attention to the individual horses; especially if a horse is young or not very fit he is likely to tire more quickly. Such horses may require more regular breaks and if they become tired it may be best to end the session on a good note rather than continuing for the full time allotted.

Soundness. Under the Animal Welfare Act, all animals should be protected from pain and suffering. If you notice that a horse is lame or in discomfort it is important that you stop the work. There may be some situations in which a horse is stiff and takes longer to warm up than most, and as long as the horse is not in discomfort and improves with time, he should be allowed to work in gradually. The difference between these two scenarios will be obvious after a few minutes work and if the horse still shows signs of lameness then he must not be used.

Rider

Physical fitness. As with horses, riders should have regular breaks and should not be overstressed. A rider who becomes tired will be less secure and more prone to an accident. Make sure that, throughout the lesson, you communicate with the rider(s) and allow breaks as required. Some riders are very determined and will push themselves hard — however, if a rider is struggling to perform an exercise, is out of breath, or losing security you should stop them.

Frame of mind. It is important to communicate with your clients; simply asking how they are before the lesson and being aware of their body language and mood can go a long way. It is important to try to gauge what frame of mind a rider is in. Sometimes a rider may be distracted by what is going on outside of their lesson time, in their home life or at work. Although their lesson is likely to be something they use to de-stress themselves, it is useful to be aware of how a person is feeling so that, if a session needs altering to suit their needs, this can be done. If a person is particularly distracted it may not be suitable to do anything too challenging.

Nutrition. Healthy eating should be promoted for both children and adults. As a coach it might not be appropriate to make suggestions about a person's diet; this is best left to dieticians who are the experts in this area. However, there are times when you might check whether a person has eaten or has drunk enough. If your rider feels faint or you notice a behavioural change you should check that they have eaten/taken in water. Of course, there may be another reason for their condition: they may be coming down with a virus or forgotten to take some necessary medication. If this happens, you should suggest that the lesson ends and appropriate action is taken.

On pony day's it is important to check that all the children have packed lunches and it is always important that everyone involved is sufficiently hydrated, especially in hot weather.

Coach

It is just as important for you, the coach, to eat regular meals and ensure that you are drinking enough throughout the day. You will often be on your feet for long periods. One other thing to be particularly aware of as a coach is looking after your voice. If you overstrain your voice you can cause lasting damage. This is easy to do, especially if teaching in open spaces. To prevent damage to your voice, try to project your voice rather than shouting, and stand closer to riders when giving instructions, especially when it is windy or in other conditions when it is hard for the riders to hear you. Drinking plenty of water can also help your voice.

> ### Liability and insurance
>
> *It is inevitable that, if a person decides to ride, they will at some point fall off. Most falls do not result in serious injuries, but in instances where a rider is injured they may seek to take action against the coach. If you are employed at a riding school you will be covered under their insurance. However, if you are working as a freelance coach, you will need to ensure you have adequate public liability insurance cover. The BHS can provide this insurance if you have achieved your Stage 3 in Complete Horsemanship and signed up to become an Accredited Professional Coach.*

What to do in the event of an accident/rider fall

It is recommended that anyone coaching riding lessons is trained in first aid and keeps their certificate up to date. If coaching at a riding school there should be a nominated first-aider available on the yard, as it may be yard policy that, in the event of an accident, that person is called. However, if you are teaching private clients it is vital that you are able to respond in the event of an accident.

If an accident occurs, stay calm, assess the situation and make sure you do not put yourself in danger. Below are some signs to look out for and examples of the procedure to follow if a rider falls off during a lesson, ©Skillbase First Aid 2017.

The following information given under this heading has been provided by SkillBase First Aid. The information is intended as a guide, and should accompany practical first aid training with a fully qualified instructor. It reflects UK first aid practice at the time of printing. Efforts have been made to ensure accuracy, however the author does not accept any responsibility for any inaccuracies or any loss, liability, injury, or damage however caused. Guidance should always be followed with caution. Ill or injured people require the help of a medical professional.

Recognising a head injury

Concussion. Concussion is where the brain has been shaken within the skull.

POSSIBLE SIGNS AND SYMPTOMS

- Briefly unconscious.
- Dizzy and confused.
- Feeling or being sick.
- Mild 'all over' headache.

- Paler than usual, clammy skin.
- Loss of memory (amnesia).

TREATMENT

- Sit the casualty in a quiet place.
- Stay with the casualty to monitor them.
- They should start to improve; but if their condition becomes worse call an ambulance.
- Treat any wounds.
- For advice call the NHS on 111 if the casualty seems drowsy, their levels of consciousness are declining, or they develop a severe headache.
- Monitor for signs of compression.
- For all head injuries an ambulance should be called.

Compression. Compression is where pressure is placed on the brain. This might be caused by bleeding or swelling inside the head, or an infection.

POSSIBLE SIGNS AND SYMPTOMS

- Possible recent head injury.
- Declining levels of consciousness or drowsiness.
- Intense headache.
- Flushed (red) dry skin and high temperature.
- Unequal pupils.
- Fitting.
- Slow, noisy breathing.

TREATMENT

- If the casualty is conscious, lie them down, elevating their head and shoulders .

- Reassure the casualty.

- Give nothing to eat or drink.

- Monitor airway and breathing.

Spinal injuries

These are a concern for all first-aiders. We must try to prevent the injury from becoming worse whenever possible. If a spinal injury has affected the spinal column, this may lead to loss of movement below the injury and, as such, can be very scary for both the casualty and the first-aider.

POSSIBLE SIGNS AND SYMPTOMS

- General signs and symptoms of a fracture.

- The casualty may be in an unnatural position.

- Loss of control of the bladder or bowel.

- Breathing difficulty.

- Pain in the neck or back.

- Loss of control of limbs (paralysis).

- Pins and needles or burning sensations in the limbs.

TREATMENT

IF THE CASUALTY IS BREATHING

- Keep the casualty in the same position, unless they are in danger.

- Call an ambulance.

- Support their head with your hands (leave any headgear on — but see note below).

- Monitor, responsiveness, airway and breathing.

- Be prepared to use your emergency plan.

- If the casualty's airway becomes compromised, e.g. through vomiting, you roll them on to their side.

WHAT TO DO IF THE CASUALTY'S AIRWAY IS BLOCKED OR THEY ARE NOT BREATHING NORMALLY

- Ensure that an ambulance has been called.

- Use a gentle but sufficient controlled head tilt/chin lift to open the airway and check for breathing.

- If the casualty is now breathing normally maintain the position and await the arrival of the emergency services.

- If the casualty is not breathing normally, start basic life support.

- If you are unsure of how to, or unwilling to open the airway or commence basic life support, recall ambulance control for advice — but do not just wait until their arrival.

Riding hat removal

As stated above, it is usual practice to leave any headgear in place. However, if the casualty is wearing a helmet and this is hindering their breathing check, you should consider careful removal. Ensure that any chinstraps have been undone and try to use other helpers to keep the head and neck still and supported during gentle removal. If you are unsure or unwilling, call ambulance control for further guidance.

Importance of air

It is important to remember that we can live with most injuries but we cannot live without air. It is therefore essential that the first-aider recognises that airway and breathing problems always need to be prioritised over other injuries.

If the casualty is not breathing, follow the DRSAB procedure:

Danger — check for dangers to you and any casualties. Make sure it's safe for you to give help ...

Response — talk to the casualty and gently tap their shoulders. If the casualty is not responding ...

Shout — for helpers if possible, but don't leave the casualty yet, whilst you attend to the ...

Airway — open the airway by tilting the head back and lifting the chin. Maintain a clear airway, while you check for ...

Breathing — by looking, listening and feeling for signs of life for up to ten seconds.

If the casualty is not responding, call 999 and

- Give thirty chest compressions, followed by two rescue breaths.

- If you are unwilling or unable to give rescue breaths, continue with chest compressions only.

- Continue with chest compressions (and rescue breaths) using the ratio of thirty compressions and two breaths.

- Only stop to recheck the casualty if they start to breath normally — otherwise don't interrupt resuscitation unnecessarily.

- If there is more than one rescuer, change over every two minutes to prevent fatigue.

Compress the chest by at least one-third of its depth using two hands. Use one or two hands for a child as needed to achieve an adequate depth of compression (at least one-third).

Coaching theory

An equestrian coach's professional knowledge can fall into two main areas. First, technical riding knowledge, including an understanding of the horse. Second, the inter-personal aspect of the relationship between coach and rider. The first can be described as the 'what to coach', the second as the 'how to coach'. Coaches will initially rely on the style of coaching and training they have received themselves as a rider; as they develop and gain practical experience their practice and style will become more personal, shaped by their own journey through the inexact nature of working in the industry. This section will focus on the second area of professional knowledge necessary for a coach; the skills necessary to develop the rider through the inter-personal relationship.

Understanding the requirements of riding

A coaching philosophy is one that describes your values and approach to your practice — this should include horse welfare and putting your riders at the centre of the process. A coaching environment is set by the coach and the organisation.

The coach's own technical knowledge of riding, and personal experience of what riding involves, should provide an understanding of the physical and mental demands that riding makes on others, and this should help the coach show empathy towards clients.

Physical

Riding is a late specialisation sport; riders can continue in the sport for as long as their health allows. Balance and coordination are key skills for the rider to develop; core strength follows closely. Strengthening muscle groups to maintain the rider's balance and coordination is a gradual process, but this should not be at the expense of maintaining the essential suppleness of joints. Supple shoulders, lower back and hips enable a rider to absorb the horse's movement and not transfer it to their head, hands and legs. Saddle hours are essential. Riding clients come in many different shapes and sizes. Fortunately, the horse does not judge the aesthetic appearance of their rider. However, it is the responsibility of the coach to be aware of the challenges of different biomechanics in the rider. Long bodies with short limbs require more balance as opposed to the ideal long-limbed short body. However, long levers (arms and legs) present their own challenges, (e.g. when jumping). Long thighs and short lower legs are challenged by some saddles. The list is endless; suffice to say that the ideal riding position is one that inconveniences the horse the least.

Mental

'What is in the brain goes down the rein'. The horse will assess the rider's mindset quicker than the coach. This uncomfortable fact is inescapable, therefore coaching strategies for developing and maintaining that golden confidence and positive mental attitude in the rider are a priority.

Generic sports coaching does not have the added dimension of interacting with a sentient being that coaching riding does; the third party in our coaching relationship is the horse. Riding coaches must, therefore, be first and foremost horse-people, to enable them to put the horse as well as the rider at the centre of the coaching process.

The rider will develop competence leading to confidence if the horse's movement and responses assist in achieving the sessional aims. The rider also needs a certain level of emotional resilience to deal with the inevitable challenges of mastering riding a horse. Primarily, time (number of saddle hours) is necessary for progress to occur. Compared to other activities, ours would be low on the score of instant gratification.

Motivation

Riders have differing reasons for taking up the sport. Common ones are an interest in the horse, and family or peer influences. Motivation can be intrinsic (coming from self) or extrinsic (coming from outside influences). Riders with intrinsic motivation tend to be more able to deal with the challenges of the sport; however the coach's persona can be a strong influence upon motivation, either positively or negatively. Maintaining intrinsic or self-motivation can be helped by the rider having input to the coaching process through good coach/rider rapport and well-managed coach/rider feedback. At the other end of the motivational scale is the child who is sent riding because the parents wish it; often siblings are dragged along to 'join in' with an older brother or sister. This is a motivational challenge for the coach. Empathic coaching, setting achievable goals and management of parental expectation by the coach can help the situation.

The goal of the coach is to encourage and foster intrinsic motivation and self-determined goals in the rider to ensure continued engagement with the sport. Participation relies on regular engagement by the riding client, driven by holistic, effective coaching and encouraging a passion for the horse.

Communication

Equestrian sport has a language of its own and it is important for the coach to be able to put into 'layman's' terms some of the basic concepts for the beginner. As the rider learns the terminology and becomes more competent and knowledgeable the language used can become more technical.

Glossary of terms and commands used in the school

THE RIDE	All horses and riders in the coached group
CLOSED ORDER	All horses working at a set distance apart in single file
ONE HORSE'S LENGTH	A measurement (approx. 3.05m/10ft) of distance between horses
LEADING FILE	The rider at the front of the ride
REAR FILE	The rider at the back of the ride
OPEN ORDER	Riders working in their own space, observing the rules of the school
LEFT REIN	Travelling anti-clockwise (left hand inside)
RIGHT REIN	Travelling clockwise (right hand inside)
TRANSITION	A change of gait
UPWARD TRANSITION	Increase in gait
DOWNWARD TRANSITION	Decrease in gait
PROGRESSIVE TRANSITIONS	Will move from one gait to the next gait e.g. walk, trot and halt
DIRECT TRANSITION	Will miss a gait e.g. canter, walk
LEAD FILE IN SUCCESSION	One at a time from the front
REAR FILE IN SUCCESSION	One at a time from the back
WHOLE RIDE	Everyone together
INWARDS TURN	Turn as a ride towards the middle of the school
FORM UP A RIDE	Make a line side by side, with stirrups aligned
FREE END OF THE SCHOOL	The end with no riders

School figure descriptions can be found in the dressage tests of a suitable level, e.g. Intro, Prelim and Novice.

Developing rapport

A rider will enjoy their experience of being coached if they feel they 'get on well' with their coach. For recreational riders a sense of 'belonging' to the sporting environment can be encouraged by an empathetic, patient approach by the coach. Establishing rapport with the rider is easier when a coach works with them on a regular basis; however in a commercial context it is important to be client-friendly from the outset. Putting the rider at ease, ensuring they are comfortable, and being quick to notice lack of confidence or signs of unease will ensure a positive start.

Encouraging feedback

A coach knowing the rider and having a rapport with them will facilitate feedback from the rider. If the rider feels sufficiently comfortable with the coach to voice their thoughts and opinions, this will result in valuable feedback. Some people are naturally vocal and opinionated and experience no problems with making the coach aware of their thoughts! However, in group situations this may discourage the less-confident individuals from being heard. Accurate, honest feedback from a rider regarding themselves and their horse is an invaluable aid to the coach. This will inform the coach and give a deeper understanding of how effective their practice is. Accurate observation and honest feedback will help the coach to progress the session appropriately, meeting the needs of both horse and rider.

Feedback can be sought from the rider at any stage of the session; after an exercise, after an explanation for clarification and, essentially, at the end of the session.

> *The coach's ethical approach to riders, and the rider's role in establishing rapport and offering feedback, are discussed further in the section Coach and Rider Behaviour in the next chapter.*

Questions and answers

For questioning to provide a valid source of information to the coach, using 'open' questions is of benefit. An open question would begin with a '*How?*', '*Why?*', '*What?*', '*When?*', '*Where?*' or '*Who?*', avoiding a yes/no answer. The coach will receive more information from the rider. However, complex questions to the beginner/novice rider can be intimidating and have the opposite effect, the rider being unwilling to show their ignorance, particularly in a group context. Questions must be framed within the rider's knowledge base and be aimed at developing rapport rather, than being an inquisition. The timing of the questions is important, and should be when the rider is in a position to produce an answer, not at a crucial moment, such as canter transition, or landing after a jump! 'Wait' time is also central to effective questioning; this means giving the rider 'think time' to formulate an answer. It is tempting for the coach to jump in and answer their own question, which is demotivating for the rider. When the rider produces an answer, the coach should be respectful of their input; the temptation for the coach to insert their own views can be demoralising for the rider and discourage them from further engagement in the Q & A session. Keeping a balance between 'too much chat' and not enough action can also be a challenge. Questioning should be kept to a minimum, during periods of intense activity.

Coach's voice

A coach's tone and pitch are highly influential, not only to the rider but to the horse as well. The coach should try to maintain a low to medium pitch with clear enunciation of all words. Emotion is conveyed through tone of voice and good control of this is important. It is a common desire to say too much too quickly; the phrase 'too much information!' should sit at the back of the coach's mind. 'Silence is golden' is another useful phrase; a coach should not be afraid of periods of quiet in which to observe and analyse the action, and the rider needs to concentrate on themselves and the horse. Constant chatter from the coach is an unnecessary distraction.

Coach's eye

Observation, analysis and evaluation of what is in front of you are important skills for a coach to perfect. Developing your eye will continue for the whole of your coaching career. Changing position frequently to ensure that you see the horse and rider from all angles will help.

As your eye develops, looking for and identifying the root causes of problems in rider and horse, rather than just the signs and superficial indicators, will improve your coaching effectiveness. For example, the rider's lower leg too far forward can often be a sign that the seat is too far back in the saddle. Just correcting the lower leg repeatedly will not fix the problem; addressing the rider's seat position will be more effective in helping the

The coach should change position where required in order to see riders from all angles.

Chapter 17

Coaching in Practice

Preparing for coaching sessions

Coaching a session – general principles

Developing the rider

Lead rein lessons

Lunge lessons

Coaching early flatwork

Progressing the rider

Coaching jumping

Teaching horse care

Summary

Preparing for coaching sessions

Necessary information

Riders

Before a coaching session can be planned, the coach needs some basic information on the riders taking part. A commercial riding school will have registration forms giving the height, weight, age and riding experience of the clients. There will also be information on any medical conditions, past injuries and relevant contact numbers. Freelance coaches would also be well advised to carry these forms. The rider's aims and reasons for booking are also relevant, although managing realistic expectation on the part of the client may be required. Rider's goals can be discussed and agreed after an initial assessment.

Horses

In a riding school context the horses are usually a known quantity to the resident coach. It is important to be aware of any changes to the horses' management that might influence their behaviour and level of work. Each horse's age, type, level of schooling and fitness will influence his suitability for a range of clients.

Horse allocation

Riding school

This is easier for a resident coach as they will have some input, allowing them to allocate a horse suitable in type, temperament and level of schooling to the rider's needs. Even so, sometimes horses and riders may not be perfectly matched. In many cases this may not mean that the combination is unsafe, but the work undertaken needs to be managed to ensure that the rider is not overstretched. This could include, for example, a rider mounted on a bouncy horse when their balance is not fully established: in this situation the lesson plan would need to be adapted and might include work to help the rider learn to absorb the movement. Work without stirrups in trot may need to be avoided. In another scenario, a rider might be on a horse who is more forward than they are used to: if the plan was to do a jumping lesson this may need to be scaled back to pole work and work to control the horse, e.g. transitions.

There may, of course, be the need to challenge a known rider, at times, in order to assist progression, but this should not be to the extent of stressing the rider with unrealistic expectations. Over-horsing a rider can be a confidence-sapping and demotivating experience and could also cause a safety issue. For this reason, when assessing a new client, horse allocation a little below the rider's stated standard is advisable as they may have overstated their ability.

Owner-riders

As encountered by those coaching Riding Club/Pony Club sessions, or working freelance. This coaching context presents a great challenge to the coach because of the unlikelihood of having much input to the client's choice of mount. Owner-riders do not always present themselves to their coach on the most suitable mount. However, they will be in love with their horse and the coach must make the best of things!

Safety of the rider remains the first concern, followed by realistic goal-setting to work within the limitations of the partnership.

Grouping riders

Ideally, riders in a group session should be of similar levels and have compatible goals. Mixed-ability groups present more of a coaching challenge to adapt exercises to meet individual needs — this is known as 'differentiation' in generic coaching terms. If this is well-managed by the coach there are some advantages to a mixed-ability group, provided the levels do not differ too wildly. The more advanced riders can prove useful for demonstrations and to work as leading file; this can build confidence and self-esteem for them and be inspirational for the less-experienced riders. Care must be taken to stretch the stronger riders suitably at times during the session.

In a commercial environment clients want to ride at their convenience, not necessarily when their group level is scheduled. Safety can be an issue in a scenario with widely different levels, e.g. first ridden clients (just off the lead rein or lunge) and canter/jump clients. Horses are herd animals and in the absence of effective direction from their rider they will inevitably follow the cantering ones!

In a freelance environment, grouping riders according to their horses' levels of schooling will make your life easier. However, this is not always possible if you are not organising the groups. Generally, mixing age groups can be unpopular. Older teenagers may not want to ride with young children and some adults may feel demeaned by riding with children.

Planning the session

This is often done at the beginning; however, you cannot plan a session effectively until you have a high proportion of the above-mentioned information.

With a known rider or group, effective planning will take into account what has gone on before, However, with a new client an assessment plan is a must, inevitably with the content a little open to allow the session to develop in line with the needs of the rider. If this must be done in a group session it is wise to have the new rider in a group a little below their stated ability. Clients sometimes display a vivid imagination regarding their ability on a horse. For insurance purposes it is important that a new client fills in the box on the ride registration form regarding their perceived experience. However, it is unwise to bring out your retired 3* horse even if they have stated that they are an event rider.

For a regular client or group the sessions should link together and follow a logical progression of gradual incremental skill acquisition. Planning is essential to ensure that you are organised and have the necessary arena and equipment prepared (e.g. bending poles, mounting block, poles, etc.) to ensure a smooth efficient session.

Always have a plan 'B' in the event of things not going according to plan 'A'. Be prepared to modify your plan if it is not proving to be safe, suitable and effective. Do not stay on a 'sinking ship'.

Plan, observe, evaluate, give feedback and then plan again. To summarise, a plan should include introduction and safety checks, warming up and assessment, session content, cooling down, summary and finally feedback.

Coaching a session — general principles

Introduction and safety checks

If you are working in the same environment regularly then risk assessments should be in place for the arena, equipment and surroundings. During the introduction, additional checks should be made to ensure that there have not been any changes, e.g. surface conditions, weather conditions, outside influences such as machinery or loose horses in adjoining paddocks.

Risk assessments are essential for freelance coaches to ensure that the area being used is suitable. The variables are many, from a client's own facilities to a corner of a muddy field. Riding Clubs and Pony Club branches often have facilities for rallies and clinics, but equally a coach can find themselves coaching in a large farmer's field, particularly in the summer months.

While you are introducing yourself to the riders, tack checks and PPE (personal protective equipment) checks can also be carried out. Health and safety issues and risk assessments were covered in detail earlier in the previous chapter.

During the introduction you have the opportunity to set the coaching climate with a calm, friendly manner, ready to engage with each rider on an individual basis within the group. Learning riders' names is important for developing rapport and promoting feedback in the early stages. A clean, tidy appearance and suitable attire (even on a wet day in an outdoor school) will reinforce your air of professionalism. It shows a form of respect to ensure that your turnout is appropriate; you do not have to be wearing top-of-the-range kit, but you should be in practical, workmanlike riding wear, with a safety helmet to hand in case of a mounted demonstration.

The warm-up and initial assessment

Generally this is carried out mounted, but if the opportunity is there, some dismounted stretches are a good idea. Owner-riders will have warmed up through preparing their horse for riding.

The point of a warm-up session for horse and rider is to promote the circulation gradually in order to prevent straining muscles, ligaments and tendons and to prepare the cardiovascular and respiratory systems for effort. Suitable working-in exercises will use all three gaits, building up gradually to the canter where appropriate for the rider and gaining feedback from the riders as to how they and their horses are feeling. During this part of the session you can observe the rider's performance and check that the intended lesson plan will be suitable.

Setting goals for a session

This is best carried out with the ride in halt, to allow the riders to concentrate fully. You should encourage feedback from the riders on how the horses are feeling and agree with the riders on the sessional goals. The theme of the lesson should be clearly explained and, if appropriate, a demonstration given. This can be mounted, or you can demonstrate on foot. The level of knowledge and understanding of the riders can be assessed through open questions (see Questions and Answers, in the previous chapter), but it is important to move on to the execution of the exercises to prevent horses and riders cooling off.

A coach discussing the goals of the session with riders in a group lesson.

It is important for the coach to engage with each rider.

Managing to deliver good-quality information and corrections, while maintaining the action and flow of the session, is a challenge for the less-experienced coach. Interspersing work as a ride and individual exercises can help the coach to engage with the individuals without losing the attention of the rest of the ride.

More complex coaching is easier in a private lesson, but this can be intense and more tiring for both horse and rider. In group sessions the riders can watch and learn from others, and both adults and children will enjoy the social aspect of a well-managed group session. Throughout the session your ongoing observation and evaluation of the rider's performance should ensure that the plan remains appropriate. 'Teach what you see in front of you' should always be in the back of any coach's mind and a flexible, democratic approach is necessary in order to respond to the ever-changing nature of a ridden session.

Cooling down and summary

Running to time is an essential skill and allowing enough time to cool down and carry out a summary to conclude the lesson is important. Sometimes it is difficult to get this timing right, but it's important always to try to end on a good note so the riders feel positive, even if they have encountered some challenges during the session.

The cool-down is a period of gradual decrease of work intensity, usually in walk, allowing the horses to stretch and work on a long rein. This allows the cardiovascular and respiratory systems to eliminate waste products from the physical exertion and prevent subsequent stiffness in both horse and rider. Riders can be encouraged to stretch when dismounting again; owner-riders will warm down when untacking and caring for their horse after work.

The session summary is an important opportunity for you to check that learning has taken place. This is achieved by encouraging feedback from the riders on their performance and engaging in open questioning to develop the rider's ability to self-reflect. A coach must endeavour to maintain a balanced discussion between positive and negative, and encourage the riders to identify their strengths as well as discussing areas for development. Owner-riders will benefit from ideas for inter-sessional homework to encourage continuity. Weekly riders may welcome non-ridden activities to improve fitness between lessons.

Coach and rider behaviour

As already mentioned, the coach's persona and manner have a major influence in setting the coaching climate. Being courteous, friendly, approachable, well-presented and organised are all desirable traits to be developed. The more experienced a coach, the easier it becomes to deal with the challenges faced in a calm, professional manner. Emotional intelligence is a term used to describe the ability to manage one's own emotions and feelings in times of stress and drama. As mentioned earlier, riding is a risk sport and the ability to keep a cool head will benefit both riders and horses.

Equity and ethics describe the coach's duty to ensure transparency and fair play at all times within their practice. All riders must be treated equally, with no favourites, and wherever possible equal attention given to all riders in the group.

Although the coach might be seen as the 'lead' in the coach-rider relationship, appropriate relationships between coach and riders are really a two-way street. Riders must engage in the coaching process, adhering to the coach's instructions to ensure their safety and enjoyment as well as the horse's welfare — e.g. listening and obeying school rules, maintaining distances and endeavouring to improve. This can be achieved while maintaining a welcoming environment suitable for all riders to enjoy their time with the horses.

Managing parents/observers

Developing coaches are often challenged by the 'expert' parent in the viewing gallery. This can be distracting and humiliating for the rider and, at worst, present a safety issue. It should be made clear by the coach that this is not acceptable behaviour and the person concerned should be invited to a discussion period at the end of the session. Parents are an important part of the coaching process and it is essential that they are encouraged to be 'onside' by open communication and discussion before and/or after the session. It should not be necessary for them to intervene during the session. Introductions, feedback and summaries can all take place within earshot of the gallery, so parents can feel part of the process — after all, they often transport and supply financial support to your riders.

Managing helpers

Helpers should help, not hinder! It is fairer to them to ensure that they are of a suitable age and are sufficiently trained to be confident, competent and courteous in their role. As such, they can be integral to the smooth running of a coaching session involving lead rein, first ridden clients, jumping sessions and mounted games and activities. Their support is also appreciated in pony care sessions and in helping with mounting, and leading less confident clients.

A level of maturity is required as helpers may need to maintain client confidentiality (e.g. awareness of medical issues). Any briefing should be done before the session and away from clients. Helpers must be aware of safety guidelines, suitable dress and equipment and the importance of their role. They must be capable of carrying out the tasks required of them, such as leading, moving and carrying equipment. Helpers can gain competence and confidence, allowing them to get further involved with horses.

Basic lesson plan (1 hour session)

Introduction and safety checks — 5 minutes

Warm-up/Assessment — 10 minutes
- Include walk, trot and canter

Feedback/Goal-setting — 5 minutes
- Move on to next stage/do not allow participants to cool down

Lesson Content — 20–30 minutes
- Could include: School figures, Transitions, Work without stirrups, Developing canter, etc.

Cool down, Feedback/Summary — 10 minutes

Developing the rider

As you continue to work with riders, you will learn more about them as individuals (and they about you), and it is at this point that an understanding of coaching and learning styles will be most fruitful.

Coaching styles

There are three main coaching approaches recognised.

Autocratic

This is where the coach dictates the aims and progression of the session, maintaining absolute control at all times with little or no input from the rider.

Although this style is thought to be 'old school' in some opinions, it should not be discounted. Riding is a risk sport and there are many scenarios where this would be a required approach. Any situation where safety of the horse and rider may be compromised would demand a rapid autocratic response from the coach. Beginners need instruction and support from their coach in order to feel safe and make progress — also, some research has shown that young children, teenage girls and nervous adults appreciate a coach who is 'instructive and supportive'.

Democratic

This is where the coach and rider jointly agree the aims and progression of the session. More experienced and confident riders often welcome this approach. Motivation theory tells us that intrinsic motivation is encouraged if the rider has some control over their actions. Different riders will vary in how 'self-determined' they require their coaching to be. It is down to the coach to identify the needs of the rider through feedback, allowing more input from the rider. In a group some riders will require more instruction and support than others. Some 'needy' personalities may require gentle encouragement to take more responsibility for their learning.

Set up and stand back (Laissez-faire)

This is where the aims and progression of the session are agreed jointly by coach and rider. The rider then takes more responsibility for the progression of work, with input from the coach where appropriate. This approach is suitable for young professionals preparing for exams and competition riders at representational or elite level. Many owner-riders will benefit from an adapted form of this style as it develops the ability in the rider to self-reflect and continue the learning process in the coach's absence, e.g. in an exam, at home or in competition.

> *All three styles of coaching are valuable provided they are used appropriately. The skill of the coach lies in identifying when to use a particular style; many sessions will contain a mix of all three.*

Learning styles

Physically, the rider takes in information in three ways, auditory (hearing), visually (seeing) and kinaesthetically (feeling). Most riders will use a blend of all three, but some may follow one more strongly. The use of explanation, demonstration and execution by the coach when introducing an exercise will meet the needs of all three. Psychologically, riders may be theorists, reflectors, activists or pragmatists. Theorists like to understand the theory, reflectors need time to process the information, activists like to get on with the job and a pragmatist will be happy to comply provided they understand the reasons why. Again, all four types of learners can be accommodated by the coach in a group environment with the use of clear explanations, sound reasoning and plenty of action. If a rider is strongly a theorist or reflector they may benefit from private lessons, which allow them more time to take in the information provided by the coach. Strongly activist riders need to be kept safe and made aware of the welfare of the horse. The pragmatic learner will require a competent, confident coach with sound reasoning skills.

> ### Recorded media
>
> *DVD and video recording can be helpful tools for learners — perhaps especially those who are primarily auditory or visual learners. If riders are recorded and then able to watch themselves, and others, they may be able to analyse and consider how to correct faults more easily; a classroom setting is a good place to do this.*

Skill acquisition

Learning to ride a horse consists of acquiring a variety of motor skills over a period of time, gradually refining the rider's ability to first balance and go with the horse's movement and then to communicate with the horse to form a partnership. The skill of the coach ensures the gradual, logical acquisition of these skills while encouraging an understanding of the horse's reactions and needs.

Three stages of skill acquisition have been recognised and will apply each time a rider progresses to the next level or tries something new.

Cognitive stage: the rider has to think about the skill and still makes many mistakes when trying to achieve the task — low confidence.

Associative stage: the rider needs to practise over and over, fewer mistakes are made, which develops confidence.

Autonomous stage: little thought required, instinctive action.

The coach's job is to maintain confidence and motivation in the rider, particularly during the first two stages, as it is discouraging for the rider to make mistakes. Also, the horse must be of a placid and forgiving nature to deal with the rider's efforts to acquire the new skill. A practical example would be when the novice rider learns the rising trot. At the cognitive stage the rise is best taught in the halt and walk to give the rider a chance to acquire the skill of rising in the saddle without the added bounce of the trot. The horse should be controlled by the coach either on the lead rein or lunge. Introducing the rise in the trot will result in loss of balance and position, just using the long sides of the school will help with this. Short, regular periods of trot to allow plenty of practice is necessary at this associative stage. Eventually the rider will be able to maintain the rise down the long side, through the short side and through school figures, only to lose it again when they have to control the horse themselves with leg aids and rein aids. Thus the skill of acquiring the rising trot for the rider requires practice and time. The coach must be instructive and supportive to achieve this.

Methods of encouragement

Positive reinforcement

It is important for the rider's engagement that the coach is motivational in approach. Praise should be given for effort as well as achievement, pointing out achievement and valuing it, however small, and maintaining a positive balance between praise and criticism. If a correction is necessary, the method of correction is fundamentally important. Just delivering criticism to a rider without any strategies for putting it right will demotivate and disengage them. A coach should try to avoid the word 'don't' and replace it with a 'doing' word. Instead of 'don't cut the corner', 'ride into your corners'.

Fun and enjoyment

Hopefully, this is why your clients come to you as a coach. They go away with a sense of achievement, having enjoyed themselves. Adults and children will have different ideas of a 'fun time'! For most adults, interacting with the horse, being out of the home or office and achieving some improvement are all forms of enjoyment. A good coach of adults will balance enough theoretical information with achievable goals, setting challenges that are realistic and time-relevant within the session. Adults and young people will enjoy pared-down adapted versions of riding activities seen in the media, such as the 'Rider's Test — a dressage test

Above all, lessons should be enjoyable – this is the reason why clients come to you.

judged on the style of the rider — recently introduced by British Riding Clubs and marked primarily on rider empathy and handling of the horse. Similarly, a simulated show including circling round as a ride before demonstrating an individual show and stripping and trotting up the horse, or swapping horses, are examples of variation on the theme of a basic coaching session.

For children, mounted games are valuable, in either pairs or small teams (transparency of team selection is important, not self-selection, as someone is always left out). The focus should be on fun and progress, rather than a 'win at all costs' mindset. Adapted versions of handy pony or, for those who jump, 'chase-me-Charlie' (fence gets higher with each round) or block elimination (using blocks, the fence gets narrower) are popular. The coach must maintain an atmosphere of safety and fair play, emphasising the fun, informal element.

Lead rein lessons

A lead rein lesson can be very useful for coaching beginner riders. It allows you to have close control of the horse and the rider, allowing the rider to develop their basic riding skills in a safe and controlled way. A nervous person will often feel more safe and secure on the lead rein while they are learning new skills, as you can be on hand to help them and they do not have sole responsibility for the control of the horse.

A large proportion of the lead rein lessons you will coach will be small children learning to ride, although you may at times use a lead rein lesson for older children and adult beginners. It is important to consider the individual person when planning your session, as the exercises you do and the language you use will vary. For small children there will be more 'doing' and having fun, with less explanation of why, whereas an adult may find explanation useful so that they understand what they are doing why they are doing it. However, for everyone it is important that they feel safe when they are learning new skills, and if they enjoy the session and feel that they have gained something from it they are much more likely to return for another lesson.

An important aspect of coaching a lead rein lesson is being able to lead and control the horse at the same time as giving the rider your attention and help. You cannot be an effective coach and develop a rapport with the person being coached if you do not look at them, but equally you do not want to fall over a cone because you are not aware of where you are walking. This is a skill that requires practice. When you are coaching a group lead rein lesson you rely a lot on the people leading for you. They are extra pairs of eyes and ears that can prevent problems and help the riders learn.

Preparation

A lead rein lesson could be in an arena or on grass, as long as ground conditions are suitable. However, it is important to remember that a large, open area may be more intimidating for a beginner, so a smaller fenced-off area would be better. It is a good idea to have the coaching area set up ready before starting the session. Equipment such as cones, poles and letters can all be useful in a lead rein lesson; however their positioning in the arena needs to be carefully considered. A beginner will find it more challenging to avoid obstacles than a more experienced rider. Any unused equipment should be stored neatly, preferably outside the arena to avoid any unnecessary 'clutter'.

The horse used for the lead rein lesson needs to be of suitable size and temperament. He should be in proportion to the rider's height and weight, with a calm and patient temperament. In addition to the usual tack, the horse will need a neckstrap or balance strap and a lead rein. It is ideal to use a headcollar under the bridle or a coupling attached to the bit to lead from; this removes the need to change the lead rope over when changing the rein and prevents uneven pressure on the bit.

Coaching session

A rider's first lesson is their first experience of riding, and maybe even horses in general. Starting with basic handling skills can be a good idea so that the rider can learn to handle and lead the horse safely. This will help to make them feel more comfortable around the horse before they ride, and also allows them to start to develop a relationship with the horse. However you, as the coach, should always be in ultimate control of the rider and the horse in order to maintain a safe learning environment. By encouraging a rider to talk to you and ask questions you can develop a relationship with two-way trust and respect, which will be of further help to a nervous rider.

You can involve the rider in checking the girth and adjusting the stirrups and this will mean they will know how to do it for themselves in future lessons. Using the mounting block, you should then teach them the correct way to mount the horse, demonstrating if necessary. If a small child cannot reach to mount in the normal way, you may need to lift them on, but it is best to let the parent know this is what you are going to do before doing it. If you need to alter the girth or stirrup leathers once the rider is mounted you will need to bear in mind that a beginner will not be used to moving around in the saddle and this may make them feel insecure. It is a good idea to talk them through what you are doing as you do it, and try to involve them where possible, e.g. ask them to hold the saddle flap up while you are altering the girth.

Mounting correctly is an important skill that should be taught from the first lesson.

You will need to show the rider how to hold the reins and how to sit, helping them into position if necessary. Before moving off it is a good idea to tell them what to feel and expect, as the motion can be a little strange to a complete beginner. You should encourage them to hold the neckstrap, balance strap or the front of the saddle to begin with, as this will provide them with some security and avoid them using the reins for balance. As they become more confident they can progress to only holding on with one hand, and then not holding on at all.

The session should aim to teach the basic aids of how to start, stop and turn. Using cones, poles or letters can help with this, giving the rider a point to stop at or to aim towards. Using exercises can help them to learn and develop these skills in an enjoyable way.

Progression

Once the rider is comfortable with the basic aids in walk and halt you can further develop their skills by introducing trot, and then rising trot. To introduce trot, ask the rider to hold the saddle and lead them for a few steps of sitting trot in a straight line. Explain that the trot is bouncier than the walk as the horse moves his legs in diagonal pairs with a moment of suspension in between each step. Rising can be introduced in the halt, paying particular attention to the position of the rider's lower leg, which will affect their balance if it moves forward or back. You might want to hold the leg gently in position while they practise. Encourage the rider to swing the hips forwards rather than stand straight up. Their upper body should incline forward slightly from the pelvis, but don't allow them to lean too far forward. Make sure they control the downward movement and don't bang on to the horse's back, and have them holding the neckstrap to stop them pulling back on the reins in an effort to rise. Once the rider has the idea, progress to rising in walk and then trot. This will be tiring for a beginner, so make sure you intersperse it with lots of walk breaks. You can allow them to rest in between trotting by mixing the periods of trot practice with periods of basic aids practice, e.g. walking over poles or walk-halt transitions. Once the rider is able to rise to the trot fluently you can introduce the idea of the correct diagonal.

As the rider is developing, you can progress them towards coming off the lead rein in walk by allowing them to be increasingly in control of the horse, with you simply being there as a 'back-up' at the end of the lead rein. Removing the lead rein but staying close can allow them another step towards becoming independent and being able to ride around the arena with minimum support. This will take different lengths of time to achieve with different people, so it is important to treat each person as an individual and work with what you see.

A quick learner may be capable of coming off the lead rein within the first or second lesson, whereas others may not feel comfortable off the lead rein until a little later. A small child may not be able to control the horse independently until they are bigger and stronger, so may be on the lead rein for a lot longer. However, you can adapt your sessions to keep them enjoyable, by using lots of games and maybe even short hacks on the lead rein (if suitable fields or bridleways are accessible). Offering group lead rein lessons can also allow small children to have fun together, although this is only possible if enough leaders are available.

Regardless of the rider's age or ability, you should encourage them to develop a relationship with the horse.

Exercises to assist progress

1. **Change of rein from letter to letter**

   AIMS AND BENEFITS

   This exercise teaches riders the aids for turning, riding straight and looking ahead.

   DESCRIPTION

   Ask the rider to ride from one letter to another, using a turn to a straight line to another turn. This can be made fun for children by giving each letter a name, e.g. A = apple and C = carrot. The exercise can be progressed by adding in a halt transition over the centre line or by linking a few changes of rein together.

2. **Halting between blocks**

   AIMS AND BENEFITS

   This exercise allows riders to practise the aids for stopping and starting by using accuracy.

A young rider halting between marker blocks.

DESCRIPTION

Ask the rider to ride forwards to halt in the area between the blocks, before counting to five (can be five caterpillars or bananas for children) and walking on again. The exercise can be progressed by making the area between the blocks smaller. Poles or other markers could be used instead of blocks.

3. **Standing up in halt**

   AIMS AND BENEFITS

   This exercise develops the rider's position, balance and security, encouraging them to take their weight into their lower leg and find a natural balance.

   DESCRIPTION

   Ask the rider to stand up while in halt, using the neckstrap, balance strap or the front of the saddle to help them balance. You may need to help them into the correct position. This exercise can be progressed by using it in walk, or over poles.

4. **Walking over poles**

A young rider being led over a series of poles.

AIMS AND BENEFITS

This exercise teaches riders to ride straight and over a certain point, allowing them to plan an approach and develop accuracy.

DESCRIPTION

Ask the rider to walk straight towards and over the centre of the pole, looking ahead as they do. This can be made fun for children by asking them to tell you their favourite food/colour/animal etc. as they walk over the pole. This could also encourage a shy child to speak more. The exercise can be progressed by linking a few poles together into a 'course', by trotting over the poles or by asking the rider to practise their balancing position over the pole.

5. **Traffic lights (for children)**

   ### AIMS AND BENEFITS

   This exercise allows the rider to practise the aids for starting and stopping in an enjoyable way.

   ### DESCRIPTION

   Ask the rider to halt when you say 'red', walk when you say 'amber' and trot when you say 'green'. This can be progressed by having less time between each command or by introducing other colours, e.g. purple for balancing position.

6. **Simon says (for children)**

   ### AIMS AND BENEFITS

   This exercise can be used as an enjoyable way to practise basic skills as well as the rider becoming more comfortable and secure moving around in the saddle.

   ### DESCRIPTION

   Give the rider instructions using 'Simon says' before them, e.g. 'Simon says place one hand on your head.' You can also introduce basic horse knowledge using this exercise, e.g. 'Simon says touch the horse's mane.' This exercise can be progressed by using more complex instructions, e.g. 'Simon says do the actions to head, shoulders, knees and toes.'

Some important skills you are aiming to develop during these early sessions are the rider's balance and coordination. There are a variety of exercises that can be used to improve these at the same time as adding variety to the session, including holding arms out to the side, arm circles, folded arm and standing in the stirrups.

A young rider doing 'head, shoulders, knees and toes'.

Lunge lessons

Lunge lessons provide an opportunity for the rider to develop their position and balance without having to control the horse. Lunge lessons are useful as a tool to help beginner riders master the basics, e.g. balance in rising trot, or for riders to improve and develop their position and security in the saddle.

Equipment

The horse should have a lunge cavesson on and a snaffle bridle with the noseband removed. A neckstrap is essential. For a beginner rider a general-purpose saddle may be suitable, but for a more experienced rider a dressage saddle is preferable to encourage a more classical dressage position. The side-reins should be attached to the girth straps in a position whereby they cannot interfere with the rider's legs. Ideally, the horse should be wearing brushing boots on all four legs, and you should be wearing gloves, hat and suitable footwear. The lunge line and whip should be of suitable length and in good condition.

Warming up the horse

Once you have introduced yourself and the horse to the rider, ask the rider to stand in a safe place, such as the corner by the mounting block, while you warm up the horse. Explain what you are going to do and make sure you interact with the rider while you are lungeing the horse.

The horse will need to be worked on the lunge without the rider before the lesson begins, to give you the chance to assess the horse and make sure he is listening to your aids, and also for the horse to warm up.

Use the warm-up to make sure the horse is listening to you and responding to your aids. Make sure the horse is on a large circle, as a small circle is harder for both horse and rider to balance on. You need to be able to keep the horse out on the circle without falling in and maintain an active rhythm and tempo in each gait. It is harder for the rider to keep their balance if the rhythm and tempo of the horse are constantly changing. Don't forget to change the rein regularly during the session.

Begin by working the horse on each rein without the side-reins. If you don't know the horse you can also carry out a quick assessment of his gaits and whether he is suitable. Then adjust and attach the side-reins and lunge the horse in walk and trot, on both reins. During this time it is important to continue to engage with the rider; if they haven't had a lunge lesson before you can discuss the reasons for warming up the horse and ask if there is anything in particular they want to work on in the session.

When warming up the horse, continue to engage with the rider.

Starting the lesson

When you are ready for the rider to mount, unclip the side-reins and move the horse over to the mounting block. Untwist the reins and recheck the girth before pulling down the stirrups. If the rider is experienced they may adjust their own stirrups before mounting; for a beginner rider, explain what you are doing and why.

The side-reins provide the contact and therefore you must ensure that the rider has a loose rein contact as, if the horse feels two opposing contacts, he may hollow or panic. For safety the side-reins should be unclipped when the rider mounts and dismounts, if the rider is doing exercises in halt, and also if the tack is being adjusted or the rider is crossing or uncrossing the stirrups over the horse's neck.

Once the rider has mounted and the stirrup leathers have been adjusted, ask them to adopt their normal position and observe them in walk and trot on both reins; this will allow the rider to warm up while you assess their position. You are looking for the imaginary straight line from the rider's ear, shoulder, hip to heel. Try to identify whether the rider tips forwards or back and whether there is any differences on each rein — it is common for riders to be stronger on one side than the other. In addition, try to see whether the rider is dropping one hip or shoulder; this can be more difficult to identify on the lunge as you cannot see the rider directly from behind.

Hold the horse while the rider mounts; ensure that the reins have been untwisted and the side-reins are unclipped.

A rider sitting in an ideal position with a vertical line from her ear, shoulder, hip to heel.

Identifying areas for improvement

It is important to note that most positional faults are a result of stiffness through the lower back and hips, and much of your work will be towards improving the rider's suppleness in these areas. If a rider is tensing and lifting their shoulders in sitting trot as a result of insecurity or stiffness through the lower back, arm circles and shoulder rolls will not improve this. The rider needs to practise the sitting trot and develop their suppleness and balance so they can absorb the movement of the horse. As this improves they will be able to 'let go' and relax their shoulders. Often the rider needs very little in the way of actual exercises and time is better focused on developing suppleness and balance in the sitting trot. Similarly, with a rider whose toes turn out, this often stems from a lack of suppleness through the hips, so they are unable to simply turn their foot towards the front and keep it there.

Below are some common positional faults.

Rounded back.

Arched back.

Leaning back and collapsing through the middle.

Tipping forward with the seat pushed to the back of the saddle.

Tensing through the shoulders.

Rider sitting to the back of the saddle with the lower leg too far forward.

Collapsing to one side.

Exercises

It is important to remember that any adjustment to a rider's normal position can feel like a big change to them, so they may need some time to get used to the feeling. It may feel 'strange' or 'wrong' to them, especially if they have a tendency to tip forward or push their seat to the back of the saddle. Mirrors can be useful in this situation; a rider who normally tips forward will feel that they are leaning back when they are sitting correctly, but by looking in the mirror they will be able to see that they are sitting correctly and this will reinforce your coaching. A beginner rider will naturally sit in an 'armchair position', with their legs out in front of them. In order to be in best balance, over time riders need to be able to develop a position with their legs further back under the body; this must be achieved from the thighs and hips rather than just pushing the lower legs back. Exercises can be used to help improve suppleness, however, when using these exercises care should be taken not to overstretch the rider, particularly with the exercises for the lower body, as these can result in cramp if the rider is not used to them.

The first step to help a rider correct their position is to help them to achieve a neutral spine position; first the rider should be encouraged to sit in the centre of the saddle with their weight equal on both seat bones. Hold the horse in halt, without the side-reins attached, and ask the rider to draw their knees up together with the aim of touching them over the pommel of the saddle (not all riders may be able to do this, so encourage the rider to do what they can). Riders who are stiff may adjust their upper body position by tipping forward or twisting in the saddle to achieve this, so once the rider has lifted their knees up, check their position in the saddle again to ensure that it is correct.

Before they drop their legs back down, ask the rider to open their knees out a little to the side and hold this position for a second (this will open the hip joints) and then drop their legs down against the saddle. Some riders may not be able to do this if they are a little stiff; if this is the case they should allow their legs to slide down gently. For this exercise to be effective the rider needs to keep the weight even on both seat bones and not twist or tip through the upper body. Over time, as they become freer through the hips, the rider will gradually find it easier to draw their legs into the correct position, but the priority should be the position of the rider's seat and back. If you force the legs back too early, it is likely that this will prop them forward off their seat bones.

With all the exercises, the rider should be asked to maintain a neutral spine and a good posture. Lower body exercises will help to open up the hips and stretch the thighs so the rider can begin to position their legs further back on the saddle.

Other exercises for improving suppleness of hips and lower body

- Legs away, back and down — the rider lifts their legs, one at a time, away from the saddle from the hip, rolls the hip back and relaxes the leg against the saddle. This exercise helps the rider to sit in the central part of the saddle, open up their hips, and begin to stretch their thighs. For riders whose toes turn out this is a useful exercise, as the rider lifts the leg off the saddle, turns the foot and leg to the front and places the leg back on the saddle.

- Swinging legs forward and back from the hip — this is a very useful exercise to free up the thighs and help the rider to move the thighs back on the saddle.

Swinging legs forward and back.

- Holding the legs out — this exercise opens the hips and stretches the thighs out. When the rider relaxes the legs back they should be reminded to rest the thighs lightly in the saddle to concentrate on the majority of their weight dropping evenly through their seat bones. The upper body should remain straight and the rider shouldn't tip forward or twist.

- Rolling the ankles — this helps to free up the ankles to encourage the feet to point forwards. The ankles should be rolled in towards the horse.

- Holding the foot up, to stretch the front of the thigh.

17 | Coaching in Practice

Holding legs out.

Holding the foot up to stretch the front of the thigh.

Exercises that concentrate on the upper body

These will help to release tension in the shoulders and neck and increase flexibility.

- Arm circles, shoulder circles or shoulder shrugs — these help to free up the shoulders, and, if the arms are circled backwards, encourage the shoulders to drop down and back.

- Turning the head to look as far to the left as possible and as far to the right as possible — to free up the neck while encouraging the rider to relax through the neck and shoulders.

- Rotate the upper body to the left and right — to increase movement through the torso and help the rider to turn in the direction of the horse's movement.

Working without stirrups

It is beneficial to spend a short time in walk at first, so the rider can begin to relax and begin to soften through their lower back before moving on to trot. Although the ultimate aim is for the rider to establish an independent seat, with their legs underneath their body, this is challenging to achieve in the trot. When beginning sitting trot it is always best to ask the rider to start by holding the front of the saddle with the outside hand. The reins can be tied in a knot and the rider can then hold the loop and does not need to worry about the position of their hands, and is less likely to use the reins to balance. If the rider is just starting to learn how to sit to the trot, they may want to hold the saddle with either one or both hands. When they are ready, they can let go with the inside hand and drop it down by their side; this will allow them to sit up straight and turn their body with the curve of the circle. It is best to start with shorter periods of trot; if the rider is in sitting trot for too long and begins to struggle they may begin to tense up and lose their position.

It is important to get feedback from the rider: by asking how they are finding the exercise you will know whether they are able to cope with more work, or need more breaks. It is also useful to ask the rider what muscles they feel are working, as it is not always easy to see whether the rider is engaging the correct muscles. In order to maintain the sitting trot, although the rider needs to relax through their lower back and hips they need to engage their core muscles (torso muscles).

This rider is working in trot on the lunge, holding the saddle with the outside hand, keeping the leg long and relaxed.

With a more established rider, you will be helping to develop their position further. This will include them learning to sit to the trot with their legs relaxed and underneath them and a good upper body position, and improving their ability to absorb the movement through their lower back, legs and seat. If they have moved their legs further back and underneath them, they may find the sitting trot more difficult at first as it will require more mobility through the lower back and hips. Therefore it is best to suggest that the rider starts by holding the saddle so they can work on their suppleness and maintain their leg position. Gradually work up to the rider letting go of the front of the saddle and maintaining their position. Placing the inside hand on the small of their back can help the rider feel the movement (or lack of it) through their back.

After working without stirrups, the rider should have the opportunity to work with their stirrups before you bring the lesson to a close. When the rider takes back their stirrups they may feel that they want to lower their stirrup leathers and this is a good sign as it means they are sitting in a better position. However, it is important that they do not put their leathers down too long. A length that feels comfortable in the walk may throw them out of balance when they come to do rising trot. With more established riders you may spend some time helping them establish their sitting trot with stirrups.

Exercises with stirrups

You may decide not to do any work without stirrups with your rider, or to do a small amount only. These could include situations where a rider struggles to ride without stirrups, or where a rider is nervous. There are exercises that can be done with stirrups that will help the rider improve:

- Standing up in the stirrups — you may need to start this in halt and help the rider to find their balance, you can then progress to practising this in walk and then trot. You can also test a rider's balance and coordination by asking them to sit for a number of strides and then rise (e.g. sit for two strides then rise for two strides) while maintaining their balance and position in the trot.

- Work without reins — working the rider without reins, particularly in the trot, is a good way to help them develop their balance independently without the reins. The rider may want to start by holding the neckstrap or saddle and take time to build confidence holding on with just one hand before letting go with both hands. The rider can hold their arms out to the side, straight in front of them or practise holding them in the correct position while maintaining balance.

A rider who has established the basics and is looking to progress can be encouraged to think about what they are feeling underneath them as the horse moves. You can include the sequence of the footfalls and ask whether they can feel the hind legs stepping underneath the horse.

Cantering on the lunge

It can be useful to work a rider in canter on the lunge — however, the circumstances must be right to do this. The horse being lunged will need to have a well-established canter and be balanced in canter on the lunge. When on the lunge, the horse is required to work on a constant circle and some horses will find it hard to maintain a steady, balanced canter while doing this. If a horse is not balanced in canter on the lunge, any work will be detrimental to the rider and may not be safe. It is important that you know the horse you are lungeing so that you know he is safe to canter on the lunge with a rider aboard. With regard to the rider, if you are lungeing a novice rider who has just learnt to canter, they are likely to find it hard to maintain their balance on a circle. In most circumstances it is best for riders to learn to canter in a straight line initially.

Coaching early flatwork

There are many methods of teaching people to ride and as you become more experienced you will start to develop your own style, philosophy and techniques that work for you and the horses and riders you teach. This section suggests subjects to cover when teaching beginners through to novice level riders on the flat, that you can build on and refine.

Your role when teaching riders at this level is to produce a rider who is confident, has a correct and balanced position, is able to apply the aids correctly to control the horse, is able to change the rein in a variety of ways, can ride a variety of school movements and exercises and is beginning to understand how they can influence the horse's way of going.

A coach teaching a group flatwork lesson.

Suitability of horses and equipment

The choice of horse for a beginner rider is crucial to ensure that they have a good experience and can develop their skills and confidence. A quiet horse with a calm temperament and who has smooth gaits will be beneficial to a rider learning to trot or canter. A horse with expressive gaits is likely to throw the rider out of the saddle and make it harder for them to balance. The horse should, however, be responsive to the aids and move forwards when asked without requiring a massive effort on the part of the rider, to allow the rider to concentrate on their position. As the rider progresses the horses used can become a little more challenging, such as one who requires stronger leg aids, or a schoolmaster who will only respond when the rider applies the aids precisely.

A general-purpose saddle is ideal for most riders to begin with, as it will offer more security than a dressage saddle, while a forward-cut jumping saddle will make it harder for the rider to achieve the correct leg position because of the position of the stirrup bars. As the rider progresses and begins to work on improving their depth of seat and refining their position, a dressage saddle would be more beneficial. The saddle should be the correct size for the rider — a small rider might feel unsecure in a big saddle and a saddle that is too small will be uncomfortable for both horse and rider.

A neckstrap is a useful item and will save the horse's mouth while the rider learns to balance.

Rider's position

When teaching the correct position you have to consider the build and suppleness of the rider. A rider with short arms is going to struggle to keep the reins short and have a bend in the elbows and therefore you have to make allowances for this without compromising the contact. A rider lacking suppleness through the hips will struggle to keep the legs and upper body in position and this will have to be developed over many sessions.

To begin with, focus on getting the rider to sit in the centre of the saddle with the weight equal on both seat bones so they are in balance with the horse. It is common for beginner riders to slouch and sit heavily on the horse's back, so explain that they need to sit up and support their own weight with the upper body 'carried' and the shoulders relaxed back and down.

Their legs should hang down underneath them and be relaxed, with the inside of the thighs against the saddle and the weight going down to their feet. The widest part of the foot should sit straight across the stirrup and the foot should face forwards. As a guide when measuring the length of stirrups, the stirrup iron should rest level with the rider's ankle bone; if the stirrup leathers are too long the rider will be reaching for them, and leathers that are significantly too short will be uncomfortable and compromise the position of a novice rider. However, it can be more comfortable for a beginner rider to have stirrup leathers that are slightly shorter than would be considered 'normal'.

A rider in a good position in halt.

The rider's arms should be carried so that the upper arms are slightly in front of the body with a bend in the elbows. Rein position can be something that a lot of riders struggle with; most people automatically want to hold the reins in the 'handlebar' position.

Make sure you view the rider from each side as well as from the front and back. Move around the school to make sure you are observing the rider from all angles. Explain to the rider about the imaginary straight line that runs from ear, shoulder, hip to heel and elbow, rein to the bit.

If you need to manoeuvre the rider's leg or arm into the correct position, always do this gently and with permission! If there are mirrors in the arena, as the rider progresses, get them to use these to check their position and make their own corrections.

You will need to explain how the rider's position will vary slightly in each gait and how the rider has to move with the horse to be able to stay in balance and keep their position. It is relatively easy to sit the rider in the correct position in halt only for them to lose it the moment the horse moves.

> **Common positional faults**
>
> - Head not straight — rider's head dropping down or tipping to one side. This can have an effect on the rest of the position.
>
> - Tipping forward — when the rider tips forward their weight is transferred from their seat bones to the pubic arch. This weakens the lower leg position and allows the legs to slide back, resulting in the rider gripping with the knees.
>
> - Gripping up — the rider gripping with the knee causes an insecure lower leg position and the heels to rise up.
>
> - Lower legs too far forward — sometimes referred to as a chair seat. The rider is sitting too far back in the saddle, with the legs out in front of them. The rider is not in balance with the horse and will probably be behind the movement.
>
> - Upper body not straight — the rider either collapses forward through the waist, or to one side over a hip. The rider can be sitting heavier on one seat bone than the other. The shoulder might also be dropped down.
>
> - Rounded back — collapsing through the middle, rounded shoulders.
>
> - Hollow back — pelvis tipping forward.
>
> - Hands turned over so the knuckles are on top, blocking the feel down the rein.
>
> - Arms straight, with no bend at the elbows.

The aids

The aids are the rider's way of communicating to the horse what they want him to do and where to go. The reins are used to control forward movement and, in conjunction with the legs, to guide the horse forwards and sideways. Initially the rider will focus on moving quietly with the horse with their seat and maintaining their position rather than using their seat aids actively. However, once they have mastered the basics you can start to introduce an understanding of how they can use their seat by making subtle changes in their position to produce weight aids in order to influence the horse.

Once the rider is confident in stopping and turning the horse, you can start to refine the aids they are using. Introduce the concept of bending the horse around turns and circles and what each of the separate aids is used for. Discuss how to apply the aids for each gait as you introduce it to the rider. Don't forget to teach the rider to reward the horse with a pat, or their voice.

Common issues

- Rider lifting the heel to kick and losing the stirrup.
- Rider not giving a firm enough leg aid.
- Rider swinging legs backwards and forwards rather than inwards to apply them.
- Rider taking hand too far to the side or pulling back when trying to steer.
- Rider pulling on the reins for balance.
- Rider lifting hands up.
- Rider leaning to one side when turning.

This rider's lower leg is too far back and she is lifting her heel to give the aid.

Gaits

For the first few sessions the focus should be on the rider maintaining their position and balance as the horse moves. In the walk the rider needs to understand how to mirror the head and neck movement of the horse with their arms and reins without restricting it. You can talk about the 'feel' of the walk in a basic way, such as what a forward, active walk feels like compared to lazy walk and, as the rider progresses, you can cover the sequence of the footfalls in all three gaits and how they differ; this is particularly useful in the trot when you are teaching the rider to rise.

Common issues

- Rider pulling back on the reins and restricting the horse's head and neck movement.
- Rider not maintaining position.
- Rider becoming tense and gripping up with legs.
- Rider losing balance.

Rising trot

It is best for riders to first master the rising trot on the lead rein or lunge. The process for teaching this has been mentioned previously in the lead rein section. However, even once rider has picked up the rhythm and is able to rise in time with the horse, there will be further development required in order that they can maintain balance and be able to control the horse while trotting. Lunge lessons are a valuable tool for helping the rider to establish their balance; ideally the rider should be able to trot without holding on to the saddle, reins or neckstrap, before they start to trot independently. However, this is not always possible, especially if the rider has opted to join group lessons. It is important to ensure that the rider's lack of balance is not detrimental to the horse; the rider should not be balancing on the reins. A good way to introduce the rider to trotting independently is for them to hold the neckstrap with one hand while also holding the reins; this will help them to keep their hands steady.

> **Common issues**
>
> - Rider pushing up from the stirrup irons, causing the lower legs to swing forward and rider to lose balance.
>
> - Rider gripping with knees, causing lower legs to swing back and upper body to tip forward.
>
> - Rider using reins to pull themselves up, or to find their balance.
>
> - Rider standing or sitting for too long.
>
> - Rider not controlling downward phase of rising trot.
>
> - Rider trying to lift themselves out of the saddle by hunching their shoulders, causing them to tip forward.
>
> - Rider not establishing the trot first before looking to check the diagonal.
>
> - Rider dropping head down or leaning over to check the horse's outside shoulder.
>
> - Rider losing balance or sitting for an extra beat when changing diagonal.
>
> - General loss of position.
>
> - Rider forgetting to use leg aids to keep the horse in trot.

Sitting trot and work without stirrups

Sitting trot requires a lot of balance, suppleness and coordination by the rider. The rider should sit softly in the saddle and be able to keep their position as they absorb the horse's movement through their seat, thighs, knees and ankles. If the rider is tense or stiff they will lose balance and often grip on with their legs. Introduce sitting trot gradually for short periods, starting with sitting for a few steps before rising again. The aim is to keep the rider relaxed so they are able to move with the horse, and then rise before they become tense or start to struggle.

Work without stirrups is beneficial to the rider to help develop sitting trot, as well as general improvement to the rider's position and balance. This has already been discussed in the lunge lesson section. Work without stirrups can also be used during flat lessons, however it should be introduced over short periods. Riders should be encouraged to hold their saddle with one hand while they are developing their suppleness so they do not bang on the horse's back.

17 | Coaching in Practice

A rider in sitting trot without stirrups, maintaining a secure position.

Common issues

- Rider tenses up and grips up with the leg, losing position and balance,

- Rider not able to absorb movement through seat and back.

- Rider tips forwards.

- Rider leans back.

- Rider uses reins for balance.

- Rider not able to keep horse forward.

Canter

The rider is ready to learn to canter when they are confident and capable of maintaining their position and balance in trot and are able to keep the horse moving forwards. Their leg position should be secure and the rider should be able to move fluently between rising and sitting trot.

Riders may struggle with the coordination of the canter aid as they now have to use their legs independently. A neckstrap is useful to stop riders pulling back on the reins to balance themselves, and for extra security. Start with short canters on a straight line. For the first canter, ask the rider to encourage the horse into a forward-going, active trot and as they approach a corner of the school to take up sitting trot, take hold of the neckstrap, and use their legs firmly, with the inside leg on the girth and the outside leg a little further back — you can use your voice here as well to tell the horse to canter. Hopefully the horse will respond and pick up canter; the rider should sit up tall and try to maintain the canter rhythm by keeping their legs against the horse's sides.

Tell the rider to ask for the downward transition into trot before the corner by sitting up and increasing the pressure down the reins slightly, trying to keep their leg gently against the horse's side until the horse trots. If the rider is holding the neckstrap ask them to let go of it with the outside hand only and use the outside rein to slow the horse. You can also use your voice (in the same way as to if you were lungeing the horse) to help encourage the horse to trot. The downward transition after the canter can be more unbalancing for the rider than the canter itself, especially if the rider has lost their position and gripped up with the legs and the horse falls or rushes into trot. Encourage the rider to take up rising trot again as soon as they can to help horse and rider rebalance. The canter transition requires practice and, once the rider has mastered the transition, you start to think about canter leads.

Common issues

- *Rider not giving a clear aid and ending up in a fast, unbalanced trot.*
- *Rider leaning forward and gripping up with lower legs.*
- *Rider losing balance in the downward transition to trot.*
- *Rider pulling back on the reins for balance.*
- *Rider slips to outside of the saddle.*
- *Rider not able to go with the movement of the horse in canter.*

This rider is gripping up with her lower leg and is tipping forward out of the saddle.

Transitions

Most of the transitions at this level will be progressive; direct transitions can be introduced later when the rider is more established. The aim of a good transition is to be clear, smooth, forward and balanced.

When the rider is first learning, your focus will be on them maintaining their position and applying the aids correctly. As the rider progresses you can encourage them to concentrate on the clarity of preparation and aids and the quality of the transition. Were the gaits active throughout? How accurate was it — did it really happen where it was supposed to? Asking the rider to make transitions at specific letters or markers is a good way to make them more aware of how much preparation they need to make that happen. Check and make any required corrections to the rider's position throughout and emphasise the need to use the legs even in the downward transitions. Transitions can be ridden anywhere in the school; to make them more challenging include them in school figures such as over the centre line on a three-loop serpentine.

> *Common issues*
>
> - Rider not using legs in the correct position.
> - Using too much rein in the downward transition and no leg, so the horse becomes unbalanced.
> - Driving with seat in an attempt to encourage the horse forward.
> - Tipping forwards in an upward transition.
> - Leaning back in a downward transition.
> - Hands coming up in the downward transitions.
> - Not able to keep horse forward through the transition.

Turns, circles and school figures

Riding turns and school figures will help to improve the rider's understanding of how to apply the aids clearly and effectively and improve their coordination and balance, as well as moving towards working in harmony with the horse.

You will need to explain that moving the horse from a straight line to a curved line requires the rider to alter their aids and position slightly. When moving on a straight line the horse's hind feet should follow the prints of the forefeet and this also applies on circles and turns. The rider needs to understand how they should apply the leg aids and why, so the inside leg is used by the girth to produce bend and the outside leg slightly behind the girth to stop the horse swinging his quarters out. The inside rein guides the horse around the turn and the outside rein controls the speed and the amount of bend through the neck. Be careful that the rider doesn't try to bring the outside hand over the neck and drop the inside hand down; the hands should stay on either side of the neck and be held level.

School figures are a sequence of turns, circles and straight lines of varying sizes and shapes. Make sure that the rider is aware of the size of the arena they are riding in so they can be accurate with the size and shape of the figures. It is helpful to use markers such as cones as a guide to help the rider to be accurate and then gradually remove the markers.

The rider is asking the horse to bend on a circle.

Common issues

- The inside rein is taken too far out to the inside, causing the horse to overbend through the neck and step sideways rather than around the turn.

- Rider pulls back on inside rein to turn.

- The rider drops the inside hand and lifts the outside hand.

- The outside leg is not moved back and therefore the quarters swing out.

- The rider doesn't use enough leg to keep the horse forward through the turn, losing the fluency.

- The circle is not round.

Progressing the rider

Once the rider has mastered the basics it is a case of hours in the saddle to gain further experience and become more proficient. Much of your focus will be on developing the security of the rider's position and the amount of control they have over the horse, and keeping the lessons interesting and varied so you can also start to increase the rider awareness of how their horse is going and how they can influence this.

The Scale of Training

The Scale of Training is used as the foundation of training horses and, although it would be too much at this level to expect the rider to be improving the horse's way of going, you can use the Scale of Training in a very basic way to start to teach the rider to think about how the horse is going and to develop their feel. You can pick one component as a theme for the lesson, or work on several together.

Rhythm

Rhythm is the regularity of the footfalls in each gait and the tempo is the speed of the footfalls. You will have already covered the sequence of the footfalls in each gait, so now you can start to teach the rider to recognise the footfalls and whether they are regular. If there is more than one horse in the lesson, ask riders to watch each other's horse and how the legs move in each gait. You can also get them to call out the beats of their horse's feet as they go. This will also start to develop the riders feel as to how the horse is moving and they should start to recognise, with your help, whether the tempo is too quick or too slow and what they need to do to change it.

Suppleness

As the rider becomes more aware of what the horse is doing, start to encourage them to feel what is happening around turns and circles. Do they find the horse easier to ride on one rein compared to the other? Can they feel if the horse is falling in or out around a circle, or drifting off a line? A horse that is lacking in suppleness may not be able to maintain a consistent rhythm through turns or changes of rein. The rider may be weaker on one side and you might want to suggest some dismounted exercises to help strengthen their core. One issue that can cause complications is if a horse and rider both have the same very 'stiff' side, or indeed, if both are very one-sided on opposite sides.

Contact

Is the rider able to keep their hands level and still and use each rein independently? Are they able to feel if the horse is heavier on one rein compared to the other?

Impulsion

Mention has been made earlier of the desirability of the horse being 'forward', which can be described as his willingness to cover the ground. Novice riders often confuse impulsion with speed, as it can difficult for them to differentiate between the two. Impulsion is the spring of the gait, or controlled energy, whereas speed is going quickly but in a flat gait, with little spring to the steps. Ask the rider to ride within a gait at various speeds so they start to get an understanding of what fast, slow and working gait feels like.

Straightness

This can be linked to suppleness and the same questions asked. Encourage the rider to think about whether the horse's head and neck are directly in front of him, or whether he leans on one rein.

Collection

All the other aspects of the scale should be established before collection should be attempted. It is very unlikely at this level that your riders will be ready to attempt this, so it can be saved for when the rider and horse are more established.

The half-halt

Teaching the half-halt requires the rider to have an independent seat so they can use the rein and leg aids separately. It should be a subtle aid between the rider and horse and is used as a way of rebalancing the horse and to prepare the horse for a movement. When first learning to ride a half-halt it is common for riders to forget to use their legs and just pull on the reins. Explain that the legs are used to develop impulsion, which is then contained by the reins, encouraging the horse to take more weight on to his hind legs.

To apply a half-halt the rider should sit up taller in the saddle and close their legs around the horse and, almost at the same time, momentarily increase the pressure down the reins and relax it again. Be careful that the rider does relax the rein aid again as, if they keep up the pressure, the horse will lean against it. A good exercise for teaching the rider how to ride the half-halt is to ride transitions from trot to walk, and walk for a specified number of steps before asking for trot again. The number of walk steps can then be reduced until the horse eventually walks for one step then trots again. This can then be adapted so the rider almost asks for walk during trot, and then this aid can be refined to a half-halt. Once the rider has established this, you can encourage them to use the half-halt as a preparation for riding turns and school movements and to help rebalance the horse before and after transitions.

> **Common issues**
>
> - Rider not using the leg to develop impulsion and just using the rein aids.
>
> - Rider not softening the hands after giving the rein aid, causing the horse to lean on the rein.
>
> - Rider forgetting to use half-halts at all.

Improving the rider's position

Developing an independent seat takes time and hours in the saddle. Riders need to build strength in their muscles as well as being supple enough to move with the horse and this can take time, especially if they ride only once a week.

- Some of the suppling exercises suggested in the lunge lesson section can be repeated in the halt, with you holding the horse.

- Working the rider without stirrups can help to lengthen the legs, but should be done for short periods to prevent the rider becoming tense, which is detrimental to their position.

- Standing up in the stirrups and balancing on their legs is a good way of strengthening the lower legs. This can be done in halt, walk and trot. Be careful that the rider doesn't lean too far forward or grip with their knees.

- A good exercise for improving coordination, and as an introduction to changing the diagonal in trot, is to ask the rider to rise for two beats and sit for one, etc. Then change it to sitting for two beats and rising for one. If the rider is unbalanced, get them to hold the neckstrap.

Work off the horse

For riders who are unable to practise between sessions, or those who struggle to find the right feeling on the horse, there are some simple things you can guide them to do on their own. Exercise balls are an excellent way of improving core stability and suppleness. There are many books and online tutorials that suggest suitable exercises for riders. A useful trick for someone who struggles to let their weight fall into their lower legs and heels is to ask them to stand on a step with the balls of their feet and their heels hanging off it. They can then experiment with the feeling of standing on their toes compared to letting the heels drop a little. By helping them to feel what is correct it may be easier for them to replicate it on the horse. There are many more things that can be done; a little imagination goes a long way.

17 | Coaching in Practice

Standing on a step and lowering the heels can help with flexibility; this is a good example of an unmounted exercise riders can do between lessons.

School figures and exercises

1. Circles (20m, 15m, 10m)

    AIMS AND BENEFIT

    1. Encourages horse to bend.

    2. Teaches the rider to be accurate.

    3. Teaches the rider to use both legs and reins to control horse.

    EQUIPMENT

    Can use markers positioned at the four tangent points of the circle, to give rider a visual aid of where to go.

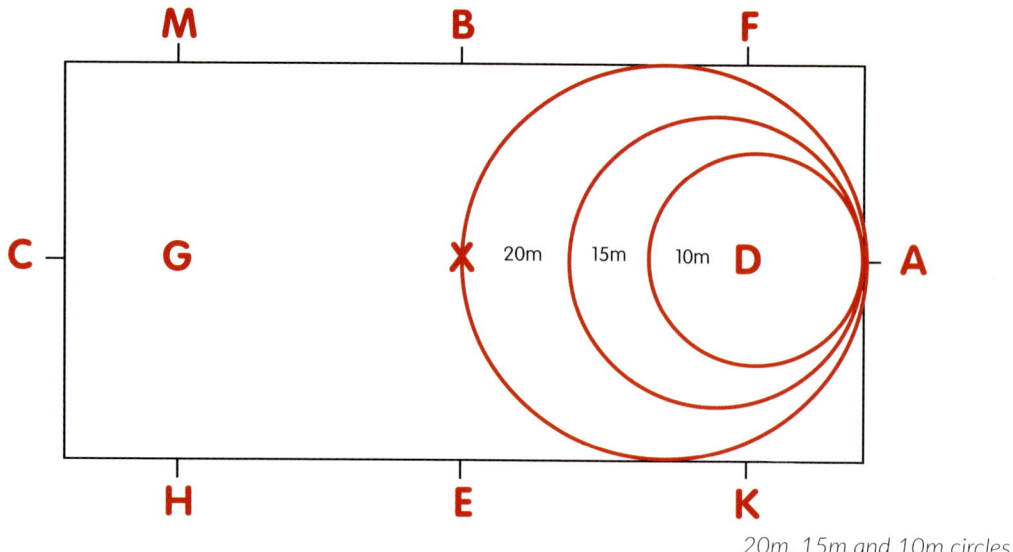

20m, 15m and 10m circles.

DESCRIPTION

When first teaching riders to ride circles it is helpful to put markers all the way around the arc of the circle to guide them, and then gradually remove the markers once riders know where they are going.

Starting at A or C is easiest when first teaching 20m and 15m circles. 10m circles are half the width of a 20m wide arena and are better first taught at E or B so the rider can use the centre line as a guide.

Explain that the horse's hind feet should follow the tracks of the forefeet so that the rider thinks about the shape the horse makes with his body rather than just turning the horse's head. The bend should remain constant around the circle. The riders inside leg produces the bend; outside leg moves slightly behind the girth to control the size of the circle; outside hand stays by the withers and controls the outside shoulder; inside hand guides the horse round the arc. Encourage the rider to turn their body slightly to move with the horse around the curve.

COMMON PROBLEMS

- Circle shape and size inaccurate.

- Rider rides around the outside track into corners and then turn across the school instead of using tangent points.

- Horse not bending.
- Rider uses too much inside rein.

2. Figure of eight

AIMS AND BENEFITS

1. Teaches the rider to plan.
2. Encourages the rider to use outside aids.
3. Creates awareness of speed, balance, bend and straightness.

EQUIPMENT

Can use markers to create two circles with their intersection at X.

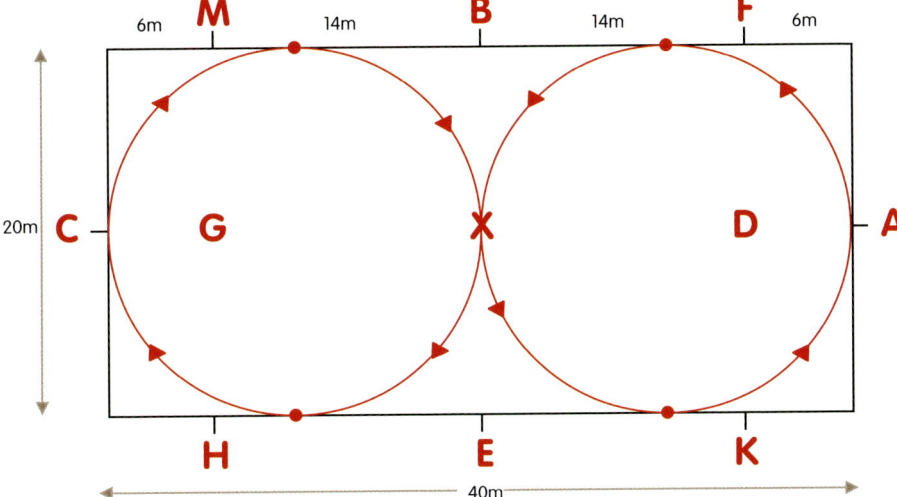

Figure of eight using 20m circles.

DESCRIPTION

Ask each rider to ride two interlinking 20m circles, making a change of bend and direction over X. Start in walk, with all the cones in place. Progress the difficulty of the exercise by removing the cones a couple at a time and increasing the gait to trot and eventually to canter with a trot transition over X.

Can increase complexity for more advanced riders by including transitions at various places around the circle, not just X.

COMMON PROBLEMS

- Rider not planning well enough.
- Circles not round.
- Horse falling in or out.
- Trot rhythm varying between circles.
- Wrong bend in second circle.
- Circles differing sizes.

3. **Half-circle and incline back to the track**

   AIMS AND BENEFIT

   1. Teaches the rider to be accurate and plan ahead.
   2. Used as a variation of a change of rein.
   3. Teaches the rider awareness of leg position and straightness.

   EQUIPMENT

   Can use markers or poles on the floor as a guide.

   DESCRIPTION

   Use the markers on the wall to help direct the rider.

   Can be ridden using 10m or 15m half-circles (e.g. at F ride a half 10m half-circle to the centre line followed by an incline reaching the track at M on the opposite rein).

   Increase the difficulty by making the inclines steeper, e.g. back to track at B.

17 | Coaching in Practice

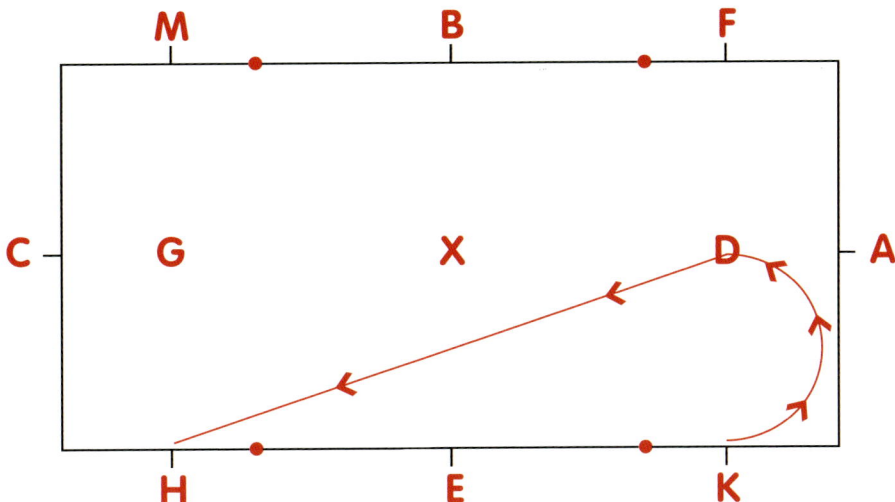

Half-circle and incline back to the track.

COMMON PROBLEMS

- Half-circle too big.
- Half-circles not round.
- Horse not straight on incline.
- Horse slows down around half-circle and speeds up on straight line.
- Rider reaches the track too early or too late.

4. **Joining two 20m half-circles to change the rein**

   AIMS AND BENEFIT

   1. Make changes of rein using half-circles.
   2. Teaches the rider to change the bend.
   3. Teaches the rider to plan ahead.

   EQUIPMENT

   Use cones/poles on centre line to help rider keep straight.

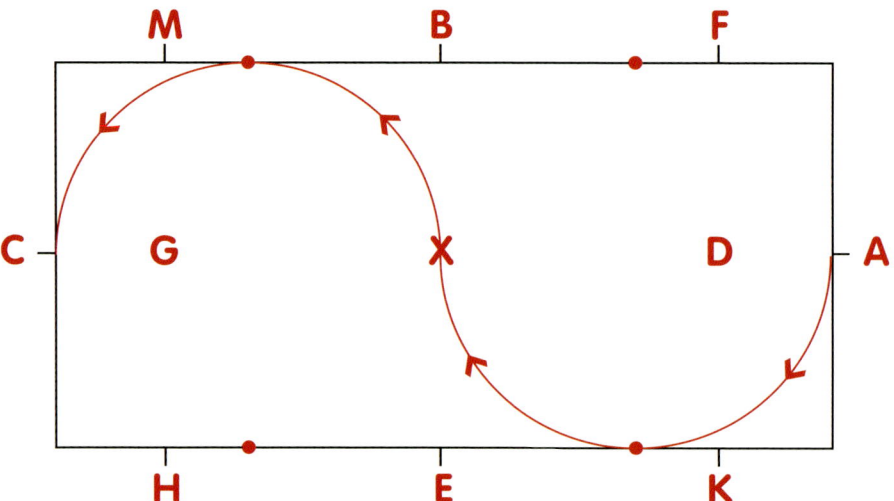

20m half-circles to change the rein.

DESCRIPTION

Can be ridden from either end of the arena.

For example starting at A ride a half-circle to X; just before X ride straight for a stride or two then change the bend and half-circle from X to C.

The trot rhythm shouldn't change between the circles.

Transitions can be ridden between walk and trot through X.

Can be ridden in canter with a change of lead through trot at X for more experienced riders.

COMMON PROBLEMS

- Circles are not equal size, or round.
- Rider doesn't ride straight over X or change the bend.
- Horse falls in or out.
- Rider rides round the outside track rather than following the circle shape.
- Transition not at X.

5. 20m half-circles across the width of the school

AIMS AND BENEFIT

1. Ride a half-circle across the width of the school.

2. Teaches the rider to plan ahead.

3. Encourages bend.

EQUIPMENT

Can use cones for guidance.

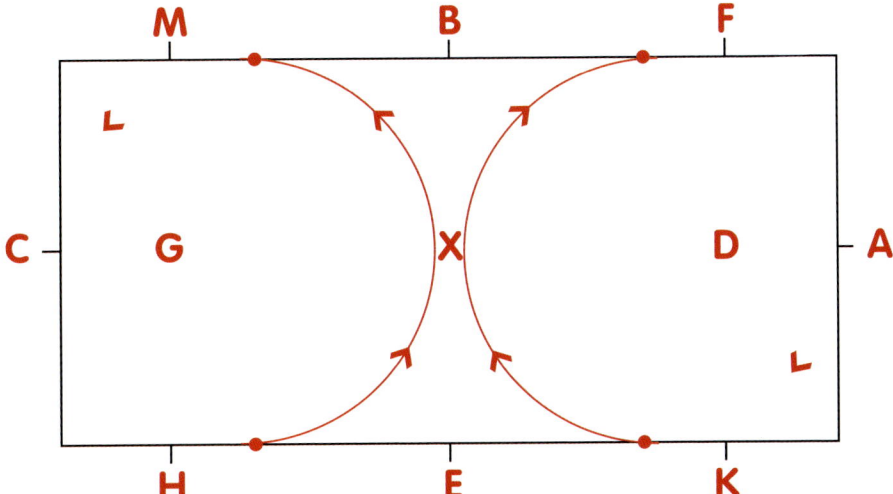

20m half-circles across the school can be ridden from various points.

DESCRIPTION

A 20m half-circle can be ridden across the school from any point on the long side that allows room to complete the arc. The widest point of the arc should be over the centre line. The shape should be symmetrical, with the rider reaching the track directly opposite the point they left.

If using this exercise with a group of riders, have them all turning from the same side, on the same rein to reduce the risk of crashing.

COMMON PROBLEMS

- Half-circles not round.
- Half-circles not symmetrical.
- Size inaccurate.
- Horse falling in or out.

6. Three-loop serpentine

AIMS AND BENEFIT

1. To ride three equal-sized loops up the length of the arena using a series of half-circles and straight lines.

2. Works the horse on both reins, is a suppling exercise, teaches accurate riding, teaches rider to use legs and reins for control of direction, is an introduction to changing bend.

3. Good to use for improving changing diagonal at trot.

EQUIPMENT

Can use poles over centre line to guide rider straight across.

Can use cones to help rider know where to turn across school.

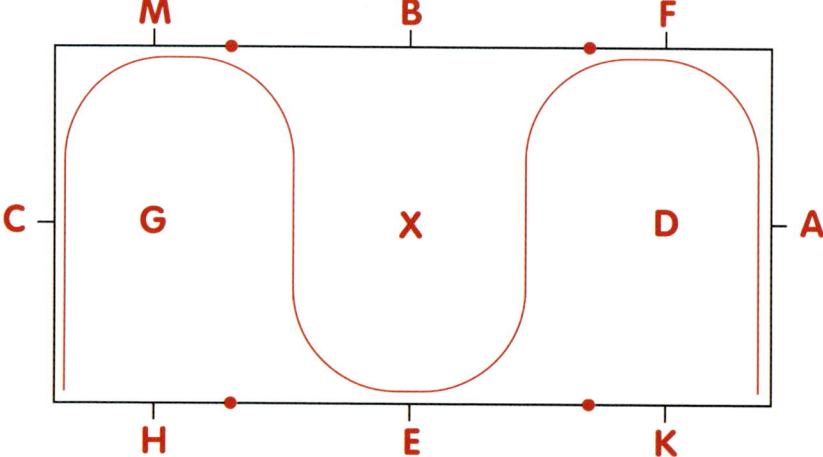

Three-loop serpentine.

DESCRIPTION

The movement starts from A or C.

The line of the serpentine should divide the school into three: in a 40m school each loop would be approximately 13m wide. The half-circles are linked by straight lines. For example, on the left rein: starting at A, ride a 13m half-circle left, then ride straight; change the rein and just before the quarter line ride a 13m half-circle to the right, then ride straight; then ride a 13m half-circle back to the left again, finishing at C and going large. The line B–E should be in the middle of the centre loop.

Can add transitions (e.g. walk/halt/walk or trot/walk/trot) over the centre line for more experienced riders.

The figure can be changed from the three-loop form by increasing the number of loops used. An equal number of loops will result in a change of rein.

COMMON PROBLEMS

- Loops are unequal in size.
- Rider does not ride straight across centre.
- Horse falls in or out around turns.
- Rider doesn't change diagonal over centre line when in trot.
- Half-circles are not correct shape.

7. 5m and 10m loops

AIMS AND BENEFIT

1. Suppling exercise for the horse.
2. Teaches the rider how to change bend.
3. Teaches the rider to plan and think ahead.

EQUIPMENT

Can use markers as a guide to how far off the track to come.

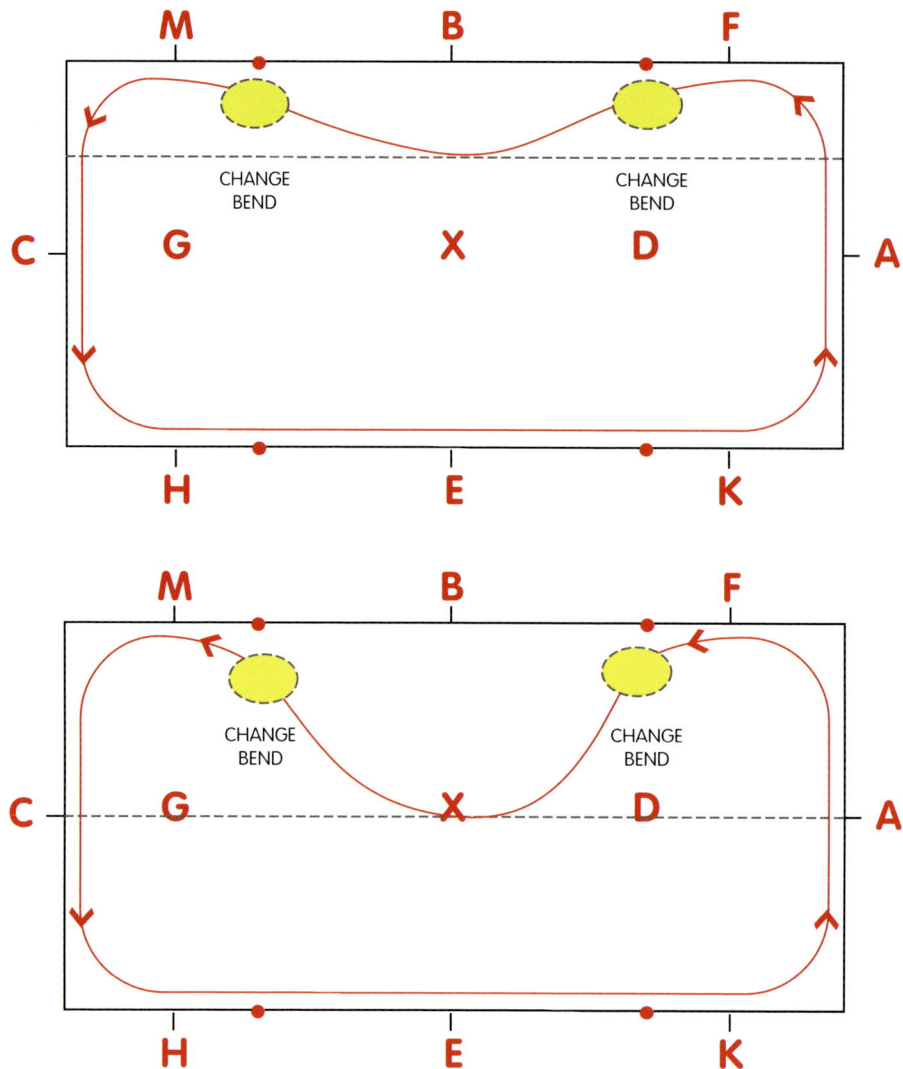

5m and 10m loops.

DESCRIPTION

Concentrate on changing the bend and encouraging the rider to use leg aids to bend the horse around the loop.

The corners at the beginning and end of the loop are part of the movement.

Can be used as an introduction to counter-canter for more advanced riders.

17 | Coaching in Practice

COMMON PROBLEMS

- Rider not using corners.
- Rider not changing bend.
- Loop too small or too big.
- Loop not symmetrical.

8. **Straight lines**

AIMS AND BENEFIT

1. Teaches the horse and rider about straightness.
2. Teaches the rider to use leg and rein aids to keep the horse straight.
3. Increases the rider's awareness of straightness in the horse.
4. Teaches the rider to think about planning for turns on to and off the line.

EQUIPMENT

Can use cones or poles as guide.

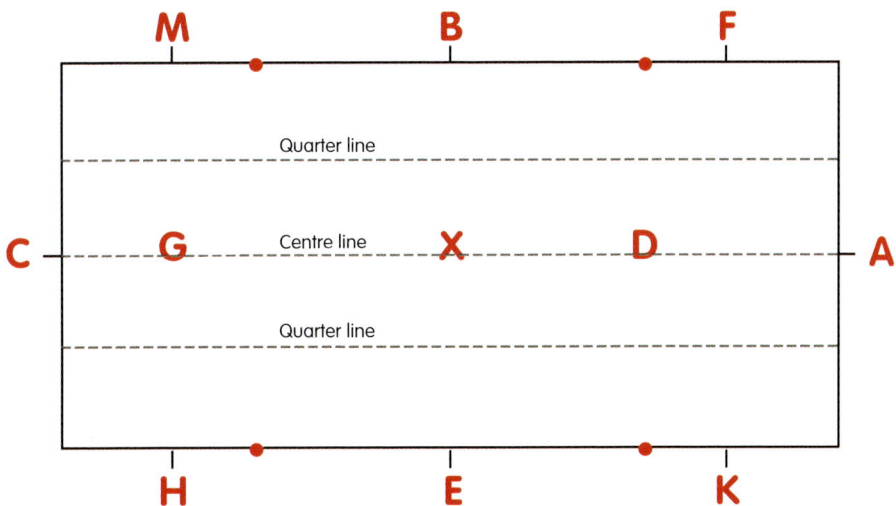

Working on straight lines.

DESCRIPTION

Straight lines can be ridden anywhere across the school, e.g. centre line, quarter line, across the middle (E–B), on a inside track,

Straight lines encourage the rider to look up and ahead where they should be going and try to use a fixed point to aim towards.

To increase the difficulty, ask the rider to ride on an inside track, where the horse may try to drift back towards the track.

COMMON PROBLEMS

- Lines/horse not straight.
- Rider overshooting or undershooting turn onto, or off the line.
- Horse drifting towards track.

Coaching jumping

Jumping can be great fun and many riders really look forward to learning this skill. As a coach it can be very tempting to introduce jumping before the rider is fully ready because the rider does not always understand why they are not ready but only sees the excitement. When a rider is keen to start jumping there are several key prerequisites that should be in place first:

- Independence from reins.

- Balance in walk, trot and canter.

- Ability to influence rhythm and speed.

- Ability to ride independently.

Once these have been established the next step should be to prepare the rider progressively, starting with shorter stirrup leathers on the flat, then working over poles before finally leaving the ground. It is beneficial at this stage if the rider has become used to riding with slightly shorter leathers and cantering in a light seat in the open — this makes it more likely that they will find the postural adaptations involved in jumping easier when they start. Rushing any stage may well mean they progress more slowly in the long run. Rider confidence is something that should be protected carefully; once lost it can be challenging to rebuild.

Suitability of horses and equipment

The right horse to teach jumping on is essential; it is important for beginners that the horse is willing to take them to the jump in a calm manner. During the early stages the rider should not have to think too much about steering or speed control (beyond basic forwardness and the right direction), allowing them to concentrate on development of balance and confidence. Once they have mastered this the use of horses who may require more encouragement or direction may be beneficial to help the rider progress. For novice riders to develop further a horse who enjoys jumping and has a good-quality canter will offer faster progression.

A neckstrap (either from a martingale or a secured stirrup leather) is a very useful piece of equipment at all levels, but particularly for beginners. This allows the rider not to rely on the reins for balance and can give confidence to them even though they may not use it. When teaching more experienced riders who have a young horse, or who occasionally struggle to see a stride it can be equally beneficial to protect horse's mouths.

The topic of saddles is an interesting one when it comes to jumping. As a result of every rider being a different shape it is rare that a general-purpose saddle works well for everyone. In reality this is what is economically possible in riding schools but there are still things that can be done to help.

Make sure you look at the rider in relation to the horse and saddle they are riding on, for example:

- Look at the length of their thighs — very tall, long-legged riders often find their knees end up over the front of the saddle when their stirrup leathers are short enough to help with balance.

- Small riders in a long saddle will be pushed to the back and have little support to keep their knees and legs in the right place to be able to balance easily.

If you are teaching someone on their own horse it is important to discuss this with them as they may be able to change the saddle for one that suits their needs better (provided it fits the horse); a good qualified saddle fitter will be able to help them. In a riding school environment, while you are unlikely to be able to change saddles, it may be that you can allocate horses differently so that you match the riders' needs better in this area. If you can't change any of these things try to think outside the box; does the saddle have moveable Velcro knee and thigh blocks that could be positioned differently? Could you use a seat saver to provide better security for a small rider in a big saddle?

Using fence-building equipment safely

Jumping as an activity is somewhat higher-risk than flatwork because of the additional balance and timing required by horse and rider. This means that it is essential to use jumping equipment in a way that minimises injury if anything goes wrong. Any broken poles or wings should be removed from the arena and not used; sharp edges can be a hazard in the unfortunate event of someone falling off into them. Always take time to risk-assess what you are planning to do, asking what could go wrong and whether there are there any changes you can make to minimise the chance of it happening.

When using ground poles you should always consider that a horse could kick or stand on them, causing them to roll in an uncontrolled way, which may trip them up further. Poles can be kept a little more stable by banking up a small amount of arena surface on either side (at the ends of the poles). When using a pole as a ground-line you must always provide a true ground-line — i.e. on the side of the fence in the direction it is to be jumped. Asking someone to jump a false ground-line might result in the horse misjudging where to take off, which could cause the horse and rider to lose balance and potentially cause an accident. Similarly, when using spread fences, make sure that the rear rail is always level or higher than the front one so the horse can see it.

If you have access to safety cups these should be used where possible, but particularly on the rear rail of spread fences. In a situation where a horse misjudges their take-off and comes down early and on to a pole, the safety cups collapse, allowing the pole to roll freely away rather than impacting on the horse's forward movement. Any spare cups that are not needed should be kept in a tub outside the arena or tucked neatly underneath the feet of jump wings so that they are not a hazard for horses to stand on or riders to fall on.

17 | Coaching in Practice

An example of a good position over a fence.

This rider has got a little 'left behind' over the fence and has not been able to allow with the hands. She has also stood up in the stirrups rather than folding from the hips; her stirrup has slipped back on her foot so she has been unable to drop her weight effectively into her heel.

Here the coach is helping the rider to find balance in the light seat position.

Introducing a more forward position for jumping and improving balance

The most important thing to ensure successful jumping is to work on the rider's balance. Initially, shorten the stirrup leathers a hole or two and introduce them to adapting their position for jumping.

Once the more forward position has been explained and demonstrated to the rider, spend time in the halt helping them to find the right balance and feel where they need to be. If you have mirrors in the teaching area make use of them so that the rider can look at themselves and learn to recognise what 'correct' looks like. This way, once they begin to move around the school they can be encouraged to check for themselves when they pass a mirror. Another way to encourage balance out of the saddle without relying on the reins is to teach an upright standing position (not to be used over a jump — simply as a balance exercise on the flat). Encourage them to find their own point of balance by standing in the stirrups, using a neckstrap to regain it when lost rather than using the reins. As their balance improves they will be able to take this position in walk and trot without reliance on the neckstrap.

Both the balanced and the upright standing position can be used initially at halt, then progressively through walk, trot and canter (with more experienced riders). This exercise can be made more difficult by increasing the length of time in the position, combining it with school figures or moving in and out of it on command. The ability to fold and react quickly will allow the rider to move with the horse over a jump.

A rider in a standing position in trot, using the neckstrap for balance.

Flatwork exercises that help prepare for jumping

Time spent practising riding with shorter stirrup leathers can be combined with developing skills required for successful jumping in the following ways.

Riding turns towards specific markers. Use pairs of cones, or blocks, to give the rider specific points in the school to aim for and ride between, simulating the process of looking for a jump, planning a turn and riding a line. This can be kept very simple or made more complex dependent on the rider's ability.

Maintaining consistent rhythm and speed. Ask the rider to count strides in either trot or canter between two school markers and ask them to match the number each time they pass between the markers. Counting out loud the beats of a trot or canter can help generate awareness (1, 2 for trot and 1, 2, 3 for canter). To help them be aware of speed encourage them to watch another rider and discuss with them when the speed is right. You could also have them purposefully ride slower and faster than they think is correct to help develop awareness of how speed feels.

Riding straight lines. Dependent on how much work the rider has done away from the track they may find it difficult to stay straight. A lesson spent completely off the track will benefit flatwork and jumping equally. Choose lines both down and across the school, initially with pairs of markers or poles at either end as a guide, progressively removing them. This will help them greatly when riding towards individual fences and over courses.

Pole work

The next stage is likely to be using ground poles. Using single poles set between wings allows all essential concepts to be taught other than the actual jump. When a horse trots over a ground pole he lifts and flexes his limbs, which gives a feeling of a bigger, rounder stride, allowing the rider to feel more movement underneath them. This gives the rider an opportunity to adjust their balance and learn to cope with the feeling of more power, helping progressively as an intermediate point before jumping.

Use poles progressively, starting with single ones, then once this is established, small lines of poles. When using poles in a line never use only two, as some horses can be tempted to jump over them as one obstacle, which can cause a safety issue. Three poles are enough to encourage most horses to negotiate them in a sensible way. Emphasising the need to employ flatwork accuracy when approaching the poles will assist when the rider progresses to approaching actual jumps.

A way to increase the complexity of pole use at this stage is to use single poles in a variety of positions around the arena. This allows you to include them during standard flatwork exercises (e.g. circles, changes of rein, serpentines) and create unique floor plans linking the poles in a way similar to riding a course of jumps. You can use poles on their own or with jumping wings/blocks at the ends. Using wings can help visually focus the horse and rider and allows the rider to become accustomed to the equipment before an actual fence is used.

When working with poles, start with one pole then progress to three. It is best not to use two poles in a row as some horses can be tempted to jump over them rather than stepping through them.

17 | Coaching in Practice

Teaching the phases of the jump

All flatwork and pole work in preparation for jumping should aim to develop the skills needed to carry out each phase of the jump effectively. The process of jumping can be broken down loosely into the following parts.

Approach

This starts from the moment the rider decides to negotiate a jump. At this point a plan needs to be made as to where in the arena to make a turn on to the true approach line (e.g. a jump on the three-quarter line next to E would require the rider to make a turn off the track on to the three-quarter line at the short end of the arena). It is essential to impress upon riders the need to ride good turns at this stage, making sure they look where they are going and keeping the horse balanced between leg and hand. If a poor turn is executed it will impact on the following phases of the jump.

A rider approaching the fence, just before take-off. She is in an upright position, ready to move forward with the horse.

Once the rider has turned on to the approach line and is heading straight toward the jump, straightness and regularity of rhythm are key. They should be encouraged to aim for the centre of the jump and look for a point beyond it to help them to stay straight afterwards.

The jump

The jump itself is made up of take-off, flight and landing, although during the early days of jumping the rider will find it hard to differentiate. They should be encouraged

The rider then folds as the horse goes over the fence.

to remain in an upright seat on the approach until they are getting close to the jump. During the early lessons it may be wise to encourage them to take a slightly forward fold and hold the neckstrap before take-off to ensure that they do not 'get left behind' and pull on the horse's mouth. This approach does, however, depend on having a suitable beginner's horse who will stay straight to the jump and help the rider. Once they feel the horse has landed and takes a stride forward after the fence they should be encouraged to regain their upright position and to concentrate on riding the getaway.

The rider sits up on landing.

Getaway

When learning, riders are often so elated to have jumped successfully that they switch off and do not continue riding the horse away and around the arena. It's really important that, even from the early attempts, they are encouraged that the exercise is not complete until they have ridden some way on around the arena then made a planned downward transition before stopping. If this is not done horses often start to anticipate, slowing to walk and stopping soon after jumping. In a way similar to the approach, the rider should be encouraged to ride a straight line to the end of the arena, ride a well-planned turn on to the track and carry on around the arena in good form.

This rider has landed after jumping and is now in an upright position, looking to the next fence.

Key issues and suggestions

1. Maintaining straightness can be challenging, so poles or cones can be used on either side of the approach and getaway lines to help centre the rider. These can be progressively removed as the rider improves their coordination. Some riders continually cut corners before the approach and at the end of the getaway, so a strategically placed cone can improve their spacial awareness.

2. Riders often look down to the base of the jump on the approach and during the jump itself. By positioning yourself at the end of the getaway line you can encourage them to look at you and ask them to watch you and tell you what they see — e.g. how many fingers you are holding up. Similarly, identifying a physical item at the end of the arena that is at rider head-height or higher for them to focus on may help.

3. For riders who like to stop immediately after a jump and don't ride a good getaway, link straight to a second exercise after the jump. For example, 'Ride a 20m circle at C', or 'Make a change of rein MXK before riding a downward transition and stopping.' This shifts the rider's focus so that they have to plan for the next element and ride more positively away from the jump.

Simple jumps and use of the arena

While riders are learning they need a reasonably long approach and getaway to allow them time to coordinate and put all the required skills together. This means that care should be taken to position poles and jumps in places that allow them to make a good job of each exercise. Dependent on the size of the arena, you may be able to use other locations, but the best initially include:

- Just off the track midway down the long side.

- On X down the centre of the school, although this does require a fairly tight turn on the approach and after the jump.

- On X across the long diagonal.

These locations also give space to stand other riders safely out of the way.

Once a rider begins to handle these initial exercises well you can move on to shorten the approach slightly, link two or more jumps together as an exercise or include some small uprights or spreads. The fences used initially will be cross-poles then small, simple uprights. (How to introduce other types of fence is explained in the Exercises section that follows.) It is important to balance making the session interesting with not overfacing the rider and making things too complicated. Often the best way to increase the difficulty of an exercise is to link it with flatwork exercises such as circles, turns and transitions, making the rider plan and think ahead more.

Group lessons

When teaching jumping to a group of riders it can be challenging to balance the amount of time a rider is busy and practising the skills with safety and being able to have more than one rider jumping at once. You must consider the following.

1. If riders follow each other through an exercise, what happens if one kicks a pole or knocks a fence down? You need to have plenty time to make adjustments to avoid the next rider's safety being compromised. If bringing riders through an exercise as a ride, they must be suitably spaced out so you can make minor adjustments confidently if needed. With more experienced riders you can brief them to circle away and wait if the rider in front alters the fence or poles.

2. It can be really boring for riders to stand and wait for their turn. Furthermore, horses

The initial stage of a gridwork lesson where riders are keeping the horses moving while taking it in turns to ride down the grid.

can switch off and become cold while waiting. Sometimes riders just appreciate a break, dependent on their fitness. It is up to you to pay attention to the riders in front of you and work out the best plan for them. There are many ways of keeping riders involved in the session, even when they are standing waiting. People learn a lot by watching and you can direct them to watch specific things while other riders are completing an exercise and then involve everyone in discussion and feedback.

3. With riders who have a little more experience it is possible to increase the pace of the lesson a little by having one rider warming up and preparing for an exercise as another is completing it; this will allow you to do more in a session. It is essential that all riders understand where they are going and who has right of way.

4. Think about where you position fences and poles. It may be possible to use the inner area of the school so that other riders can carry on moving and working while a individual moves in to complete an exercise. This depends on the ability of the riders you have. If you plan to have riders waiting for their turn, make sure you build an exercise where the riders can stand safely facing it, allowing both them and their horses to see what is going on.

5. Remember that, within a group, you will have a range of abilities, especially when teaching for the Pony Club or a Riding Club. When you plan your session try to think of ways that the same exercise can be made more interesting for the better riders so they still feel challenged. For example, combining transitions and school movements before or after a jump can increase the degree of difficulty. Through more directed questioning you can encourage riders to analyse their own performance more and work harder mentally.

Some useful exercises

1. Linking fences together (a simple course)

AIMS AND BENEFITS

Once a rider is competent jumping a single fence, the next step is to link a few fences together. The rider will now need to learn to react a little quicker and to look ahead to their next fence when landing, learn to ride good turns and lines to each fence and change the canter lead as required. This exercise will start to develop the rider coordination between fences.

EQUIPMENT

Three fences — minimum three pairs of wings and cups and six poles.

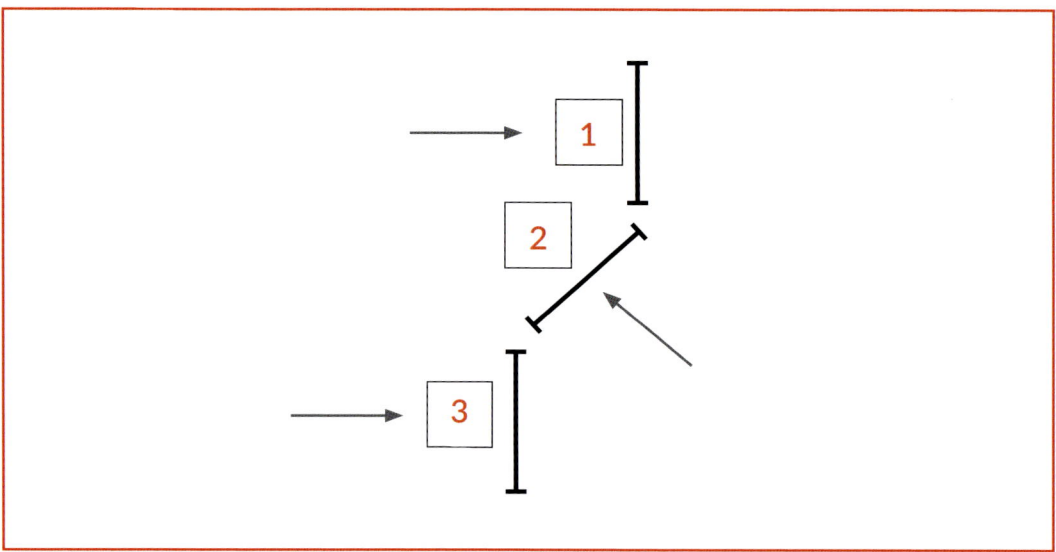

Layout for a course of three fences.

DESCRIPTION

The exercise will build up to the rider being able to ride a simple course of three fences. The session could start with the rider riding the course with poles on the ground in the position of the fences. They could do this in trot first to practise lines and turns before progressing into canter. Once they are riding over the poles in canter you can begin to develop the rider's awareness of canter leads. Particularly after the pole on the diagonal the rider will need to return to trot and then ask for the new canter lead when changing the rein. Once the rider is happy with this, the fences can be built one at a time so the riders first links two fences together and then three.

COMMON PROBLEMS

1. Riders cutting corners to get to their next fence. Riders can be become eager to get to the next fence, but they will need to be encouraged to ride away from their first fence on a straight line and use as much space in the school as possible to then ride around the corner in order to line up to the diagonal fence, and then do the same to get a good approach to the final fence.

2. Riders may find it difficult to organise themselves quickly enough after fences, so if the rider lands on the wrong canter lead and is not able to correct this quickly enough, encourage them to ride a circle, ask for trot and then give the aids to establish the correct canter lead. As they become more practised they will be able to do this more quickly but, at this stage, it is important that they are able to approach each fence in balance.

2. Basic gridwork

AIMS AND BENEFITS

There are many reasons why grids may be used as part of training the rider to jump. The real benefit is that, through setting up a combination of jumping efforts and poles, a schooled horse should jump consistently and take off and land in a predictable way, provided that the rider still rides him forward from the leg. This makes things somewhat easier for the rider, allowing the focus to be on them developing skills such as:

- Maintaining a rhythm.
- Keeping sufficient energy in the gait.
- Recognising where the take-off point is.
- Timing and coordination.
- Positional adaptation during jumps (including suppleness).
- Confidence — often riders will happily jump a bigger fence at the end of a grid because of it being set up for them.

EQUIPMENT

Three fences — minimum three pairs of wings and cups, seven poles (including placing pole)

DESCRIPTION

You ideally want to keep the grid simple and make sure that the rider does not have to think about much other than moving with the horse and folding well. A grid that is progressively built to have three simple jumping efforts with one or two strides between each would be sufficient. By approaching from trot with a placing pole before the first fence they should naturally meet it on a good stride, allowing them to think about moving with the horse as he takes off. If the horse then canters forward away from the first fence, the second and then third jumps should happen easily and in a predictable way. Add one fence at a time once the first has been ridden well. You can progressively raise the height of the fences (within reason) and possibly add a spread pole to the last one at the end of the session. Hopefully, the rider will leave the session feeling more confident and in better balance with the horse.

There are infinite combinations of poles and fence layouts with which to build a grid and what you use depends on the desired outcome. However, make sure you use a grid wisely and really consider how it will help (or not). Distances should be chosen in the same way as for building simple combinations and be appropriate for the horse's stride length (see Table of Distances and Striding at end of section). A grid built with poor distances may work against you and inhibit a rider's confidence and feel. (It is not a good idea to try to use grids with groups of very different horses and ponies.) In general, if using a trot approach or working with less experienced/confident riders, distances will need to be shortened slightly as they are less likely to be travelling forwards well (evaluate each horse/rider individually). You must also be careful about the use of trot or canter poles on the way into the grid; if a horse trips or stumbles it can be almost impossible for them to complete the grid without further mishap. If you do wish to use poles at the front then leave a couple of non-jumping strides after them before the fence to allow recovery time if needed. In general with less experienced riders, less is more — remember, if they lose balance early on then every subsequent jump may make the situation worse. It's better that they have sufficient time between jumps to recover.

COMMON PROBLEMS

1. The horse is not forward enough or does not quite meet the first fence right and then struggles to make the distance between the fences. At this stage the fences should be small enough that the horse will be able to clear them even if he has to fit in an extra stride, or take off from further away. Encourage the rider to keep riding positively forward then, on the next approach, show them how they can correct their mistake. If they have lost confidence you can put the fences back down to poles and gradually rebuild the grid to three fences, supporting them to ride a correct approach.

2. Lack of straightness through the grid. If a rider does not keep the horse straight through the grid this can alter the distance between the fences (usually making them longer) and may cause the horse to have to take off further away from the fence. To help the rider to keep the horse straight you can put poles alongside the grid.

3. **Introducing different types of fences**

   To include spreads, basic fillers and doubles.

   AIMS AND BENEFITS

   Introduce the rider to different types of fences, and incorporate them into courses.

   EQUIPMENT

   Material for four fences — five pairs of wings and cups, minimum of nine poles, filler material.

DESCRIPTION

These different types of fences can be introduced over several sessions, eventually building up to a course containing them. Spreads are best introduced using a cross-pole, and then adding the back rail. The cross-pole helps the rider to ride to the centre of the fence and will make the fence look more welcoming. When the rider is confident, you can make the fence into an ascending oxer with a straight front rail (back rail will be slightly higher). Riders can sometimes become worried about spreads and how wide they are, however, at this level the horse in unlikely to be jumping any bigger than when the fence is an upright. Horses usually find it easier to judge the take-off to a spread, especially if it has a ground-line, so they are usually more inviting for the horse.

A basic spread; a cross-pole with a back rail is an inviting fence and will encourage the rider to aim for the centre.

When introducing fillers, it is important that the first ones you introduce are simple. Ideally, use two matching fillers; these can initially be pulled apart so the horse jumps the fence with the fillers placed to either side. These can then be gradually pulled inwards until the rider is jumping the fillers. (This is often how you would introduce fillers to a young horse, but it is also useful to introduce them to the rider this way.) Some horses will jump bigger over the fence when there are fillers underneath so the rider needs to be ready for this.

Throughout all of the rider's jumping work, they should have some time dedicated to improving their balance and security. Work in light seat at the start of a session is useful to help develop this. By developing their strength and security in this way, when a horse jumps a bigger fence the rider will be better equipped to be able to absorb this effort and remain in balance.

A fence with fillers; these could easily be pulled out to the side of the fence initially and then gradually moved inwards.

Hopefully at this point the rider will already have done some simple gridwork, so will be familiar with two or three jumps in a row. When introducing a double on its own, the first element should be inviting — e.g. a cross-pole with a back rail (simple spread) — then the second element an upright. The rider should be encouraged to ride straight and sit up briefly after the first element before folding for the second one. It is always best to keep the second element as simple as possible to reduce the risk of the horse jumping the first one and refusing the second.

As mentioned earlier, it may be best to introduce these different types of fences over several sessions so that the rider becomes confident with each fence individually before they are all incorporated into a course.

COMMON PROBLEMS

Rider backing off a fence that they deem to be more difficult. It is important to introduce different types of fences gradually, so the rider builds confidence. Ideally, the rider should be on an experienced horse when these fences are introduced to further build their confidence.

Table of distances and striding

Jump distances can be measured in Feet or Metres. An average human stride is approximately one Yard (1yd) which is 3ft.

	Pony		Cob/small horse		Competition/large horse	
Trot poles	1.22m	4ft	1.37m	4ft 6in	1.52m	5ft
Trot place pole	2.44m	8ft	2.74m	9ft	3.05m	10ft
Canter place pole	2.44–2.74m	8–9ft	2.74–3.05m	9–10ft	3.05–3.66m	10–12ft
Bounce	2.74m	9ft	3.05–3.35m	10–11ft	3.66m	12ft
Upright to upright – one non-jumping stride.	6.40m	21ft	6.70–7m	22–23ft	7.32–8.08m	24–26½ft (max)
Spread to upright	6.10m	20ft	6.40–6.70m	21–22ft	7–7.32m	23–24ft
Upright to spread	As above					
Trot approach deduct 2–3ft (85–95cms) from all distances						
Upright to upright on two non-jumping strides	9.60m	10½yds	10m	11yds	11m	36ft
Spread to upright	9.14m	10yds	9.45–9.75m	10–10½yds	10–10.40m	11–11⅓yds
Upright to spread	As above					
Trot approach deduct 2–3ft (85–95cms) from all distances						
Related on three non-jumping	12.80m	14yd	13.76m	15yd	14.63m	16yd
Related on four non-jumping	16.46m	18yd	17.37m	19yd	18.29m	20yd
Related on five non-jumping	19.20m	21yd	20.57m	22½yd	21.95m	24yd

Related distances — walk total number of human strides (1yd each), deduct between three (pony) and four for landing and take-off combined, divide remainder by four for competition distance (for school ponies divide by three), to get number of strides.

One human stride will measure about 1yd (3ft): 0.91m

Teaching horse care

Learning about horse care is just as important as learning to ride, and these topics often go hand in hand. Many of the people you will teach may go on to have their own horse, so they need to know how to keep their horse healthy and happy. Owning a horse is a major commitment and it is a good idea that the person knows exactly what they should expect (including the costs involved) and what they need to do to look after their horse's welfare.

Horse care sessions can provide people with important skills and knowledge that will help them to develop in the horse world, in whatever area that may be. (Unmounted sessions do not have to be for just horse care topics, they could also be used for teaching riding theory. It can be easier for someone to learn when they are not thinking about controlling their horse at the same time.)

For a freelance coach, teaching unmounted sessions could provide an extra source of income, or provide an alternative to a riding lesson when riding is not possible (e.g. adverse weather). In riding schools, holding unmounted sessions can be a way to use the horses in a different way, giving them more variety in their daily routine. When teaching for a Pony Club, unmounted sessions can make up a large proportion of the teaching, especially during winter months when the lack of daylight and facilities may mean less riding.

Preparation

Location

The location of your session will depend on the topic you are teaching, but it should ideally allow the session to be as practical and visual as possible. Suitable locations for horse care sessions could include:

- A stable.
- The tack room.
- The feed room.
- An arena.

There may be times when a classroom could be used for some or all of the session, e.g. when it is cold and wet, or when you are teaching technical subjects where diagrams or drawings would be helpful to the learners. Using a whiteboard to draw on can often help learners to visualise what you are teaching them, e.g. drawing the bones of the horse's leg on a whiteboard, or even on a large piece of paper, gives people a better idea than simply looking at the outside of a horse's leg. DVDs can be used to teach some parts of topics and even to develop riding skills, as mentioned earlier under Learning Styles. Being able to access wider resources such as online video clips or DVDs can add further strength to a session.

If you have a tired group of children (e.g. on a 'pony day' or at camp) it can be beneficial to do an activity that allows them to have a break but still learn, e.g. asking younger children to draw/colour an ideal field. This allows them to sit quietly and they will learn without even realising it. If using a classroom environment for teaching horse care (no matter what the topic), it is important to keep it as visual as possible and involve the learners wherever you can, rather than just giving a lecture.

Regardless of the location, you need to think about keeping yourself and the learners safe throughout the session. The number of people may have a bearing on the location, as you would not want too many of them in the same stable with a horse. There has to be room for everyone to have a clear view of what is happening without them being too close to the horse, which could put them at risk. The horse could perhaps be tied up outside the stable to allow more room and learners should always be briefed about any potential hazards. The weather should also be taken into account. You do not want people to get cold, so you should encourage them to bring plenty of warm clothing, and include plenty of 'doing' in your session. It is a good idea to be prepared to adapt your session if necessary for really adverse weather. This may mean changing the location or the topic of the session, depending on the circumstances.

Equipment

Learners will need a hat, gloves and suitable footwear if they are going to handle or lead a horse as part of the session. It is a good idea to think ahead and advise them if they will need to bring anything specific for the session. This could include:

- Hat.
- Gloves.
- Suitable footwear.
- Clothing suitable for the weather, and spare clothing.
- Notepad and pen.

Before the session you should check that you have enough of any equipment needed and that it is safe and suitable for those who will use it. You do not want to get part-way through a session to find the grooming kit is missing a hoofpick or the stitching on the bridle is coming undone. The equipment should be placed neatly in a safe place, ready to use in the session.

Structuring the session

The length of time given to teaching a session will depend partly on the age and level of the learners. Small children may not be able to concentrate for more than half an hour at a time, whereas an adult should be able concentrate for a longer period. If the session includes lots of practical involvement people will often be able to cope with longer sessions than if they are sitting in a classroom environment just listening. Variety within a session will help to keep everyone interested and engaged.

To plan a session effectively, you need to break it down into stages, as shown:

Introduction

- Explain purpose and importance of the topic (why they should learn about it).
- Outline the structure of the session.

Explanation/demonstration

- Explain/demonstrate slowly enough for the participants to take in and learn.
- Break the topic down into sections if needed.
- Use visual aids where appropriate.
- Repeat/clarify where needed.

Learner practice time

- Allow plenty of time for the learners to have a go and practise.
- Offer help/guidance if needed.
- Re-demonstrate if needed.

Summarise and check learning

- Summarise the session.
- Ask open questions to assess learning.
- Ask if anyone has any questions.
- Direct to further learning if appropriate.
- Outline the link to further sessions.

17 | Coaching in Practice

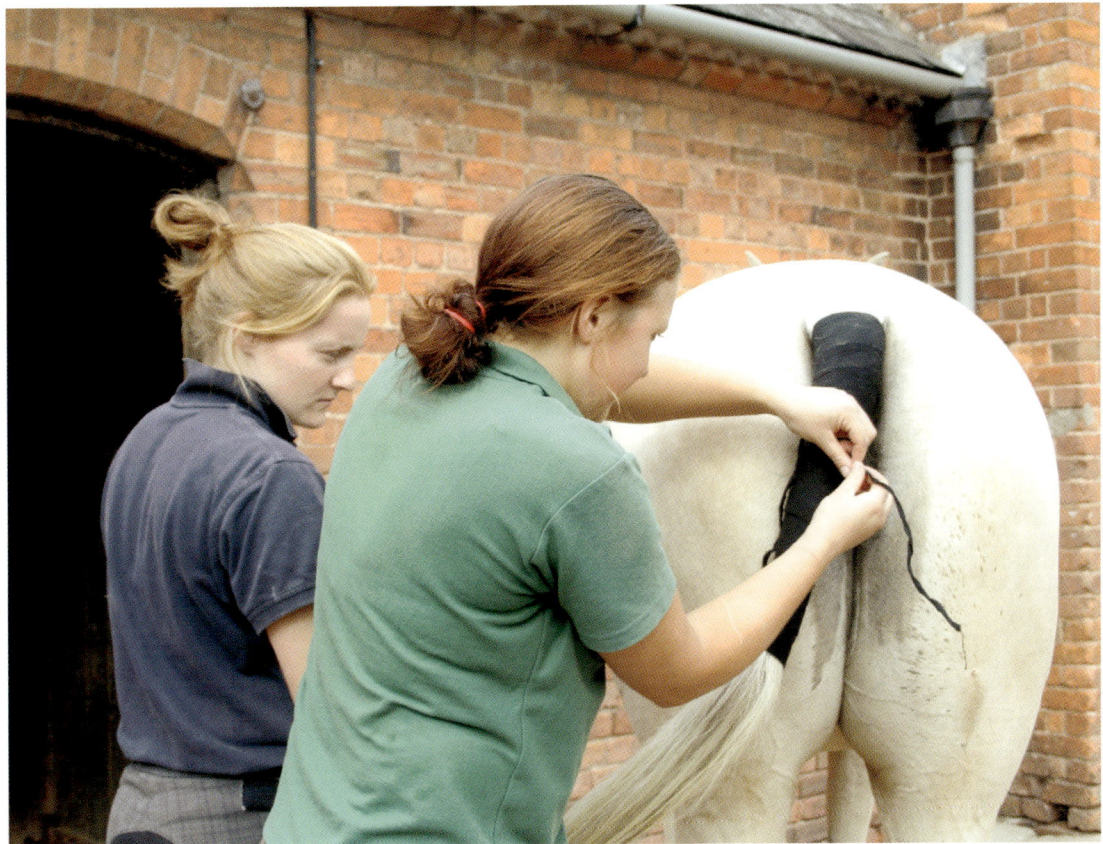

As part of a practical session, participants should be given time to practise the task with support from the coach.

Example sessions

Some common topics that might be taught in horse care sessions are:

- Tacking up.

- Care of tack.

- Grooming.

- Rugs and rugging.

- Stable bandages.

- Tail bandage.

- Mucking out.

- Point of the horse, colours and markings.

Each of these topics can be delivered by being broken down into the same four stages. By finding ways to make the session interesting, learners will get the most benefit when they are engaged and enjoying themselves. Using grooming as an example, here are some suggestions how to make different areas interesting or fun:

- Write the reasons for grooming on flash cards, and include a few red herrings. Give learners 2 minutes to pick out the correct reasons. This could lead on to a discussion about each card.

- Blindfold a person and ask them to guess which brush you have given them.

- Write the items of grooming kit on paper and stick them to each person's forehead. One by one they can ask the others questions to try to figure out which item they are (the questions can only be answered with 'yes' or 'no'), e.g. 'Can I be used on a clipped horse?'

- Split the group into two teams and have a relay race where each person has to bring back a certain item of grooming kit, e.g. the first person brings back a dandy brush, the second person brings back a body brush, and so on. This can be useful for keeping energetic children engaged.

- Split the group into two teams and give each team a horse to groom. The team with the best-groomed horse wins.

There may be some topics that require a lot of practice, e.g. bandaging. Bandaging their friend or family member's leg could be a good way for someone to practise when they don't have access to a horse.

Summary

- As your experience of teaching increases, you should gain more practical knowledge of coaching and learning styles, and be able to apply this to ever-greater effect in your communication with riders.

- Before any session it is a good idea to have a plan of what you are going to do. The plan can always be adjusted to suit the rider(s), in terms of factors such as horse allocation and the overall situation on the day. The plan should include as main elements the warm-up, content of the session and cooling down.

- There are several different types of lessons you are likely to teach, these include lead rein lessons, lunge lessons, flat lessons, jumping lessons and stable management lessons.

- Lead rein lessons are used for complete beginners and small children. Adult beginners will often progress over a few sessions to be able to do some riding independently. However, small children are often not strong enough to ride on their own, so you will need to have lots of exercises to keep them interested.

- Lunge lessons are very useful, as the rider is able to work solely on their position and balance without having to control the horse. This type of lesson is equally useful for both the novice rider (where the session may focus on developing the rising trot) and the more experienced rider who may work on developing their position or correcting positional faults.

- Development of good foundations in flatwork is essential for any discipline. The development of the horse and rider should follow the elements of the Scale of Training; rhythm, suppleness, contact, straightness, impulsion and, in time, collection.

- It is important not to introduce jumping too soon. Once the rider is ready to start jumping, it should be introduced gradually, with the focus on the rider's balance and security to ensure that the rider gains confidence along with the skills required for jumping.

- Stable management sessions may be used as part of a course for adults, or can be used as part of 'pony days' for children. When teaching a practical skill the format of the session should include an introduction, then an explanation and demonstration of the task. The participants should then have the opportunity to practise the task with support, and then the session can be summed up.

- After all coaching sessions, you should summarise with your pupils so they are clear as to what they have learnt and can discuss what to work on and what to expect in their next session. This is a useful time to get feedback as to what they found useful and what was not so useful in the session. From this information you can tailor their next session in a way to suit them best, as well as reflecting on your own coaching performance. You can then consider things to work on to improve your own coaching practice.

TRAINING TIPS

The tips mentioned in the previous chapter on Coaching Concepts are equally valid as you move from theory to practice:

1. Watch more experienced coaches teaching different types of lessons and observe how they put coaching theory into practice.

2. Put together a number of different lesson plans and put them into practice in your coaching sessions.

3. Try to take note of how your own coach structures your lessons.

4. It is also important to coach in sensible, progressive increments, for example:

    - Progressing riders through lead rein, lungeing, basic flatwork as appropriate.

    - Working through the elements of the Scale of Training as riders become capable of addressing them.

    - Ensuring the riders have a reasonable grounding in flatwork before jumping is attempted.

5. Remembering the value of summarising and feedback.

What's Next?

What's Next?

Whether you have read the entirety of this volume or dipped into the areas that interest you, we hope you have been inspired to pursue a career in the equine industry, or to continue to learn about the fundamentals of complete horsemanship.

If you are considering a career take a look at what the BHS Equine Excellence Pathways offer you. This Volume will help those looking for a career in grooming, in professional riding, in coaching and specifically supports candidates looking to achieve the following awards: Stage 2 Care, Stage 2 Lunge, Stage 2 Ride, and Stage 2 Teach. We have developed our qualifications following extensive consultation with varied professionals in the equine industry and we believe this Volume should be of benefit to people seeking any type of equine career.

BHS Coach in Complete Horsemanship Pathway

Career pathway	What qualifications do I need to study?				
BHS Stage 1 Complete Horsemanship	Stage 1 Care	+	Stage 1 Ride	+	—
BHS Stage 2 Complete Horsemanship	Stage 2 Care + Stage 2 Lunge	+	Stage 2 Ride	+	Stage 2 Teach
BHS Stage 3 Coach in Complete Horsemanship	Stage 3 Care + Stage 3 Lunge	+	Stage 3 Ride (Dressage)	Stage 3 Ride (Jump) +	Stage 3 Teach
BHS Stage 4 Senior Coach in Complete Horsemanship	Stage 4 Care & Management + Stage 4 Lunge	+	Stage 4 Ride (Dressage)	Stage 4 Ride (Jump) +	Stage 4 Teach
BHS Stage 5 Performance Coach in Complete Horsemanship	Stage 5 Care & Management + Stage 5 Lunge	+	Stage 5 Ride (Dressage)	Stage 5 Ride (Jump) +	Stage 5 Teach

Fellow

Please note: Complete Horsemanship pathways in dressage and jumping are available from Stage 3 onwards.

What's Next?

BHS Groom Pathway

Career pathway	What qualifications do I need to study?		
BHS Stage 1 Care	Stage 1 Care		
BHS Stage 2 Foundation Groom	Stage 2 Care	+	Stage 2 Lunge
BHS Stage 3 Groom	Stage 3 Care	+	Stage 3 Lunge
BHS Stage 4 Senior Groom	Stage 4 Care & Management	+	Stage 4 Lunge
BHS Stage 5 Stable Manager	Stage 5 Care & Management	+	Stage 5 Lunge

BHS Professional Rider Pathway

Career pathway	What qualifications do I need to study?		
BHS Stage 1 Ride	Stage 1 Ride		
BHS Stage 2 Foundation Rider	Stage 2 Ride		
BHS Stage 3 Rider	Stage 3 Ride (Dressage)	+	Stage 3 Ride (Jump)
BHS Stage 4 Senior Rider	Stage 4 Ride (Dressage)	+	Stage 4 Ride (Jump)
BHS Stage 5 Performance Rider	Stage 5 Ride (Dressage)	+	Stage 5 Ride (Jump)

Please note: Ride pathways in dressage and jumping are available from Stage 3 onwards.

We encourage you to take basic qualifications, whichever career path you choose to go down. The BHS Ride Safe, Stage 1 and 2 qualifications are the ideal way to begin your journey. You can start Ride Safe at 11 years old, Stage 1 at 14 years old, and Stage 2 at 16 years old. Stage 1 and 2 will compliment other qualifications you may undertake such as Apprenticeships, Work Based Diploma (WBD) or Scottish Vocational Qualifications (SVQ). Stage 1 and 2 will provide practical skills and knowledge that will prepare you well for almost any career with horses.

A recent survey reported that BHS assessments are chosen by the majority of equestrian employers.

All of the Society's Stage 1, 2 and 3 assessments have been revisited in 2017 to provide the most up to date, robust and high-quality method of exploring candidates' knowledge of riding, horse care and coaching skills, catering for every level from novice owners and beginners through to international experts.

Assessments are available at BHS Approved Centres throughout the majority of the year and are a friendly, supportive introduction to the equestrian industry.

The BHS Equine Excellence Pathway team will be happy to guide you through the assessment structure. Browse our site www.bhs.org.uk/pathways, email pathways@bhs.org.uk or give the team a call on 02476 840508. Advice, guidelines and a syllabus are available for every level, so you can be confident in what you will be asked to do, and these resources will also help you make sure you are making the right choices — whatever they are!

Good luck!